W9-BWI-801

RICHARD BARBER

Edward, Prince of Wales and Aquitaine

A BIOGRAPHY OF THE BLACK PRINCE

CHARLES SCRIBNER'S SONS
New York

Printed in Great Britain
Library of Congress Catalog Card Number 78-54019
ISBN 0-684-15864-7

1-19-79

CONTENTS

LIST OF PLATES

LIST OF MAPS

Preface

To attempt to write a biography of Edward 'the Black Prince', a legendary paragon of chivalry, without turning first to the chronicler of chivalry *par excellence*, Jean Froissart, may seem self-defeating, particularly as there is so little light to be shed on the prince's character from other sources. But the classic stories of the school textbooks and romantic histories have held sway for too long without being challenged, and I have therefore tried to work outwards from accounts and 'official' chronicles to arrive at an account of Edward, prince of Wales and Aquitaine, and in particular of the group of men who were his companions-in-arms. Space and time have not allowed me to do as much work on the latter as I would have wished, but I hope that I have been able to show both the prince and his father as part of a close-knit, brilliant group of knights rather than as isolated figures, and to capture something of the prince's life as a great baron and as an almost sovereign ruler in Aquitaine.

I am indebted to many people for their courtesy in patiently answering queries on a number of topics, and for assistance with points of research. I should like to thank in particular the following: Dr Derek Brewer, Miss Elizabeth Danbury, Mrs Madeleine Ginsburg, Mr Simon Jervis, Dr Richard Marks, Mrs Stella Newton, Dr Peter Rickard, Miss Anne Riches, Mr Brian Spencer, Dr Pamela Tudor-Craig and Dr Marcia Vale. For access to manuscripts or for providing microfilm I am grateful to Mr Graham

Haslam of the Duchy of Cornwall office, Dr R. I. Page of Corpus Christi College, Cambridge, and the librarian of Corpus Christi College, Oxford. Professor A. R. Myers kindly read the manuscript and made a number of helpful suggestions. I should like to acknowledge the courtesy of the staffs of the British Library, the Public Record Office, the various archival collections on which I have drawn, the Bodleian Library and last, but far from least, and indispensable to anyone working on such topics outside London, the ever-patient members of the staff of the London Library.

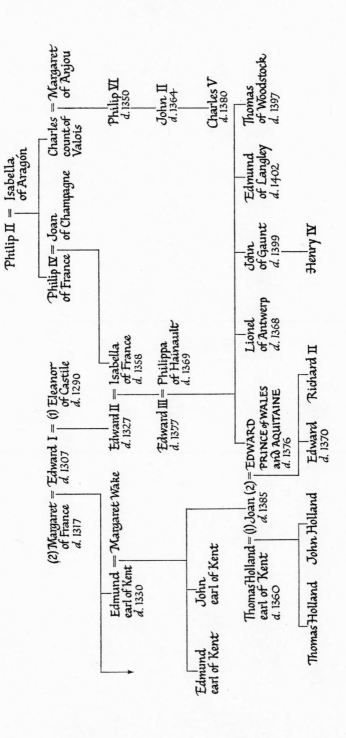

The King's Eldest Son

◄────►

I

When the eldest son of Edward III, called Edward after his father, grandfather and great-grandfather, was born in 1330, England was a weak and divided country. Edward III himself was only seventeen years old, and was in the power of his mother and her lover. Harassed in the north by the Scots, the English had recently lost much of Ireland, and the vast inheritance of Henry II's domains in France was reduced to a mere parcel of lands around Bordeaux. The intermittent civil war and intrigues of two decades showed no sign of ending. Much of the blame for this sorry state of affairs must be laid on Edward II, whose distaste for matters of government was notorious. He had inherited his father's superb physique, but none of his political skill: favourites – some worthless, such as Piers Gaveston, some with higher aims, such as the Despensers – had ruled in his place, while he preferred either an empty ceremonial pomp or humble rustic pursuits such as digging pits or thatching barns. Isabella, his wife, daughter of Philip the Fair of France, had suffered much from his favourites: Edward is said to have given all her father's wedding presents to Gaveston. She was equally harshly treated by the Despensers when they in turn became Edward's confidants: her estates were confiscated and she was kept under close guard because she was suspected of encouraging the barons to oppose the king. In 1325, when she was allowed to go to France to negotiate over the war which had broken out between French and English in Gascony, she refused to return to England.

As her eldest son Edward was with her, her bargaining position was strong, and the more headstrong members of the dissident barons gathered round her. At Paris she met Roger Mortimer, who became her lover. As Isabella's power grew, so she seemed to imitate her husband's failings: the Despensers were balanced by Mortimer, Edward's dislike of government by Isabella's rapacity for money. But Isabella was the more determined character – the chroniclers called her the 'she-wolf of France' – and this determination led her to plan an invasion of England, with the help of troops from Hainault. She had secured this alliance by betrothing her son to Philippa, daughter of count William of Hainault, and the count's brother John was joint-commander of the army with Roger Mortimer.

Isabella landed at Harwich on 24 September; by 15 October, her forces were successful enough to encourage the Londoners to rebel in her favour; and by the end of the year she was the effective ruler of England. On 7 January 1327 a parliament at London formally deposed Edward II and recognized Edward III as king, aged fourteen. The three years that followed were a return to the uncertainties of the rule of Edward II's favourites, although Isabella had gathered some far from incompetent administrators around her, such as Adam Orleton, her chief agent and bishop of Hereford, and Henry Burghersh, bishop of Lincoln. The weakness lay in the centre: Isabella's policies might have been designed to arouse popular resentment, while she was reputed to have appropriated two thirds of the royal revenue, besides all the forfeit lands of the Despensers. Her open flaunting of her relationship with Mortimer was another tactical error. Peace was made with France and Scotland, but on disadvantageous terms; such money as was paid by the Scots for the English surrender of their claim to be overlords of Scotland went into Isabella's coffers. Nor did the murder of Edward II, unpopular though he had been, help her cause.

Meanwhile, the marriage alliance with Hainault, which had been the key to Isabella's success, had yet to be completed. The betrothal seems to have been more than merely political, if we are to believe Froissart, who says of Edward's stay at Hainault in 1326:

William, the count, had four daughters, Margaret, Philippa, Joan and Isabel. Of whom, the young Edward, who was later king of England, preferred and was more inclined to esteem and love

Philippa than the others. And the girl was more familiar and friendly with him than any of her sisters. So I heard the good lady who was later queen of England say, at whose side I lived and served.[1]

The following year, ambassadors were sent requesting the fulfil-ment of the betrothal, but a papal dispensation was needed before the marriage could take place, since Edward and Philippa had a common great-grandfather (Philip III of France). This was procured by Edward from Pope John XXII, and in October Roger North-burgh, bishop of Lichfield, went to Hainault to carry out a proxy marriage and to arrange the dowry. Jean Le Bel notes that Philippa was provided by her father with a wardrobe befitting her new station as queen of England. On 20 November, Bartholomew Burghersh and William Clinton (later earl of Huntingdon) were sent to bring her from France. Edward was in the north, occupied by negotiations with Scotland, and Philippa was met at Dover on 23 December by her uncle, John of Hainault. They travelled to Canterbury, stopping to make offerings at St Thomas's shrine, and then to London. Immediately after Christmas, she left for York to meet the king; on 24 January, the full marriage ceremony took place, Edward being sixteen, Philippa probably fourteen.[2]

The alliance with Hainault was to be important in a number of ways. It had already helped Isabella to depose Edward II: when Edward III came to fight his campaigns against France, it gave him a secure base on the north-eastern frontier from which to conduct operations. Through Philippa, Edward was connected with the German emperor, Louis of Bavaria, and the marquis of Juliers, both of whom were potentially valuable allies. At a humbler level, many knights from Hainault distinguished themselves on the English side, notably Froissart's hero Walter Mauny. And both Jean Le Bel and Froissart, to whose chronicles we owe many of the livelier – if not always accurate – descriptions of contemporary events, were from Hainault and spent some time in England because of the link between the two countries.

From April 1330, Philippa was given a separate household, financed from her own estates. This was necessary because she and Edward were frequently kept apart by affairs of state. Indeed, it is her presence at so many great occasions, voyages abroad and even campaigns that is remarkable. For some reason, her coronation as queen did not take place until 4 March 1330 at Westminster: normally this ceremony was carried out within a month of a king's marriage, unless he himself had not been crowned, in which case the queen would be crowned at the same time as the king. By the time of her coronation, Philippa was expecting her first child, and this may have been the reason for carrying out the ceremony. In June she was at Woodstock in Oxfordshire, at the palace built by Henry II and Henry III with its pavilion or summer house grouped round three pools, and it was here on 15 June, the feasts of St Vitus and St Modestus, that Edward, her first son, was born. Philippa is reputed to have breast-fed him, but there is no contemporary evidence to confirm this. A nurse was found for him from near-by Oxford, and a nursemaid was appointed to attend his cradle. Both were later rewarded with considerable pensions, Joan of Oxford receiving £10 a year and Matilda Plumpton £6 13s. 4d. The prince remembered Joan in later years, sending her a tun of wine in June 1357. Matilda Plumpton may have been elderly, as three years later she was pensioned off at the convent of St Augustine's in Bristol, 'to receive maintenance for life'; but she reappears as nurse to Edmund of Langley, the king's third son, twelve years later.[3]

Henry earl of Lancaster, leader of the barons who opposed Isabella and Mortimer, was also delighted by the news, and gave Peter Eketon, his messenger, 10 marks a year for having brought word of the prince's birth. The baby was baptized by Henry Burghersh, bishop of Lincoln, member of a family which was to be closely associated with the prince in later years. Edward III was evidently elsewhere at the time, as the news was brought to him by Catherine Montacute, later countess of Salisbury, and by Thomas Prior: again, substantial rewards were forthcoming, Prior receiving 40 marks (£26 13s. 4d.) a year for life for this one errand.

From his birth, the prince was regarded as future earl of Chester, the traditional estate of the king's eldest son since 1254. Provision was made for him and his attendants by a grant of 500 marks (£333 13s. 4d.), about half the total revenue of Cheshire, made on 16 September 1330, by which time a keeper of the prince's wardrobe had already been appointed. For the moment, however, his household was to all effects part of that of the queen, and he travelled with her on her journeys round England.[4]

Whatever Edward III's pleasure at the birth of his heir, it was soon overshadowed by a revival of the underlying dissensions in the kingdom. Mortimer had succeeded in suppressing a rebellion by

Lancaster in 1329, which had cost Lancaster a massive fine of £11,000 for his pardon: but Mortimer had not learnt his lesson, and although there were no recriminations at the time, in March 1330 he encompassed the death of the earl of Kent. Lancaster saw that he was likely to be Mortimer's next victim, and enlisted two members of the king's household to help him encourage the king to throw off Mortimer's yoke. These were Richard Bury, who had been Edward's tutor and was now keeper of the privy seal, and William Montacute, later earl of Salisbury, whose wife had brought Edward news of the prince's birth, news which seems to have encouraged both the king and Lancaster to act. The Pope's support was enlisted by means of a secret interview at which Montacute explained the true situation in England and the king's desire to rid himself of Mortimer. It was agreed that only royal letters including the words *pater sancte* should be regarded as coming from Edward himself, any others being from Mortimer's minions. By October, Montacute felt sufficiently sure of support to plan a definite move against Mortimer; but Mortimer was suspicious, and when a great council of magnates met at Northampton on 15 October, he was on his guard. He and queen Isabella barricaded themselves into the castle, but the constable of the castle admitted Montacute by a secret passage. Edward himself joined the small band of knights as they crossed the courtyard; Mortimer's room was broken open, and he was seized. Despite Isabella's pleas for 'pity on gentle Mortimer', he was taken out of the castle and hurried to London under close arrest. On 29 November, his crimes were declared to be notorious by his peers and he met a traitor's death. Isabella was allowed a discreet retirement, on an income of £3,000 a year: her vast lands, and those of Mortimer, went to the crown, but many of Isabella's castles, towns and honours went to Philippa, who was finding a dowry of £3,000 a year inadequate for a growing establishment. Even the baby prince's revenues had to be increased: on 25 February 1331 all the revenue of Chester was granted to Philippa for his maintenance and that of the king's sister Eleanor, 'from the time of the arrest of Roger Mortimer'. Curiously, although Edward had not yet been formally created earl of Chester, the letters patent use that title, so traditional was it for the king's eldest son.[5]

The young earl became a figure on the political scene just after his first birthday, when a marriage alliance with France was under discussion. In July, envoys were named to negotiate a marriage between the prince and a daughter of the king of France; but despite further plans in November 1331, for negotiations about this and about a crusade, and in April 1332 when Joan was named as the prospective bride, nothing came of the scheme. Such a match was a part of any major treaty of alliance, and Edward's name was later to be linked in similar fashion with other princesses whenever a suitable diplomatic occasion arose. He and his mother were often away from the court during these early years; the queen's household, which had no very particular reasons for moving round the country, seems to have been as peripatetic as the king's, spending time at different royal residences, Woodstock remaining a particular favourite. The members of the royal household and court changed surprisingly little as a result of the fall of Mortimer. Adam Orleton and Henry Burghersh, bishops of Hereford and Lincoln, survived the disgrace of Isabella, and the nephew of Henry Burghersh was to become a close friend of the prince. Other associates of Mortimer were temporarily disgraced and then restored to office, though none of them ever became close councillors of the king. His own friends and advisers now held power: men such as William Montacute, William Clinton and Henry of Grosmont, heir to Henry of Lancaster. Edward III, in contrast to his father, was both interested in politics and shared the outlook of the barons, which accounts for much of the contrast between the two reigns. In particular, he was very fond of tournaments, which in the past had been a continual source of trouble, since small armies could be gathered under pretext of holding a joust. Edward III encouraged tournaments, but only under his own patronage and control. He also frequently used them as a display to delight the London crowds. The first of a number of London tournaments was held at Cheapside in September 1331, and the event was marred by the collapse of a scaffold from which the queen was watching. The king was only restrained from punishing the carpenters responsible by Philippa's pleading and the fact that none of the royal party was seriously hurt.

The details of the earliest years of Edward's life are few and far between. In June 1332 his sister Isabella was born, and another sister, Joan, in late 1333 at the Tower of London, while his nearest brother was William of Hatfield, born in 1336. On 18 March 1333 he was officially created earl of Chester; however, the revenues of the earldom, which had been paid to his own keeper of the wardrobe, were now to go to his mother for as long as he was living in her household. At the end of the following year, he and his sisters seem to have been at the Tower for Christmas, because the citizens of London sent him a present worth over £7. They also presented a glass to Elizabeth St Omer, described in the queen's accounts for the same year as 'mistress and guardian of the lord earl of Chester and his sister'. Her husband, William, was steward of the earl's household, though he only ranked as an esquire. John Burnham was established as treasurer, and Edward even had his own almoner, responsible for alms and offerings. At the same time, we meet for the first time William Stratton, his tailor, who was supplied with nearly nine yards of silk and twenty-two yards of taffeta to make the earl summer robes for Whitsun, which he spent with his mother at Woodstock. At Christmas he was at York (which was the administrative capital of England during Edward III's Scottish campaigns, until 1337): for this feast the allowance was nine yards of cloth, two furs, a plain hood and a fur hood for his winter robe. One curious detail is the presence of a page in charge of hares, probably kept as pets.[6]

In the following year, deteriorating relations with France led to fears of a French invasion, and on 18 August William St Omer and John Burnham were ordered to take the earl and his household to Nottingham castle, 'because on account of news which has reached the king touching him and the state of his realm, he wishes the earl to be brought to some safe place, to stay there until further order'. Here he and his sisters remained, in the care of William and Elizabeth St Omer, probably until the following spring, while the queen went north to Scotland. He attended his first tournament in the following year, 1336, for a cloak was provided by his tailor for the occasion, trimmed with fur.[7]

The king's brother, John of Eltham, died in September 1336, and as he had no heir, the earldom of Cornwall reverted to the crown. This unexpected addition to the royal revenue was used to solve a problem which had become increasingly acute, that of the young earl's household expenses. A hundred pounds had to be found in May 1336, and a further £500 in November, 'to be paid at once'. Some of the money seems to have gone on business from abroad, as Paolo de Montefiore was paid over £1,300 in August for 'various things to be bought abroad for the use of queen Philippa and Edward earl of Chester'. However, the transfer of the Cornish revenues proved far from simple, as a large assignment had been made against the revenues from tin, 1,000 marks a year to William

Montacute. Since this amounted to almost a third of the yield of the Cornish estates, other provisions had to be made for Edward from the revenues of Exeter, Mere and Wallingford. Thomas West also claimed £100 a year from the same source, which the king had forgotten when he granted the tin revenue, or stannary, to Edward. And the king's own urgent need for money led to a payment of £7,200 out of the same revenues in June, 'notwithstanding the king's grant to Edward his eldest son'. Politically it was also important to provide a suitable style for the king's eldest son; and Edward III, not content with a mere earldom for the purpose, created him duke of Cornwall, the first time that this title had been used in England. This was put into effect at a parliament on 9 February 1337, and as was traditional on such occasions, a number of other peerages were conferred at the same time. Four of those so honoured had been important figures in Edward's assumption of power in 1330: Henry, son of the duke of Lancaster, became earl of Derby, William Montacute became earl of Salisbury, William Clinton earl of Huntingdon and Robert Ufford earl of Suffolk. William Bohun, the twenty-five-year-old brother of the earl of Essex, became earl of Northampton, and Hugh Audeley earl of Gloucester. Twenty-four knights were also dubbed at the same time; one chronicler reports that these were made by the new duke himself, though in strict practice he could not have done so, as he himself was not yet a knight.[8]

About this time, Walter Burley, queen Philippa's almoner, was possibly appointed tutor to the young prince. The evidence for his education is very slight, and depends largely on late sources. Walter Burley, a distinguished scholar, is said to have been his tutor from the age when Edward was 'of age to goo to scole', which implies that the duke was seven or eight at the time. Burley was a close friend of Richard Bury, Edward III's tutor; he was an old man of over sixty, and he died about 1343, so his period of tuition must have been relatively brief; and recent biographers of Burley are doubtful whether he ever taught the prince. Whoever his teacher was, the lessons would have been confined to relatively simple matters, reading, writing, Latin and arithmetic, sufficient to equip the prince for the business of government. It is unlikely that much of Burley's scholastic work, on philosophy and in particular on Aristotle, ever reached the prince's attention, though it is just conceivable that Burley's most popular work, *On the Lives and Morals of Philosophers*, might have been written with the prince in mind. It contains some 120 short lives of philosophers and poets, with a brief summary of their opinions to form a kind of popular history of philosophy. Burley's immense reputation in his lifetime was due to his work as a philosopher; and in the late fifteenth century it was this book, printed in edition after edition, which continued his fame.[9]

A seventeenth-century tradition claims that the Black Prince attended Queen's College, Oxford. The story first appears in a patriotic speech in the 1630s, and is almost certainly an invention based on his mother's undoubted connection with the college, founded by her chaplain, Robert Eglesfeld. The foundation charter was issued in January 1341, and the statutes in the following month. These specify a body consisting of a provost, twelve scholars or fellows in theology and up to seventy poor boys to receive instruction in the hall. Such an institution would have nothing to recommend it to the king's son, who was already provided with one of the greatest scholars in England as his tutor, and was expected to choose his companions from the sons of the great lords of the realm. Neither Edward nor his father showed any signs of interest in learned matters: even the books of romances which other kings collected eagerly are missing from the records of their possessions. When queen Isabella died in 1358, her small collection of books went to her sister, the queen of Scotland, or to the monks at Easton Royal: it included three Arthurian romances, three romances from the Charlemagne cycle, one romance on the Trojan War, a genealogy and two church service books. A list of books belonging to Simon Burley, a close friend of Edward and a relative of Walter Burley, who was educated with him, shows a similar taste, though Burley's collection of twenty-one books, including eight romances, was exceptionally large. But books were not the only way in which Edward might have come to know the romances; they were still recited or read aloud, and the tournaments of the 1340s often had elements in them from Arthurian stories, which implies that the knights who took part were familiar with the original tales.[10]

At the same time as his intellectual education, such as it was, Edward now began to train for knightly pursuits. By 1338 he was the possessor of a quantity of armour: one harness, two bascinets, two pieces of plate armour, poleyns, a pair of plate gauntlets, a pair of armpieces, a pisane, a ventail, vambraces and rerebraces. These amounted to a complete suit of armour, with a spare helmet (bascinet), which may have been for tilting, the other being for war. He also had his own small canvas tent with a central post. All of these, though obviously scaled down to suit his age, were probably made in the same way as the equivalent adult pieces: they were not toys, but real war equipment.[11]

Edward now took an active part in state occasions, if only as the king's representative. In late 1337, he went to meet the two cardinals who had been sent to try and prevent the threatened war between France and England. Arrayed in a new robe of purple velvet and a hat specially made for the occasion with a scarlet border sewn with pearls, he met them outside London, and escorted them into the City with a great company of nobles and others. His wardrobe generally was lavish, probably with a view to other such appearances: jewels and fine clothes were to be a lifelong passion, and he evidently acquired this taste at an early age. Beside scarlet hats embroidered with silver roses and a broad ribbon belt with 37 enamelled plaques and 234 pearls sewn on it, he also had tapestries, which implies that he had a suite of large rooms or even a town house for his own use. The most impressive tapestry had a design of branches on a brown background, with roses and mermaids bearing the duke's arms. His household staff now included a number of pages and valets, and a butler, John Skirbek. For his illnesses, he had the attention of John Gaddesden, one of the greatest physicians of the time; he was given a barrel of wine in 1338, and there was also the gift of a coat to 'a minstrel who was with the duke when he was ill'.[12]

The visit of the cardinals led to a truce which held off the outbreak of hostilities with France until the summer of 1338. With the coming of war, Edward was to take up his first official duties; but we must first turn to the complex roots of the quarrel which was to dominate his life and career.

The Conflict with France

─────

2

The conflict between England and France in the fourteenth century, which was to overshadow the whole of Edward's life, had two distinct but interrelated subjects. The first concerned the lands in France inherited by the English kings, their extent, and the terms on which they were held from the French king. The second, which, had it not been for the first, might well have lapsed without any action being taken, was a claim to the throne of France itself by Edward III.[1]

To understand this conflict, and with it many of the details of the prince's life, we must turn to the history of the English lands in France going back to the Norman conquest. Once William I had won the English throne, he found himself in the anomalous position of being a sovereign who was another king's vassal – sovereign in England, a vassal in Normandy. The anomaly became even greater when, under Henry II, the English domains in France grew to embrace not only Normandy but also Anjou, Maine, Poitou and Gascony, with claims to overlordship as far afield as Toulouse and Brittany. The vassal-king was now far more powerful than his overlord; but the very existence of that overlordship was an immensely valuable weapon, as Philip Augustus proved when he succeeded in driving John out of Normandy in 1204, having declared his lands forfeit. The English kings had continued to hold Gascony, though the area under their rule had ebbed and flowed with the fortunes of war. A settlement appeared to have been reached in 1259, between St Louis and Henry III; and it seemed to have eliminated the English kings' claim to Normandy, Maine, Anjou and Poitou in return for confirmation of their entitlement to Bordeaux, Bayonne and Gascony, as vassals of the king of France, and peers of the realm in France. But considerable uncertainty remained over the central areas of France along the Dordogne, Lot and Garonne valleys: complicated arrangements were made but never fully executed.

The execution of the treaty of Paris was one problem; but during the years after 1259 two others became apparent. Any vassal had the right in French law to appeal from his lord to his overlord; therefore a Gascon lord dissatisfied with the English king's verdict could appeal to Paris. This right of appeal, or *ressort*, was intended as a check on the rapacity of ordinary barons; but it could also be, and was, used as a method of deliberately disturbing the orderly government of Gascony if particular royal edicts did not meet with approval. Further, there was an increasing tendency to distinguish between the king's person and the crown as an office of state; Gascony was held to belong to the English crown, which could not be a vassal in the way that the king in person might be. Hence there were good reasons why the English kings should seek a solution which would give them their French lands in full sovereignty, even at the expense of renouncing some of their out-lying claims. The French kings, on the other hand, were anxious to keep in check this powerful vassal, and to erode the English power wherever possible. None the less, the treaty of 1259 produced thirty-five years of peace until, in 1293-4, Philip the Fair saw an opportunity to attempt a confiscation of Gascony as a result of a dispute involving the sailors of the Cinque Ports, Gascony and Normandy. Edward I's ambassador, Edmund of Lancaster, was deceived into surrendering seizin of the duchy for forty days, on the assurance that the lands would be returned at the end of this period, and that the French king would be satisfied with this. At the end of forty days, Philip refused to return the duchy to Edward. Five years of war and four of truce led to another treaty in 1303: but again 'the states of Gascony had become involved in a network of juristic learning; the boundaries were not clearly fixed; old disputes had not been settled'. All that the peace really meant was that Edward was fully engaged by Scottish affairs, Philip by the aftermath of his defeat by the Flemish at Courtrai.[2]

Attempts to define the treaties and to extract the necessary homage from the English king dragged on for the next twenty years, until a minor border dispute developed into a more serious episode, the so-called war of Saint-Sardos. Once again the duchy was declared forfeit, and once again it was returned, showing that French policy did not envisage a permanent occupation, because at this moment the internal weakness of England would have made Gascony an easy prey. But as part of the settlement the young prince Edward did homage for the duchy. Isabella, who owed much to the support of her brother, Charles IV, pursued a pro-French policy during her three years' rule, and by so doing yet further complicated the issue, for in 1328 Charles IV died without an heir: his wife was pregnant, and the regency was placed in the hands of Philip of Valois until such time as the child was born. It proved to be a daughter.

For the first time in three centuries, there was no male heir to the French throne who was either brother or son to the previous king. This meant that the cousins and nephews of the last king were the claimants. Assuming that women could not inherit the throne in their own right, which seems to have been universally accepted, there were three possible candidates: Charles of Navarre, the young grandson of Louis X, eldest of the last three kings of France (grand-nephew); Edward III as son of the sister of the king (nephew); and Philip of Valois, son of Charles of Valois, the king's uncle (first cousin). In practical terms there was only one possible choice for the French themselves, and Philip was crowned as Philip VI on 29 May 1328. Both Charles and Edward were too young, and Edward, as a powerful ruler in his own right, was in any case unlikely to be welcome to the French barons. But the theoretical argument remained: could the inheritance of the French throne descend through a woman? There was no precedent, no clear ruling.

Isabella, though she regarded Philip as 'the foundling king', was not prepared to challenge the French ruler against the advice of the other magnates of England. Edward was sent with a magnificent entourage to Amiens to do homage in 1329. But the lawyers had not yet finished: the form of the homage was regarded as too vague, and in 1330 Edward was summoned to the French court to explain what was meant by his homage. Was it the loose, general form or the more specific liege homage, which implied a close link between lord and vassal? Liege homage also bound the vassal to do military service for his lands. Again, Edward III was not in a position to quarrel with Philip over a mere form of words, and an agreement was sealed in Paris on 30 March 1331, acknowledging that the duchy of Aquitaine was held by liege homage, and specifying the oath to be used:

> The king of England, the duke of Guienne, shall place his hands between the hands of the king of France, whose spokesman shall thus address the king of England: 'Sir, will you become the liegeman of the king of France, as duke of Guienne and a peer of France, and will you promise to bear faith and loyalty to him?' The king of England shall answer, 'I will'. And then the king of France shall receive the king of England to the said liege homage and fealty with the kiss of peace, saving his right.[3]

This concession was followed by a secret meeting between the two kings in April at Pont-Sainte-Maxence, at which the possibility of a marriage between Edward earl of Chester and Philip's daughter was mooted, and it was agreed that other problems, largely of boundary disputes, were to be settled by negotiation.

Yet, within four years, war was in the air, and by the end of the decade huge English and French armies, supported by complex alliances, faced each other in Flanders. What had happened in the intervening years?

There seem to have been three main reasons why peace could not be maintained. First, the maintenance of peace between two rivals whose interests were fundamentally opposed depended on one of the two being relatively weak. Edward III's growing success in Scotland, from the victory of Halidon Hill in 1333 onwards, meant that the French rallied to the support of the Scots, particularly after the arrival in France of David Bruce as an exile in 1334. This success stemmed in turn from a second change in the political mood in England: Isabella and Mortimer had advocated a pacifist approach, signing unfavourable treaties with France and Scotland, and this had been one of the main reasons for their unpopularity. Edward III was enabled to overthrow them by men whose aspirations were quite different, barons trained and ready for war. Whatever the outward diplomatic face that England presented to her neighbours, the transfer of power in the autumn of 1330 was from the peace party to the war party. We shall meet Edward III's fellow conspirators at Nottingham again, as his commanders in war. The third reason was that the problems in both Gascony and Scotland – and the two have to be considered together after Philip's declaration in 1334 that Scotland had to be included in any *Gascon* settlement – were too intractable to admit of a diplomatic solution, however much goodwill existed on either side. Royal or ducal power still depended on the acquiescence of a majority of the local lords: in Scotland, there was an underlying resentment of the English, in Gascony a reluctance to admit any authority at all, particularly in the border areas under dispute. It may be too much to say that peace could never have been fully established; but it certainly could not have been maintained. The growth of nationalist feeling further complicated English claims in France and Scotland. Although the rise of nationalism is by its very nature difficult to chart, there is undoubtedly nationalist feeling behind the verses which Jubinal addressed to Philip in 1338, despite their use of feudal terms:

> Make them see that Gascony is held from you, and make yourself acknowledged as lord of everything on this side of the sea: the sea shall be the border and dividing line between England and France.[4]

In another sense, Philip's unequivocal linking of French and Scottish affairs was the turning point. Philip was using Edward III's position as his vassal to interfere in Edward's own relations with the king of Scotland, who, according to Edward, owed homage to the English king. The exact pretext on which Philip ordered the confiscation of Gascony in 1337 was not, in fact, directly linked with Scotland, but with the reception by Edward III of Robert of Artois, banished from France as a 'capital enemy' of the French king. To shelter such an outlaw was, in the French view, a breach of Edward's duty as a vassal. On these grounds, on 24 May 1337, Philip ordered the seneschal of Périgord and the bailiff of Amiens to seize Aquitaine and Ponthieu respectively. The impossibility of Edward III's dual status as both sovereign and vassal was once more underlined. The same problem had arisen at the end of Edward I's reign, in 1295, when the Franco–Scottish alliance was first created, and Edward III seems to have consciously turned to the records of his grandfather's time to see how these problems had then been handled.[5]

Until the beginning of the fourteenth century, the French had had a virtual monopoly of skilled legal advice on the dispute with the English kings. But from the settlement of 1303 onwards, the English had begun to accumulate experience in such matters, much of it learnt in the various rounds of negotiations ('processes') and in the French *parlement* where appeals from Gascony were heard. An English official had been put in charge of these negotiations and lawsuits, with the title 'keeper of the process', and this office had been held by one man, Elias Joneston, from 1306 to 1336. So the English were equipped to produce a legalistic answer to the problem. If the liege homage of 1331 represents the *ne plus ultra* of the French lawyers' attempts to define the status of Aquitaine, the English counterblast was to come in 1337. The English lawyers and diplomats seem to have realized that the 1331 settlement left very little room for manoeuvre: in legal terms it was precise and valid, even if the 'duchy of Aquitaine' was an imprecise term. Whatever the exact extent of the lands of the duchy might be, the king of England was liegeman of the French king, subject to his jurisdiction. He could be treated as an unruly vassal whenever the English and French policy was in conflict, and the danger of confiscation, already invoked twice (1294 and 1323), would continue to be a real one.

The way out of the impasse in which the English found themselves was simple and dramatic. It was to call in question the French king's own title, and to advance Edward III's claim to the throne as nearest surviving relative of Charles IV. The homage paid in 1329 and 1331 was rejected as having been done under duress while the king was a minor. Edward III's exact intentions in making the claim have long been disputed, because some of his subsequent actions imply that he really meant to obtain the throne for himself. The most probable explanation is that in 1337–8 this claim was put forward as a diplomatic gambit and as propaganda, but that with the series of English victories which ensued, Edward began to believe his own title to be a good one: hence the attempt in 1359–60 to seize Rheims and have himself crowned.

In summary, then, there are three phases in the English attitude to French overlordship of Gascony: the first, from 1331 to 1334, is a genuine acceptance of the terms of 1331 and an attempt to make them work. The second, from 1334 to 1338, begins as a defensive effort to counter French moves in Scotland and ends as a diplomatic offensive leading to war. The third stage varies between a genuine, sporadic attempt to seize the French throne and the purely diplomatic use of Edward III's claim as a bargaining counter, depending on circumstances.

War actually broke out, despite intensive efforts by the Pope to prevent it, in the autumn of 1339. Edward III, after long and exceedingly expensive preparations, invaded the north-east of France, with the nominal support, purchased at great cost, of the German emperor and several magnates of the Low Countries, chiefly those with whom he was connected by marriage through the house of Hainault. He had been abroad since July 1338, leaving the young Edward as guardian of England, *custos Angliae*; all government acts were witnessed in the latter's name, and he was, in name only, the ruler of England during his father's absence. In effect this meant that he appeared at certain state occasions, and the royal court centred around him. His mother and sisters were also in Flanders, presumably because it was on Philippa's relations that much of Edward III's planning depended, and her presence was a reminder of their dynastic obligations.

For much of the period of his father's absence Edward stayed at the Tower, attended by the earls of Arundel and Huntingdon and Sir Ralph Neville; on 20 July, orders were made for its provisioning and for a garrison of twenty men-at-arms and fifty archers, while the defences were strengthened by a plank palisade. Fears of a French invasion had been growing since March, when Portsmouth was attacked, possibly with Spanish help; in October the city authorities in London were ordered to drive piles into the bed of the Thames to inhibit enemy ships. At the end of July, Edward presided over a parliament at Northampton, summoned to discuss defence measures; but French raiders none the less inflicted heavy damage on Southampton in October. The real function of the council was to supply the king's needs in Flanders, and the taxes they raised provoked considerable resentment.[6]

Messengers went constantly back and forth across the Channel; the documents they carried were mostly official (usually pleas for money from the king and desperate explanations from the council as to why it could not be obtained). One letter has survived from Edward to his mother, doubtless written for him by one of his clerks, but even so of interest. Writing on 21 October 1338 from Kennington, his manor south of the Thames, he says:

My dearest and most respected lady, I humbly commend myself to your highness with all the reverence I know, and ask for your blessing. My most respected lady, I am much comforted by the news that you are well and I pray to God that he will long protect you by his grace. And, my dearest lady, as to what you lately ordered me in your letters, that I should apply all possible care and speed to hasten the sending of the money and wool due to be sent to my lord the king outside his kingdom of England. May it please you to know, most honoured lady, that I and the council of my lord have put such efforts into carrying out your orders that the last wool is completely collected and will be sent to him as quickly as anyone can with all the money. But no other [financial] aid can be raised by any means, and I have written to him to tell him this in my other letters. My most respected lady, may the Holy Spirit have you in his keeping.

Edward's household for the winter of 1338, as reflected in the list of winter robes distributed by his wardrobe keeper, William of Hoo, was now part of the court: there are gifts to judges as well as to William St Omer and other established servants like John Bradeston and John Skirbek, John Gaddesden, his doctor, and Merlin the minstrel.[7]

The following year opened with a series of French raids along the coast, beginning at Harwich on 24 March; though attacks at Southampton and other south coast ports were resisted, at Plymouth the town was burnt before Hugh Courtenay, the elderly earl of Devonshire, was able to drive off the invaders, killing 500 of them. But this was far from being the greatest of the council's problems. If the queen had had to write personally to the young Edward in the previous year about money, the situation was far worse in 1339. The immense payments made to Continental princes as the price of their alliance were on the point of exhausting the English exchequer, despite the king's intervention in the wool trade as a means of raising funds: wool was bought at artificially low prices in England and shipped to Flanders, where it was used to pay debts already incurred, the creditors being the great Italian banking concern of the Bardi. Their representatives in England were on the list of recipients of winter robes from Prince Edward's wardrobe, so important had they become in the king's schemes; but in the end his debts brought about their collapse. Short of money, fearful that his allies would disband, the king embarked on an autumn campaign in September, and Philip moved to meet him, with little intention of engaging him. To cover his real purpose, Philip challenged the English to a pitched battle at

Buironfosse, but retreated before Edward could engage him, claiming that the English had failed to meet him as agreed.[8]

Edward wrote to the prince from Brussels on 1 November, trying to make some kind of tactical victory out of his failure to engage the French; but he knew that in reality his campaign had failed and that his alliances would not survive the winter without further lavish subsidies. Whether he could afford such subsidies depended on the outcome of a parliament which had begun on 13 October. He had sent archbishop Stratford, the newly appointed 'principal councillor to Edward, duke of Cornwall, keeper of the realm' and effective head of the administration in England, to this meeting to say that, without exaggeration, he needed £300,000 to settle his debts alone. The session was a stormy one, and it was only after two delays, first until January, and then until after the king's return, in March 1340, that a grant was obtained. But for the first time the grant of aid to the king was made conditional on reforms designed to control the massive increases in royal spending. A permanent committee was planned, to control the expenditure of the money granted by parliament; and it was to consist of magnates chosen by parliament. The actual composition of the committee, once it had been set up, was in fact hardly likely to trouble the king, archbishop Stratford being its central figure. But parliament had actually put the archbishop in an impossible position: he held office from the king primarily to ensure that the king's needs for money were met, while at the same time he was given responsibility by parliament to minimize the effect of war taxes. The result, not unexpectedly, was that Stratford was unable to provide the necessary money. The generous grants of the spring, estimated to yield £100,000, had realized only £15,000 by the autumn; and a grant of a loan of wool, made in the summer of 1340 in anticipation of the taxes (which, being paid in corn and wool, could only be collected from the summer onwards), proved uncollectable in twelve counties. One chronicler wrote that, because of the tax, 'the ynnere love of the peple was turned to hate, and the commune prayrs into cursinge, for cause that the commune peple were strongliche ygreved'. Meanwhile, the campaigns of 1339–40 had cost the astronomical sum of £386,546.[9]

All this was despite the king's personal intervention; he had returned from Flanders on 21 February, thus bringing Edward's first period as 'keeper of the realm' to an end. For most of 1339 Edward had been at Westminster or Windsor, or at his manors of

Berkhamsted and Kennington; the first had come to him as part of the duchy of Cornwall estates, while the second was granted 'for the increase of the duchy of Cornwall' on 4 September 1337. Two other grants, to become effective on queen Isabella's death (Castle Rising in Norfolk and Cheylesmore in Warwickshire) were made on 1 October; but his official expenses were too much for the revenues immediately available to him, and additional payments had to be made at intervals: £1,000 was needed by August 1340 merely to acquit the debts he had run up because of 'the great charges which it behoved the Keeper of the realm to support'. Other provisions were made for him as well, on less businesslike matters: when the forest laws, governing the preservation of game in the royal forests, were proclaimed to the sheriffs in July 1339, a rider was added that 'it is the king's intention that Edward duke of Cornwall shall hunt therein'.[10]

Edward III's return to England was only temporary. Affairs in Flanders urgently required his presence, and he had had to leave behind the queen, his other children and the earls of Derby and Salisbury as pledges for payment of his debts. He was eager to embark on a new campaign, despite all financial obstacles, because he had succeeded in negotiating a new alliance with the Flemish, under their leader Jacob van Artevelde. The count of Flanders, who favoured the French cause, had been forced to flee, and the townsmen who now governed the country were anxious to ensure that the English wool on which their weaving industry depended continued to be available to them. Lest they should be accused of betraying their overlord, the king of France, Edward III solemnly reiterated his title to the French throne, and had it proclaimed in the chief towns of Flanders, altering his great seal at the same time. The proclamation was also issued in England and Aquitaine, and copies sent to France, while his case was put before the Pope at Avignon. It was made clear, however, that there was room for negotiation; in August, and again in November, the English envoys suggested that the king would be willing to drop his claim in return for Aquitaine in full sovereignty, free of French overlordship. A rather less serious note was provided by the king's letter to the Venetian senate, in which he says that he has challenged Philip, who is occupying lands that are rightfully his, to fight a pitched battle; 'or that, if he be true king of France as asserted by him, he should stand the test of braving ravenous lions who in no wise harm a true king, or perform the miracle of touching for the evil; if unable, to be considered unworthy of the kingdom of France'. A more practical effort had resulted in an alliance with Brabant; and on 3 May, John duke of Lorraine and Brabant was promised 'the marriage of the king's son the duke of Cornwall for Margaret daughter of the said John', the dowry to be repaid twofold if the marriage did not take place.[11]

So, by Whitsun, the king was ready to return to the Continent and went to Ipswich; but intelligence reports from the Channel indicated that a huge French fleet was being gathered to prevent him. The French had been active in the Channel throughout the previous year, harrying English shipping, and elaborate plans had been laid for an invasion of England itself, for which an *ordonnance* had been issued by Philip VI on 23 March 1339. This was to repeat the Norman conquest of England: the French king's son, the duke of Normandy, was to lead a force of 4,000 men-at-arms, 20,000 footsoldiers and 5,000 crossbowmen from the province, and was to hold the conquered land in his own name. The *ordonnance* prudently specified that the same arrangements were to hold should it be necessary to postpone the invasion until the following year. The ships prepared for this invasion fleet were now redeployed under the admirals Nicolas Quiéret and Béhuchet to prevent the English king's crossing, and a contingent of galleys hired from Genoa under the Genoese admiral Barbanera joined them.

The king was intending to sail with a relatively small contingent of forty ships; but archbishop Stratford opposed his departure, ostensibly on the grounds of the possibility of his being captured by the French, but perhaps hoping to delay more war expenditure for a time. He was supported by the two commanders of the English fleet, Robert Morley and John Crabbe, who declared that it would be very dangerous. None the less, rather than stay at home while the king sailed alone, they would go with him, even if it meant that they would be killed. The king was at first furious; but confirmation of his advisers' fears came from the marquis of Juliers, and possibly also from messengers from Bruges and Ypres, and he collected a fleet, apparently in considerable haste.[12]

Edward was near his father from early June onwards, with his headquarters at Babewell Priory outside Bury St Edmunds. For once, we have detailed accounts which tell us a great deal about his activities and movements. At the end of April he was at Byfleet, playing at single-stick or gambling with his companions: he lost 12d. to John Chandos on 2 May, the first appearance of his most famous companion-in-arms. On 25 May, he was at Kennington, where he presented the marquis of Juliers, one of his father's chief allies in Flanders who had just been created earl of Cambridge (with an annual pension of £1,000), with a gilt and enamelled cup, bought from a London goldsmith, but (rather inappropriately) 'of Paris work', though this referred to the style rather than the place of manufacture. From Babewell, where he stayed on 6–7 June, he went to Bury St Edmunds to make an offering at the shrine of St Edmund and before various relics in the abbey church. The following week he was at Holbrook, overlooking the Stour estuary near its confluence with the Orwell, where his father's fleet was gathering. On 22 June, the fleet had gathered and the king was ready to leave. The prince was rowed out to the king's ship by some of the crew, presumably to say good-bye to his father, who sailed that day; and on 25 June he travelled back towards London, through Colchester, Chelmsford and Crowndon (near Writtle), tipping the park-keepers of the various landowners as he went. One of his messengers, John Dagenet, was left behind at Harwich until 27 June, 'to find out about the rumours about the king's crossing and about his enemies', hiring boats to get any news that was to be had. Another, Roger Pope, spent six days at Orford on a similar mission. Evidently there was considerable uncertainty, indeed considerable anxiety, about the king's safety.[13]

On 28 June, the prince was at Waltham Abbey, and it was here that he received news of his father's victory over the French fleet at Sluys on the 24th. He at once passed on the king's letter to the archbishop of Canterbury, in the form of an order for public thanksgiving for this great victory.

> God, by his miraculous power, gave us victory over our enemies, and we thank Him as devoutly as we can for it. And we tell you that the number of ships, galleys and great barges of our enemy amounted to 190, all of which were captured, except twenty-four in all which fled, and some were later captured at sea. And the number of men at arms and other armed men amounted to 35,000, out of whom 5,000 escaped; and the rest, as we are told by some whom we captured alive, are dead and their bodies are all along the Flemish coast. Besides this, all our ships, namely the *Christopher* and the others which were taken at Middelburgh, are now retaken, and we have won in this sea-battle three or four as large as the *Christopher*.[14]

The king's letter was really designed for publication in England, and while it hardly exaggerates the scale of the victory, it left out much of the detail. The French fleet had not been encountered at sea, as expected, but in the mouth of the Swijn.* A French chronicler says that when the English were sighted, Barbanera advised the French admiral to set sail at once in the hope of reaching the high seas before the English arrived; but Nicholas Béhuchet, 'who was better at drawing up a bill than making war at sea' (he had made his career as an administrator, not a warrior), replied scornfully, at which Barbanera took four of his galleys and set out to sea. Quiéret and Béhuchet seem also to have quarrelled between themselves over a question of rank. The king, whose scouts had sighted the French fleet the previous evening and had noted the presence of nineteen large ships, realized that he had the French at a disadvantage, and attacked at once, just after dawn, despite an offer from the men of Bruges to help him with a hundred ships and galleys. The technique of naval warfare was similar to that on land, and Edward was able to deploy his archers to good effect: a hail of arrows would be directed at the enemy ship about to be attacked, and this would be followed by grappling and an assault by men-at-arms, rather as though each ship was a miniature fortress to be stormed. Edward's fleet was about 120 ships, while the French fleet was about 200 ships. They had lowered their sails, and arranged themselves in four battle lines, linked by great chains to hinder the enemy's manoeuvres. At the masthead they had erected wooden crows'-nests, filled with crossbowmen, while small boats full of stones were hung half-way up the mast, to be cut loose on top of boarding parties. The English ships, wind and tide in their favour, attacked one by one: Robert Morley was followed by the earls of Huntingdon and Northampton and Sir Walter Mauny. Four 'great ships' from the royal squadron were placed in front of the French fleet, so that the brunt of the attack would fall on their experienced crews rather than on the local levies. A ship full of English squires who hoped to be knighted was taken and sunk by a Norman ship, Le Riche de Leure.[15]

A hard-fought and indecisive struggle now followed, watched by the local inhabitants from the shore, who had suffered from raids by the French sailors and favoured the English. Most of the fighting was hand to hand, and the contest continued until well into the

* This is now an insignificant canal; the river was silted up in succeeding centuries and its estuary reclaimed.

afternoon. Edward III was in the thick of it, and is said to have been wounded in the thigh by the French admiral Béhuchet, while other individual deeds of prowess were recorded on both sides. But by the afternoon the four great French ships were in English hands, and Edward had brought up a reserve of fifty fresh ships. They came down on the French fleet under full sail, with the tide in their favour; and as the exhausted French crews tried to repulse this new attack, the Flemish blocked off the other mouths of the Swijn which might have allowed them to escape, so that they were trapped. The French were now caught inside the estuary, and the remaining lines of battle were overwhelmed. A few galleys and one or two royal ships escaped, possibly thirty in all; and by nightfall the English king was sure of victory.[16]

The losses on both sides were enormous; as usual the chroniclers' figures are not to be trusted, but the French force was said to be 20,000 strong and not many more than 5,000 escaped. The English, whose archers did much damage but suffered few casualties, also had more experienced fighting men than those who made up the French crews: their losses seem to have been proportionately lower than those of the French, but the ship containing the king's wardrobe was taken, and twelve ladies of queen Philippa's retinue killed. In terms of prestige, however, the victory was an overwhelming triumph for the English. It was their first major feat of arms on the Continent for longer than anyone could remember, and the French courtiers hardly dared tell the French king. In the end, it was said that the royal fool had to break the news, by jesting about the English reluctance to jump overboard as the Normans had done at the battle.[17]

The victory was more important in psychological than in tactical terms. It showed that the much smaller resources of the English were not necessarily a handicap: the well-organized French fleet was lost by bad generalship in the face of the combination of the king's boldness and the superiority of the English archers over the Genoese crossbowmen. Froissart is more than usually unreliable about the details of the battle, but he does bring out one important feature: the way in which the attack was led by the group of knights of the king's own age who commanded the English fleet. The English 'high command' throughout this period was a coherent group of men who worked well together: the French commanders all too often quarrelled, and lacked the same unity of purpose – whether chivalric, as Froissart would have it, or merely strategic.

In this case, a Genoese mercenary, an admiralty official and a relatively humble knight could hardly be a match for the English lords. The English contempt for the French commanders, whom they regarded as mere pirates, is underlined by Edward's action in hanging Béhuchet after the battle, reputedly because Béhuchet struck Edward after he was captured. The blow is more likely to have been a metaphorical one, namely the raids carried out by Béhuchet in 1338-9, especially that on Portsmouth: but the ignominious death of an enemy captain in this way is a far cry from the mutual respect shown in other Anglo-French battles.[18]

Edward III's campaigning by land met with rather less success that summer, for the same reasons as before: lack of money and resources. The prince, as keeper of England, remained near London throughout the summer: on 29 July he was at the Tower; the following day he went to Kennington. Letters from his father reached him at Oseney in early August, and he then went to Eynsham, Wallingford and Reading. His accounts note gifts to messengers bringing such things as three dozen arrows, a grey palfrey and a number of white hares – six or more from three different sources in early September, presumably as pets. For amusement, there was John the fool of Eltham – an idiot rather than a wit, for he reappears five years later with his 'master', but just as entertaining to the unpitying medieval eye – and there was a minstrel who played a small organ. On 1 September, Edward was at Salisbury and offered a mark at the shrine of the Virgin in the Cathedral. In the same month he went to Berkeley, to visit Thomas, Lord Berkeley, who presented him with six hounds. On the way back, a boy had to be paid to guide the prince's party as it left Berkeley – a vivid reminder of the difficulties of medieval travel, when there were no made-up roads. He spent some time at Andover during September, returning to London in mid October. October and November were spent at Wallingford and Reading; Berkhamsted, where he spent August and which was later to be his chief country residence, was now being repaired, as an entry for the purchase of £90 worth of timber in October shows.[19]

By this time, the king's financial position had become acute. By the end of the campaigning season little had been accomplished; a truce had been signed at Esplechin in September, but his fragile web of alliances could no longer stand the strains imposed by his inability to meet his financial promises. For this lack of funds, he blamed his ministers in England; and in November, urged on by his captains in Flanders, he decided to return without warning. He landed at the Tower of London, unannounced, on the night of 30 November, and proceeded to remove almost all the major officials who had formed Edward's council as guardian of the realm. That Edward had been no more than a figurehead becomes clear when his name is not even mentioned in the elaborate defence put up by archbishop Stratford against the king's charges of mal-administration amounting to treachery. But it is none the less ironic, in the wake of this great financial crisis, that we should find the ten-year-old Edward playing at dice with the queen at Shene at some time in January, and losing the enormous sum of 37s., as opposed to his more usual 12d. per session. Gambling, and a general carelessness about expenditure, were to be a hallmark of the prince's character. Not for him the cautious ways of a magnate like the earl of Arundel, who at his death in 1376 left £60,000 in cash and very few debts: indeed, he borrowed large sums from Arundel on several occasions. He was also beginning to buy jewels and expensive equipment for himself: such payments include a silver-gilt cup for 113s. 4d. in October, and 21s. for a saddle for his war-horse decorated with the arms of Nicholas de la Beche and those of his two-year-old brother, Lionel. One of his favourite pastimes appears on 5 December, when the falconers of Nicholas Cantilupe (who had just returned from Flanders) received gifts for flying their hawks in his presence. John Chandos reappears among Edward's entourage early in November: it is not clear whether he had been with Edward all summer, or whether, as Froissart claims, he had fought at Sluys and returned before the king. Knightly exercises, with companions such as Chandos, took up an increasing part of the young Edward's time: a long case was bought for his bow, and a short case for his arrows, as well as a case for one of his helmets.[20]

Meanwhile his father was gradually resolving the most serious domestic crisis for ten years: archbishop Stratford had become leader of the group who opposed new taxes to pay for the Flemish wars, and had defended himself skilfully against the king's attacks. He had succeeded in getting the king to summon a parliament in April 1341, and with the help of a group of peers who disliked the new councillors the king had chosen, he succeeded in obtaining a reconciliation with him. He had protested throughout that he desired nothing more than the king's good will; and within two years he was once more the monarch's most trusted councillor. The parliament of April–May 1341 repeated the provision of the

previous year, that a committee should be appointed to control the
spending of money raised by taxation; but the king unilaterally
repealed this in October, as something that he had agreed to under
duress. He had succeeded sufficiently in re-establishing the rapport
between himself and the magnates for there to be no protest over
the repeal: and this rapport was to endure until the closing years of
his reign. Only the commons, to whom the spoils of war were less
accessible and less attractive, continued to strive for controls on
taxation and expenditure, but alternate royal propaganda announce-
ments of national triumph and national emergency were sufficient
to keep their demands in check.[21]

Of the next four years of Prince Edward's life we know relatively
little. His period as keeper had left him deep in debt: in April 1341
he was given a licence to export wool, normally a royal monopoly,
'in aid of paying certain great sums in which he is bound to certain
persons'. Part of his problem was that even when revenue was due,
it was difficult to collect: the royal records have a number of
entries noting that Edward's stewards in different counties owed the
prince sums varying from £40 to £1,000, these being arrears of
revenue which were treated as a personal debt. Sometimes the note
of such a debt was little more than a formality: but some payments
were never realized or took as long as six years to collect. To assist
with future expenses, an additional group of manors in Northamp-
tonshire, Dorset and Devon were granted to him in July 1342, but
later that year, on 4 November, justices had to be sent to Cornwall
to enforce the duke's rights of shipwreck and tin-mining, and even
to protect his deer parks, all of which had caused a loss of over
£1,000 in revenue. On the other hand, this was nothing unusual
in royal finances, and the sums involved were minute compared to
his father's huge accumulation of debts in the early years of the war
with France.[22]

A very few details of Edward's life and household can be gleaned
from a fragment of his accounts for the period 1344-5. Apart from
the usual details of the administration of his estates (including a
payment of 55s. 4d. for fetching £232 in cash under guard from
Wales), there are notes of substantial payments for buying horses
abroad: Peter Gildesburgh went to Brabant to buy thirty-two
horses in all, chiefly destriers and coursers. Ordinary nags were
bought from Ireland, and a little horse called Wilifrid was bought
by William St Omer for the prince's own use. If the prince was
not yet old enough for tournaments and crusades, his household

knights were: Sir Robert Bradeston set off for the Holy Land in the hope of crusading there, while he and Sir John Chandos were given money to arm themselves for a tournament at Winchester which the prince seems to have attended. His household was now a large organization, ranging from Bartholomew Burghersh the elder, its master, down through such lesser officers as the household steward, Thomas Peytevin, and the master of the prince's barge, to the trumpeter, nightwatchman, and the valets and scullery-boys – in all about 120 men.[23]

The king's next military venture was to Brittany, where a dispute over the inheritance of the duchy offered an opportunity for military intervention. The two claimants were John de Montfort, supported by the English, and Charles de Blois, supported by Philip. Although John was captured in the autumn of 1341, his wife Joan continued to fight on his behalf. The king mounted an expedition to help her, which was ready in October 1342. Edward was appointed keeper of the realm on 5 October; after a council meeting at Westminster on the 16th, at which Edward was present, the king set sail on the 23rd. The expedition was successful in capturing much of the duchy, and laid siege to the town of Vannes; on 5 December the king wrote a long report to Edward (telling him to show the letter to the archbishop of Canterbury and his council) describing the campaign, listing the towns taken and the lords who had changed to his side, and adding the usual plea for money to be sent. He also mentioned that two cardinals were coming to see him: 'yet, though it is right that the cardinals should be allowed to come to see us, we have no intention of giving up our aim or accepting delays; for we can remember other occasions when they have held us up with their negotiations'. However, with the appearance of a large French army early in January, the king's firmness of purpose abated somewhat, and the campaign ended with the truce of Malestroit on 19 January; on 2 March the king was back in England, after a very rough voyage in which one of his ships was lost.[24]

Edward's period of guardianship had been uneventful; a council, at which he was present, had been held on 14 December at Westminster, but he had spent Christmas and the early months of 1343 at Kennington, Berkhamsted and Byfleet. This was his last appointment as guardian of the realm. In future he was to accompany his father on his expeditions overseas, because he was now regarded as being of sufficient age. He was also now old enough, at twelve, to be granted the title of prince of Wales, which had been created for his grandfather, but which his father had never held. At a parliament at Westminster which began on 28 April, he was formally invested with the principality: a coronet was placed on his head, a ring put on his finger, and he was given a silver rod 'according to the custom'. With the title he was also granted the royal lordships in Wales, which consisted of the lands conquered in royal expeditions in the previous century and those which had fallen to the crown under feudal procedures. The rest of Wales was either in the hands of native lords or had been won by conquest on their own account by the marcher lords, and the result was a varying degree of administrative control. Coupled with the grant were two commissions to one of the king's clerks, William Emeldon. The first empowered him to effect the transfer of lands; the second to survey the state of defence of the territory. The transfer of lands was carried out during August; unlike Chester, where a new survey had to be commissioned a year after the transfer to the prince, there was little problem of definition of territorial rights, though the charter itself was not very precise over other rights, which led to later disputes between the prince and the king. Wales was never to be as important territorially to the prince as Cornwall and Chester, and he never visited the principality. What it did provide was a valuable recruiting-ground for his armies. The expansion in the prince's territories meant that his administrative staff had to be expanded; and in the following year Peter Gildesburgh, who had entered the prince's service in 1342 from the royal exchequer, became 'keeper of the prince's exchequer and receiver-general' – in other words, head of a central accounting department. Another important change in the prince's household had been the departure in 1343 of Nicholas de la Beche, to become seneschal of Aquitaine.[25]

Meanwhile the king was making provision for the possibility of a renewal of the war in France: though the truce of Esplechin was to last until Michaelmas 1346, the diplomatic position was complicated by the collapse of all his alliances, except those with Flanders and Brittany. While peace talks were in progress at Avignon, William Trussell and William Stury were sent to try to negotiate a treaty with Castile, whose king controlled a powerful naval force, probably the best in Europe.

A Franco-Castilian alliance had been sealed in 1336, and in 1338 Castilian ships had aided the French marauders in the Channel. But Philip had failed to pay them, and aid had ceased the following year. The presence of the earl of Derby and an English contingent at Alfonso XI's triumphant siege of Algeciras that year helped the English cause, but no treaty was signed. Instead, the following year, a new treaty with France was agreed, thanks to pressure from the Pope; but Alfonso then seems to have changed his mind and sought an English alliance instead. The seeds of English involvement in Spain had been sown, but little of positive value for the war with France had emerged.[26]

At home, the king took his ease; the series of tournaments which had been held at intervals since 1331 were continued. They had been held even in the critical months of 1340–41; there was a tournament at Reading after Christmas, early in 1341, and another on 2 February at Langley in honour of a group of Gascon nobles whom the king had just knighted. The following year there was one on 11 February at Dunstable in which 230 knights took part, and in which the king fought 'like a simple knight': the younger generation of great magnates all took part – Derby, Warwick, Northampton, Pembroke, Oxford, Suffolk. However, it was not a complete success, because the start was delayed, with the result that 'night came on and prevented almost all the sport'; and ten horses were lost or stolen. On 14 April another tournament at Northampton ended with one knight, John de Beaumont, killed, many nobles badly hurt and many horses lost. At a tournament at Eltham on about 9 May, in honour of the count of Hainault, the prince's uncle, the count was wounded in the arm. But this catalogue of disasters comes from the pen of a royal clerk who regarded tournaments as a frivolous diversion from more weighty political and spiritual matters; the young prince, who probably attended all of them, would have taken a very different view. In 1343, after his return, the king went on pilgrimage, on foot to Canterbury and to Gloucester and Walsingham on horseback with a small retinue, and then dispatched affairs of state in the parliament beginning on 28 April. After this he turned again to tournaments: at Smithfield soon after midsummer he and his knights took the field dressed as the Pope and twelve cardinals, challenging all-comers; the earl of Warwick particularly distinguished himself. This was followed by other tournaments, at Canterbury, Hereford and elsewhere, and hunting parties which continued until Michaelmas. The culmination of this series of festivals was the one, announced well in advance both in England and abroad, which was held at Windsor on 19 January 1344. In addition to knights, all the ladies from the south of England and wives of the citizens of London were invited. Elaborate preparations had been made, including the provision of special robes – a long and a short robe of furred red velvet for the king, 16 tunics for his minstrels, 202 tunics for his squires and servants at arms. The proceedings began with a great banquet for the ladies in the castle hall, the guests of honour (and the only men present) being two French knights, the only ones to appear from across the Channel. Among the guests were two queens (Philippa and Isabella) and nine countesses. Meanwhile, the prince of Wales, earls, barons and knights ate in tents. In the evening there was dancing, and the tournament opened on the following day. The king and nineteen other knights fought against all-comers for three days. The king himself was generally acclaimed as the hero of the tournament, 'not out of flattery, but because of his hard work and good luck'. Three different knights led the challengers on the different days: Miles Stapleton on the first day, Philip Despenser on the second, John Blount on the third. When the jousts had ended, the king ordered that no one was to leave, but all were to remain for the following day. Early the following morning the king, dressed in his royal robes, with the velvet surcoat already mentioned and wearing his crown, accompanied by the queen, similarly attired, went to the castle chapel and heard mass in the presence of all the lords. After mass, preceded by the seneschal of England, the earl of Derby, and the marshal, the earl of Salisbury, the king went in procession to the appointed gathering-place. Here he swore on the gospels that he would found a Round Table 'of the same kind and status as that laid down by lord Arthur once king of England, that is to the number of three hundred knights . . .'. The earls of Derby, Salisbury, Warwick, Arundel and Pembroke swore a similar oath. Then, to the sound of drums and trumpets, everyone retired to a great feast; and the following day the company dispersed. The king 'fixed the day for holding the said Round Table as Whitsun* the following year . . .' He later ordered that a handsome building should be built there, in which the Round Table could be held at the appointed date. He appointed masons and carpenters and other workmen, and ordered wood and stone to be provided regardless of labour and expense. This Round Table was an association of a kind already familiar. The earliest example known dates

---

* Whitsun was the date of the great assemblies of Arthur's court at the Round Table in the romances; the king's ideas have a clear basis in Arthurian stories.

from as early as 1235, and consisted of a temporary fellowship, bound by an oath for the duration of the tournament of mutual friendship and the observation of certain safety rules such as the use of blunted weapons. Edward III seems to have had something more durable in mind, but exactly what his plans were we do not know: other events intervened before the meeting planned for 1345 could take place. Even the building operations, which cost £100 a week and which were regarded as urgent in the autumn of that year, came to an end 'for certain reasons' some time in 1345. Surviving accounts of the work imply a building somewhat like an Elizabethan theatre, with two concentric walls enclosing an open central space. The king, and probably the prince, spent All Saints at Long Melford and Christmas at Norwich.[27]

The Avignon peace talks of 1344 had ended in failure: the English envoys had continued to press the king's claim to the French throne, probably as a bargaining point against an equally intransigent French team, but a scheme was also suggested whereby prince Edward should hold Aquitaine in his own right directly from the French king. This was unpalatable to the Gascons, because separation from the English crown would leave them more open to the overlordship of France. Early in 1345, the king, who had at first agreed to make a further attempt to negotiate a peace, decided that Aquitaine could only be regained by force of arms. The weakness of the English position, which had deteriorated steadily since 1337, was underlined in 1344 by the appointment of Philip's eldest son John as duke of Guyenne; John was able to take homage from many of the lords in the north and east of Aquitaine in the spring of that year. The king, however, had already made counter-plans: he sent the earl of Derby and the earl of Arundel as his lieutenants to Aquitaine at about the same time as John appeared in the duchy, and in August the next year the earl of Derby returned with a substantial army as sole lieutenant, with instructions to begin military operations.

This, however, was only part of the king's plans: an army also went to Brittany under the command of the earl of Northampton, and the king and the prince set out for Flanders, intending to reopen hostilities on the Flemish front. The prince was accompanied by members of his household, including William St Omer, Edmund Wauncy, Richard de la Bere and Roland Daneys, as well as his master cook, Richard Raven. They left Sandwich harbour during the afternoon of 3 July and made for Sluys, where they met van

Artevelde, the Flemish leader, to discuss the forthcoming campaign. The French believed that more sinister plots were afoot and that the king was trying to get the Flemish to agree to accept the prince as count of Flanders in place of their pro-French lord who had taken refuge at Paris. However, these rumours were untrue: there were indeed discussions about the lordship of Flanders, but these ended in the preparation of a document on 19 July declaring that Edward III, as king of France and overlord of Flanders, would receive the count graciously, despite his hostile behaviour in the past, if he came to do homage. Any other plans which may have been prepared were nullified by the assassination of van Artevelde on 24 July, following riots at Ghent. His murder was not directly inspired by particular political events, though he had become increasingly unpopular over his policy of alliance with England: it was rather the settlement of a personal vendetta by one of his followers whom he had dismissed. The political effects were even so very considerable: Flanders was no longer a secure base, though the Anglo-Flemish alliance survived Artevelde's death because of the reliance of the Flemish cloth-manufacturing towns on English wool. The nobility were generally pro-French, and looked to the count as their leader.[28]

The king and the prince returned at once to England when news of van Artevelde's death reached them, having been away just over three weeks. On his return, the king wrote to the sheriffs throughout England, assuring them that matters in Flanders had been settled in such a way that the alliance had never been stronger, and explaining his hasty return by a sudden storm which had blown his fleet back to England just as he was on his way to attack France. The letter continued by outlining plans for a major expedition to aid the royal armies in Brittany and Gascony, to set out as soon as possible. What exactly the king's plans were at this juncture is difficult to discover: commissions of array for Welsh troops were put in hand on 29 September, to be at Portsmouth in three weeks' time, so there may have been ideas of an autumn campaign, or at least of sending reinforcements to the two armies already active in France. The first summons for ships was on 1 January 1346: the fleet was to assemble at Portsmouth by 16 February. Postponements moved the date back to early March, then mid-Lent; 'fearful storms' dispersed English coastal shipping, and the date went back yet again to 30 April because the fleet could not now be gathered before that date. In the meanwhile, the king and his knights amused themselves with a tournament at Lichfield, on 9 April. The king and eleven knights of his chamber took part, perhaps as defenders against challengers led by Henry earl of Derby, who had just succeeded his father as earl of Lancaster.[29]

The military preparations were accompanied by suitable propaganda releases: the clergy were to institute processions and prayers for the king, and on 15 March, the provincial of the Friars Preachers and the prior of St Augustine's, London (Greyfriars), were instructed to expound the king's claim to the crown of France to the people at large. Rumours of a rift between the king and his nobles were to be suppressed at all costs. On the diplomatic front, efforts to secure alliances in Castile and Portugal continued, a marriage between Edward and Leonor, daughter of the Portuguese king, being sought. Defence measures were taken at Southampton and along the coast, in case the king's absence should invite French raids. The prince took precautions of a different kind as well: on 26 June, he was given leave to make his will. It is possible that the large quantity of jewels bought on 24 June were intended for use as bequests: in the event, they were used as New Year gifts the next year. About this time, he also went on pilgrimage to the shrine of our Lady at Walsingham, going by way of the abbey at Bury St Edmunds, and to Canterbury with the king on the way to Portsmouth. They went down the Thames by boat, playing dice to while away the time.[30]

The Crécy Campaign

◆━━━━━◆

3

The force that finally assembled at Portsmouth during May and June was an impressive one, particularly as two English armies were already in the field and Flemish troops from Ghent, Ypres and Bruges under English leadership were also expected to mount an attack. Edward's strategy is impossible to determine: the fleet sailed under conditions of strict secrecy, and various rumours later circulated as to the king's original intentions. A letter written by Bartholomew Burghersh on about 15 July, after the landing in France, supports Froissart's story that the destination of the fleet was changed because of adverse winds:

> When the king had arrayed and victualled all the ships for a fortnight, intending to go to Gascony, and had set out that way, intending to pass the Needles at the end of the Isle of Wight, and thus hold a direct course towards the haven, the wind was so adverse that he was quite unable to hold this course, though he waited for a long while, to see if God would give him fair weather for the crossing; and since it did not please God for him to go in that direction, he turned and landed wherever God would favour him, and arrived in good health and condition with all the fleet in the country called the Cotentin of Normandy.

There were indeed delays, but of a rather different nature. Edward himself left Portsmouth on 3 July, and anchored off Yarmouth on the Isle of Wight: any debate about the destination of the fleet, which may well have been intended for Gascony when it was originally summoned, had been settled by this time. On 5 July, the army commanders sailed down together to Yarmouth, the wind being between easterly and southerly. Here they waited for more ships to join them, 'until they stretched as far as the mouth of the haven of the island, called the Needles'. On the 8th, however, the wind veered south-west, making this anchorage unsafe, and the king ordered the fleet back to Portsmouth. Here the south-westerly wind prevented them from getting to sea on the 9th and 10th, though attempts were made each day. On the 11th, the wind had evidently slackened or veered to the west, and the fleet assembled at sea off St Helens. Led by the king, who had issued sealed orders to the captains which were only to be opened if the fleet separated, the thousand or so ships of varying sizes set out towards the coast of Normandy. With favourable winds and tides, the crossing took under a day; by early the next morning the fleet was anchored off Saint-Marcon in the port of Saint-Vaast-la-Hogue.[1]

Edward's arrival was far from unexpected: the French had been making preparations against such an attack since 18 March. But there was too much uncertainty about Edward's intentions to allow for effective counter-measures. A general state of alert was declared throughout Normandy and Picardy; but the active defence of such a long coastline was impossible. Furthermore, a fleet of Genoese galleys which had been engaged in January only arrived in mid August. The king was therefore able to land unopposed. He found fourteen ships equipped for an attack on England, eight heavily armed, which were burnt, and learned that a small force of Genoese mercenaries had just left the area because they had not been paid.[2]

The army which had been brought across the Channel was a formidable one. As always with medieval armies, its exact size, even discounting the wilder guesses of the chroniclers, is difficult to determine. The best estimates are that just under 10,000 men landed at Saint-Vaast-la-Hogue, and that the number diminished to about 7,000 by the time the campaign ended at Calais the following year. The king and his company disembarked at midday, and climbed a near-by hill to survey the scene. Here, to mark the beginning of the prince's first active service, he and a number of other young noblemen were knighted. Among those were William Montacute, earl of Salisbury, aged eighteen, who had succeeded his father two years earlier; Roger Mortimer, grandson of the infamous earl, who may have been a schoolfellow of the prince and was gradually regaining the family estates; William Ros, a young baron from the Scottish border: Roger de la Warre, heir to the de la Warre barony; and Richard de la Bere, a member of the prince's household who had accompanied him to Flanders in 1345 and later became his chamberlain. As was customary on such occasions, the newly knighted prince at once exercised his right to make other knights.[3]

The town had already been deserted by the inhabitants, and was now sacked and burnt, with little resistance from the few French soldiers in the area. Meanwhile the king found a higher vantage point from which to examine the countryside and plan his strategy; this done, the royal party chose a small village two miles from the port for their lodgings. On the way, the earl of Warwick was ambushed by French troops, but fought his way out. This was the last action by the enemy for some days, because although Robert Bertrand, marshal of France, had raised the local nobles and militia, he prudently withdrew when he realized that he had to face an army led by the king himself. Some attempt was made to block the channel in the port with stakes.[4]

Disembarking such a large force was a slow process. In the interval, raiding parties began to fan out over the countryside and 'boldly set fire to the countryside around, until the sky itself glowed with a fiery colour'. The king was quick to issue strict orders to check excesses by his troops. No towns or manors were to be burnt, no churches or holy places sacked, and the old, women and children were to be spared, on pain of life or limb. Anyone who caught a soldier red-handed and brought him to the king was offered 40s. reward. However, this had relatively little effect on the events of the campaign which followed: in some cases towns put up a show of resistance and were therefore fair game, but all too often it was impossible to restrain troops whose main object was to pillage.[5]

On the 13th, the king was near Barfleur, a town 'as good and large as Sandwich', a few miles from Saint-Vaast; the following day, a raiding party under the earl of Warwick and Lord Stafford took some of the English ships and attacked the town from seawards. They found it partly deserted and pillaged it, took a number of prisoners and then, in defiance of the king's edict, set fire to it. Nine warships, heavily armed, with 'castles' fore and aft, were burnt in the harbour. The booty was reputed to be such that only gold, silver and jewels were taken, furs and fine robes being spurned. Further raids took place on the next three days, before the army was properly organized, and the king had to order the earl of Northampton and the earl of Warwick, as constable and marshal respectively, to enforce discipline; it may have been at this point that the edict about pillage was issued. By the 18th, the disembarkation had been completed, the horses rested after the crossing and supplies organized; in particular, bread for the next few days had been baked. The king was now ready to set out, and the army was put into marching order.[6]

Two main problems confronted the king and his commanders: few, if any, of them knew the area; and the army was too large to march in a single body, since it would have to live off the land to a large extent, and forage would be needed for horses. The first problem was partly solved by the presence of Sir Godfrey d'Harcourt in the English army, a Norman knight whose independent, not to say treacherous, ways had earned him a sentence of banishment from France in 1344. He was lord of Saint-Sauveur, at the base of the Cotentin peninsula, and was therefore familiar with the territory: Froissart claims that it was his advice that had led to the diversion of the fleet to Normandy, and portrays him as leading the army's scouts. The second problem was solved by dividing the army into three columns. The vanguard, nominally under the prince but actually commanded by Northampton and Warwick, contained Bartholomew Burghersh the elder, John Mohun, Burghersh's son-in-law, Robert Bourchier, the former chancellor, Sir Thomas Ughtred, a commander with long experience in Scotland and Flanders, John lord Fitzwalter, Sir William Kirdeston, William St Amand, and Sir Roger Say. Sir Richard de la Bere and Sir Richard Stafford, later the prince's chamberlain and steward respectively, were also in this group. The central column was commanded by the king, the rearguard by the bishop of Durham.[7]

On 18 July the army left Saint-Vaast-la-Hogue. A march through thick woods and along narrow lanes brought them to Valognes that night. Here the inhabitants came out to meet the king, and pleaded for mercy; the king granted this, and ordered his edict about burning and attacks on civilians to be repeated. He lodged that night in a house belonging to the duke of Normandy, while the prince occupied the bishop of Coutances's house. The following day, despite the king's orders, some of the less disciplined troops set fire to villages along the road, including the near-by town of Montebourg. Some of the army stopped at Saint-Côme-du-Mont, some

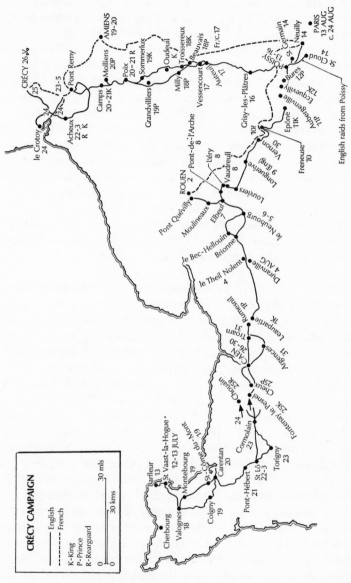

Map 1. The Crécy campaign

at Coigny, about five miles away. Here news came that the bridge over the river Douve, which separated them from Carentan, the town towards which they were making, had been broken. Scouts were unable to find a ford as the land was marshy, and there was only a narrow causeway across the marshes. So a team of carpenters was set to work to repair the bridge overnight; this was achieved, and the army crossed to Carentan the next day. Michael Northburgh, one of the king's council, described the town as being as large as Leicester, and well stocked with food and wine. Much of this was wasted by the footsoldiers, who also flouted the king's orders again and set fire to the town. The waste of food was serious, because there was no certainty that enough food for the army would be available at each halt; and the king now ordered that this should be an offence punished in the same way as unlicensed arson and pillage. The garrison of the castle, according to the French chroniclers, sold the castle to the English; they were left in charge of the town when the English left, but were captured by French troops soon afterwards and taken to Paris to be beheaded as traitors.[8]

The next day's march took them across the marsh by a causeway and bridges; the nature of the terrain meant that they had to make a long day's march on the 21st to Pont-Hébert before they could halt. Here the bridge across the river Vire had been broken by the men of the near-by town of Saint-Lô, but a party from the prince's division repaired it that evening. Rumours of the presence in the neighbourhood of enemy troops under Robert Bertrand, marshal of France, meant that precautions had to be taken. The vanguard was not allowed to cross until daylight and at once took up battle positions on a near-by hill in case of attack. As was customary before a battle, squires were knighted: on this occasion, Henry Burghersh was dubbed a knight by the prince. However, Bertrand and his men, who had intended to hold Saint-Lô against the English, thought better of it, and left on the night of the 21st: the town was taken without resistance. Again, plenty of food was found in the town, as well as over a thousand barrels of wine. The Belgian chronicler, Jean Le Bel, describes the sacking of the town in very similar terms to that of Barfleur; in fact his account is a kind of set-piece, the literary equivalent of the formal miniatures of warfare which embellished manuscripts:

No man alive can imagine – or believe, if he were told – the riches which were plundered and gained there, nor the vast quantities of cloth found there; it was a good market for whoever wanted to buy it, anyone could take it from wherever he wanted, but few did so, because they were more anxious to get gold and silver, of which there was enough to be found. And they were so intent on this that the town was not burnt. Many of the rich citizens were taken prisoner and sent to England to be ransomed; many of the humbler people were killed when the English first entered the town, and several pretty women of the town and their daughters raped, which was a great pity.

The king was still very much on the alert for enemy troops: at dawn on the 23rd orders were given that the army should march to the great Cistercian abbey at Torigny, and an advance party set out. Rumours of enemy activity near Torigny caused a change of plan, however, and that day's march ended at Cormolain. The advance party, sent to arrange quarters at Torigny and to reserve houses for the nobles, was left to catch up with the king as best it could: as they left Torigny they set fire to the town, and Cormolain was also burnt as the army departed. The next two nights were spent in small villages in the countryside after fairly short marches, and the army seems to have spread out: the rearguard halted on the 25th only just beyond the place where the vanguard had spent the previous night. The king was evidently proceeding cautiously and trying to obtain definite news of the enemy. By the evening of the 24th he had discovered that a large enemy force had assembled at Caen, the largest town in western Normandy. The following day, having made plans to attack the town, he encamped at Fontenay-Pesnel, while the prince was at Cheux, two miles to the west, and the rearguard at Maupertuis. The plan seems to have been to attack the town in separate columns.[9]

Caen was a substantial town: Michael Northburgh thought it larger than any town in England except London. But its site, in the level river plain of the Orne, had little natural defence except in the shallow tidal river itself. There were artificial defences: a wooden wall and ditch to landward, a stone wall on the side where marshes came up to the edge of the town, and more substantial fortifications around the castle on the northern edge. The defending forces were commanded by Raoul d'Eu, constable of France as well as the lord of Tancarville: they had under their command a body of Genoese archers, probably those who had retreated from the coast just before the English landing, a number of knights and men at arms from Normandy, and the local militia. The total was probably about 4,000, of whom not more than 800 were knights or men-at-arms; a quarter of the latter were detailed to garrison the castle.[10]

The English forces were therefore greatly superior in numbers, and the only advantage the defenders had was the strength of the castle. Yet the French commanders took a defiant line from the beginning. On the 25th the king sent an envoy, Geoffrey of Maldon, an Augustinian friar, with letters urging them to surrender in return for immunity for their goods and persons. Such a messenger, according to the customs of war, should have been immune from arrest; but the French seized him and threw him in chains into the castle dungeon.

At dawn on the 26th the prince's men signalled their departure by setting fire to their lodgings. They and the king's column approached the town, apparently from separate directions, the prince from the north-east, the king from the west. The prince's column, evidently the smaller of the two, was made to seem more impressive by including the cartkeepers and other camp followers in the rear. The rearguard remained outside the town, at good vantage points. The prince himself was officially in command of his men, though he evidently acted on Warwick and Northampton's advice.

The outskirts of the town were occupied without encountering any opposition, and the prince established his headquarters at the Abbaye aux Dames. The king found a suitable manor house in the suburbs, while the rearguard pitched tents. All this took place in the early hours of the morning, and by 8 a.m. the army had been given lodgings and everyone had been fed. Meanwhile the townspeople had withdrawn to the island of Saint-Jean; the bridge linking the island and the castle guarded by thirty ships and a number of men at arms; and barriers put up. The English attacked in disorderly fashion and without much plan of action; but after a first skirmish the two earls, who were in the thick of the fighting, realized that a direct assault was useless. They therefore sent a party of Welshmen and archers to cross the river by fording it, and thus to attack the bridges from the other side. This stratagem succeeded, and the French abandoned the bridges. Two of the French ships were burnt by the archers, and the rest withdrew, leaving the way clear for the English to cross in boats. In the confusion that followed, the archers and footsoldiers killed many French knights who might have been ransomed. Froissart has a tale about the two French commanders despairing of their lives, until they saw Sir Thomas Holland, whom they had known on crusade with the Teutonic Knights in Poland, and surrendered to him. In fact, only the count of Eu surrendered to Holland, who later sold his captive to the king for 80,000 florins. The lord of Tancarville was captured by Sir Thomas Daniel, one of the prince's retinue, 'so that he is my lord's [the prince's] prisoner'. Daniel was richly rewarded by the prince after the campaign for this and later services. Ninety-five noble captives were taken in all, and the English chroniclers claimed French losses of 2,500. English losses were mainly footsoldiers: Northburgh claims that only one squire died.[11]

The town was pillaged, but apart from a few houses burnt in the first onslaught, no burning took place; the king's edict was read out once again. The booty from this stage of the campaign does genuinely seem to have been enormous. Two hundred ships from the English fleet which had followed the king along the coast had been doing some plundering on their own account. They had burned Cherbourg and Ouistreham, and destroyed sixty-one warships. Now they were so laden that they were unable to transport all the plunder back across the Channel. One William Braye made off home with money, goods and jewels belonging to the prince and his men just after they left Caen: these were presumably part of their share of the booty. Richard Wynkeley, the king's confessor, said that the town had been 'stripped to the bare walls'. The prisoners were sent back to England under the charge of the earl of Huntingdon, who had been taken ill; and the fleet also left the army to return home.[12]

A rest of five days followed, but this enforced idleness was not entirely welcome to the army. On the 28th the countryside around was set on fire, and the following day these terrorizing tactics brought fifteen leading citizens of Bayeux to surrender the town to the king. No attempt seems to have been made during this time to take the castle, but when the king departed on 31 July he left a small force there, either to attempt to take the castle or, more probably, to prevent the garrison from escaping. In the event, they were set upon by the garrison and killed.[13]

The king now seems to have intended to attempt an attack on Rouen. On 31 July the army spread once again over the countryside, encamping that night at Troarn and Argences, about four miles apart. The next night it had moved towards the city of Lisieux, again in scattered columns: encampments were at Rumesnil, Leau-partie and Saint-Pierre-de-Jonque. The next day the king entered Lisieux. Here he found two cardinals, sent by the Pope to negotiate peace between himself and Philip, and learnt for the first time of Philip's preparations to counter his attack. So far the fighting had been entirely against local levies, but the king must have known that news of his landing had reached Philip not later than 18 July, and that counter-measures must be imminent. The next two days were spent in negotiations with the cardinals, but nothing definite was agreed except that they should seek an interview with Philip and see what proposals could be made. The king regarded the cardinals' mission as futile, but treated them politely: when his unruly Welsh troops stole twenty horses from them, he promptly restored them. The English army left Lisieux on 4 August and continued its march due east; on the 6th the king ordered a halt, and as there was a change of direction towards Rouen the following day, a council of war was probably held. From the army's position some miles west of the Seine, a march on either Paris or Rouen was possible. As it happened, Rouen was chosen, and the next day, 7 August, the army was at Elbeuf on the Seine.[14]

The king still seems to have been uncertain of the exact where-abouts of Philip, though he must have had some idea that the French forces were grouping in the area between Rouen and Paris. He may have hoped to reach Rouen and find the city undefended, but Philip had not been inactive. News of the English landing probably reached Philip as early as 16 July, when he was not far from Paris. He spent the next week in the Paris area, evidently organizing the raising of troops: on the 22nd or 23rd he went to the abbey of Saint-Denis to take the great standard of France, the *oriflamme*, from the abbey for use in the campaign. By the 25th he had evidently raised sufficient troops to set out. Philip's prime object was to prevent Edward from seizing Rouen, and he therefore made his way down the Seine. At first he moved slowly, to allow further reinforcements to catch up with him; on 30 July he was still only forty miles from Paris, at Vernon. By then the whereabouts of the English forces was well known, for the cardinals were able to find the king on 2 August. Philip therefore moved swiftly to Rouen, covering thirty-five miles in two days, to arrive there while the English were still at Lisieux.

Five days later, the English sent Godfrey d'Harcourt to recon-noitre and see how well-defended Rouen was. While the army waited near Moulineaux, Godfrey rode on through the forest until he came to the leper hospital at Petit-Quévilly. Here one of the inmates told him that Philip and the French army were in Rouen, and that the bridge had been broken down. The king probably expected news of this sort, but confirmation of the enemy's successful interception must have been unwelcome. Having failed in his immediate objective, he now had two possible strategies open to him: to march on Paris, relying on the absence of Philip to gain the city by a surprise attack, or to try to cross the Seine and join his Flemish allies in Picardy. Both meant that he would have to turn inland along the south bank of the river. There are hints of both objectives in the chronicles, but the latter is the more probable, as the Flemish seem to have been informed of the English movements up to this point at least. Furthermore, there seems to have been an immediate attempt to cross at Elbeuf: some of the Welsh soldiers swam the river and seized small boats moored on the other bank, but all that resulted was a skirmish with Norman troops, the bridge being too badly damaged to repair. The king next attempted to take Pont de l'Arche, but this was too well defended. Philip moved out from Rouen and kept track of the English forces from the other bank, hoping to resist attempts to cross. The English, realizing this, now took the most direct route, cutting across the meanders of the river, through Léry, Vaudreuil and Louviers, the latter being burnt. Gaillon was also burnt, and a strong castle on the Seine was unsuccessfully attacked, Sir Richard Talbot and Sir Thomas Holland being wounded. On the 9th, the king reached Vernon, where Philip had been ten days earlier; an attack on the suburbs was unsuccessful. The next day a raiding party led by Robert de Ferrers crossed the Seine and attacked the fortress of La Roche-Guyon. It was reputedly impossible to capture, and a song of the times ran: 'When Rocheguyon is bled, the fleur-de-lis will lose its name.' However, the English forced their way into the outer bailey and took the keep by assault, killing or capturing forty French knights, though Sir Edward Bois was killed by a stone hurled by the defenders.[15]

The army had separated again into two columns, because the prince encamped at Mounceux and the king at Freneuse. Here the cardinals returned with Philip's offers for peace: these were Aquitaine, to be held as his father had held it, and the possibility of a marriage alliance with the French royal house. The king rejected these, and as Philip had left the cardinals with the impression that he was unwilling to negotiate further, the cardinals withdrew. Meanwhile the vanguard of the French army had occupied Mantes, and the English had to skirt this town. There were now only a limited number of crossing points before Paris, and all had to be attempted. A detachment was sent from the prince's column, led by the earls of Warwick and Northampton (but apparently without the prince himself), to see if it was possible to seize the bridge at Meulan. When they reached the bridge they found that it was defended by a strong tower on the near bank, which was well garrisoned. The French hurled insults at their would-be attackers and a fierce skirmish ensued in which the English were driven off, several nobles being wounded by crossbow bolts. Meanwhile Philip and his army continued to shadow the English troops from the opposite bank, refusing to be lured across the river to attack. He was seriously concerned about the possibility of an assault on Paris, and on the 13th he and his army returned to the capital.[16]

There was now no likelihood of finding a bridge which could be seized intact for the crossing, and the king therefore decided to attempt to rebuild one of the broken bridges. He chose that at Poissy, which had been destroyed only the previous day on Philip's orders. The inhabitants of the town, including Philip's sister, who was prioress of a Dominican convent there, were evacuated to Paris with the French army. As they arrived in Paris the English army reached Poissy, and repair work on the bridge was at once begun, while the king and the prince took up lodgings in the town, the king in the new royal palace, the prince in the old royal palace. By afternoon, materials had been found for the carpenters and a single beam sixty feet long and a foot wide had been thrown across the breach. At this point a small enemy force appeared, but enough English troops managed to cross the beam in time to drive them off: twenty-five banners were raised by the English on the other side of the river, and after a first sharp attack, the French were soon put to flight, abandoning the carts of ammunition and provisions which they had brought, and even riding off on the carthorses, two or three astride. The carts, twenty-one in all, were emptied and burnt. Later that day repairs on the bridge were completed, sufficient for a horse and cart to be driven across it. At this point Edward's tactics seem obscure. Instead of crossing immediately, he now waited for two days, apparently awaiting some move from Philip, if not his actual arrival at Poissy. The army was allowed to lay waste the countryside round Paris in the meanwhile, burning two of Philip's palaces, at Montjoie and Saint-Germain-en-Laye, as well as small towns and villages, among them Saint-Cloud and Neuilly, at the gates of Paris itself. The following day, the Feast of the Assumption, all activity of this kind was forbidden, out of respect for the feast day. On the 16th, the army moved off again; as a feint, marauders were sent to burn villages in the direction of Chartres, to give the impression that the king was heading south to Gascony. The town at Poissy was also burnt as the army left, but the priory was spared. The king's real intention was now to join his Flemish allies as quickly as possible, and to re-establish his supply links with England, for despite the large amount of captured stores, it was impossible for so large an army to continue to live off the land. The day's marches were much longer: the five or six miles a day of the early part of the campaign now became fifteen miles. On the night of the 16th, the king stopped at 'Moliaux' and the prince at Grisy-les-Plâtres, fifteen miles due north of Poissy. Another march of similar length brought them to Auteuil and Vessancourt respectively on the next day. At Auteuil the king replied formally to letters from Philip which had reached him on either the 15th or 16th, challenging him to battle and offering a place to the north-east of Paris (between Franconville and Pontoise) or to the south (between Saint-Germain-des-Prés and Vaugirard). French sources claim that he had told the archbishop of Besançon, who brought the letters, that he would meet Philip at Montfort, south-west of Paris and on the way to Chartres. The French, however, did not take the feint in that direction seriously, and the king himself probably only regarded it as a delaying tactic. Equally, the king's protestation in his letter written on the 17th, that he had waited in vain for three days for Philip at Poissy, cannot be taken entirely seriously. It was only now that he had put what he imagined to be a safe distance between himself and the French army that he made this retrospective challenge.

Philip, criticized by the Parisians for his apparent inaction, now moved with commendable speed. His troops, reinforced by contingents from the count of Luxembourg, and the kings of Bohemia and Majorca, were fresh, and he was able to make forced marches which matched those of the English. Edward was having difficulty in enforcing the change of tactics; as the vanguard passed Beauvais, a well-garrisoned and fortified town,

the prince of Wales and his division stayed longer than they should have done before the town; and indeed he dearly wanted to obtain permission for his men to attack from his father the king. But he did not dare carry it out, for the king told him that he was likely to meet the enemy shortly, and he did not want to lose any men in such an attack.

The prince, despite the delay at Beauvais, continued to lead the way, and spent that night at Milly, and the king at Troissereux. The following day, 19 August, the small town of Oudeuil and other villages were attacked; the prince lodged at Grandvilliers, while the king was at the abbey of Sommereux two miles to the north-east. On the 20th, the king reached Camps-en-Amienois, fifteen miles south of the river Somme and the same distance east of Amiens; the prince lodged at Molliens, two miles away. The rearguard, however, spent that day, and possibly the following day as well, besieging and taking Poix, eight miles to the south, despite repeated messages from the king to call off the attack and continue on the way north. The king now had to wait for the rearguard to catch up: only six miles' progress was made on the 21st, and the next day the king halted.[17]

There were other reasons for delay apart from the rearguard action at Poix. Philip's army had come up on a parallel course about fifteen miles to the east, heading towards Amiens, where a large body of local troops had been gathering since 4 August. Philip, whose caution so far must be ascribed to a lack of sufficient men, was now sure of his superiority in numbers, and his one object was to bring the English to bay. The countryside had been laid waste on his orders, and the bridges over the Somme were broken. Skirmishes between the two armies took place on the 21st. On the 22nd, the king sent out scouts; at the same time, some of the army continued north-eastwards to Acheux and a considerable force under Godfrey d'Harcourt attempted to take the bridge at Pont-Remy. They were resisted by men from the king of Bohemia's contingent, sent there from Amiens, and the English troops retired to Airaines to rejoin the king. The next day Philip decided to set out in hot pursuit; his scouts had doubtless reported that the English army was short of food and clothing, and he was now eager to settle matters.[18]

Edward's scouts, however, warned him of the approach of the enemy, and he was able to put twelve miles between himself and the French by midday. To do this he had taken the easiest road, due west, away from the river and the French garrison at Abbeville; and he now reached Oisemont, which was defended by the local lords. Only when it had been taken did he catch up with the contingent sent on to Acheux and completely reassemble his forces. The chances of crossing between Abbeville and the sea must have seemed slight; but the king now learnt of a tidal causeway across the shallow mouth of the Somme. The traditional version tells how a prisoner named Gobin Agace betrayed the whereabouts of the causeway in return for his freedom and a reward of a hundred gold ecus. More reliable sources say that it was a squire in the retinue of Oliver Ghistels, a Flemish knight in English service; but the most interesting version is that of the Meaux chronicle, which says that an Englishman born in north Yorkshire on the abbey's lands, from Ruston near Nafferton, who had lived 'in those parts' for sixteen years,* told the king of the causeway. There is reason to believe that the Meaux account is based on a contemporary summary of the campaign, and the details are too specific to be lightly set aside.[19]

Whoever may have told Edward about the ford, it was a difficult place to take an entire army across. The Flemish chronicler Jean Le Bel was probably better informed on the crossing itself: according to him, Edward arrived at the causeway (called Blanchetaque, or 'the white spot', because of an outcrop of chalk on the river bed which gave a firm passage) and had to wait until the tide had ebbed sufficiently. The English army crossed at about 9 a.m., which is close to modern calculations for low tide (8 a.m.). The crossing was certainly something of a feat, because Michael Northburgh, who used the ford with the rest of the army, believed that no one had ever crossed there before. Edward himself, in a letter to Thomas Lucy, says that 'a thousand men crossed in line abreast, where only three or four usually went'. The Meaux chronicler, quoting this, adds that the crossing only took an hour in all, the king choosing a route a mile or two to seaward from the rest of the army.[20]

Philip had realized that a crossing might be attempted between Abbeville and the sea, and had ordered a knight named Godemar du Fay to defend the north bank of the river. He managed to discover the whereabouts of the English in time to arrive just as the first troops began to cross. His force, however, was small in comparison with the English, probably 500 men at arms and 3,000 assorted footsoldiers, many of them raised hurriedly from the neighbouring towns. He also had a body of Genoese archers. The

---

* Ponthieu, of which the Somme was the southern boundary, had been English territory until the confiscation of 1337, so there is nothing inherently unlikely about this.

archers seem to have caused the most casualties, because the English were unable to retaliate from the water: but an advance party under Hugh Despenser, Reginald Cobham and the earl of Northampton none the less managed to reach dry land and come to grips with the enemy. A fierce, brief conflict followed, at the end of which the French were driven off with heavy losses, estimated by an English writer at 2,000, including 300 Genoese. Meanwhile the main army had begun to cross, and by the time the rearguard came up, the fighting had ended; and the vanguard under Despenser went off to plunder the near-by town of Le Crotoy. Then, as the last English troops reached the north bank, the main French army appeared on the other side. Philip had made a rapid march from Abbeville, though he arrived too late to trap the English; any further pursuit was prevented by the rising tide. Edward hoped that they might repeat their venture to cross that evening or the next morning, and waited on the southern edge of the forest of Crécy in case such an attempt was made. Philip, however, returned to Abbeville, and on the next day, 25 August, Edward crossed the forest to the little village of Crécy and encamped again.

The 25th was St Louis's day, and Philip spent it at Abbeville waiting for reinforcements. What is surprising is that neither side moved very far during the two days following the crossing of the Somme by the English. Edward could have made two forced marches to get well beyond Philip's reach, and he would then have been that much nearer to his Flemish allies. Equally, Philip had been ready to attack on the 24th; there was no urgent need to swell the numbers of his army when such a delay might have allowed the enemy to escape. The Italian chronicler Villani is probably right when he explains that the English decided to select a good position and await an enemy attack because they were extremely short of food (though they had found supplies at Le Crotoy), and since even their shoes were worn out, long marches were out of the question. If Philip knew this, as he may well have done, he too would have been anxious to make sure that he was as well prepared as possible for the approaching battle. One English chronicler asserts that when Philip approached Blanchetaque, 'King Edward sent to the French king, offering him free passage over the ford, if he would come and choose a place apt to fight a field in; but this Philip went to another place of passage.'[21]

The broad outlines of what happened at Crécy on 26 August are easy enough to establish; but the details are confusing and con-

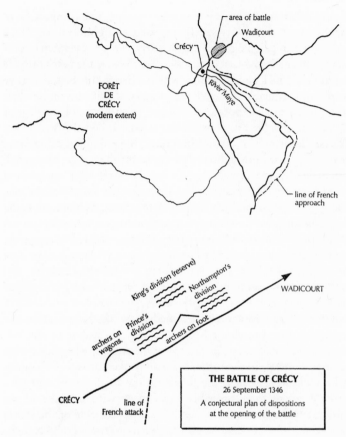

Map 2. The battle of Crécy

tradictory. The chroniclers who recorded the English progress across Normandy so carefully have little to tell us, while Froissart offers a series of classic vignettes which may or may not contain an element of truth.[22]

The English army consisted of probably 9,000 to 10,000 men (but possibly as many as 14,000), one third of these being knights and men-at-arms, who would normally have fought on horseback. The remainder were archers and infantry. They were far from well-equipped and provisioned, and had marched over 300 miles in the previous month; recent forced marches had been as far as eighteen or twenty miles a day. Against this, they had rested for the previous day, and the battle order was drawn up at leisure on the morning of the 26th, before the enemy was even in sight. Most important of all, they were a well-organized, experienced fighting force which had been campaigning as a single army for six weeks; its commanders were a close-knit group who knew and trusted each other.[23]

The king had chosen a site which offered the best defensive possibilities available in a rolling countryside with no outstanding physical features. He positioned his army just north of the village of Crécy, on a slight hill above what is now called the Vallée aux Clercs. The army was divided into three, the groupings being more or less those used throughout the campaign: the vanguard was led, nominally by the prince, in fact by the earls of Warwick and Northampton. The rearguard was under the command of the bishop of Durham and the earls of Arundel and Suffolk, while the king commanded the centre. The vanguard was placed nearest to Crécy, on the line on which the French were expected to approach; the rearguard was to the north, while the king's division lay a little back from the others as a reserve force. All the troops fought dismounted; the horses were put in a kind of *laager* of carts, on the right flank of the army. In front of the army, a series of pits was dug, a foot wide and a foot deep, designed to break the charge of the French knights, just as the Scots had dug pits against the English horses at Bannockburn. The placing of the archers, who played such an important role in the battle, is a matter of controversy. Geoffrey Baker, whose account is the fullest on the English side, and who wrote in about 1358, probably from an eyewitness record of the battle, says that the archers were placed to each side of the army, like wings, rather than with the men-at-arms. Froissart talks obscurely about a 'harrow' pattern, but the two can be reconciled if each corps had its archers on the flanks, facing slightly inwards and thus providing a covering cross-fire against any approaching charge. As a further precaution, if we are to believe the French chroniclers, trees were cut down, perhaps to block roads leading to the flanks.[24]

The French army left Abbeville some time during the morning. Reinforcements were continuing to come in up to the time of departure, and the strength of Philip's army is even more difficult to determine than that of the English. Edward himself and Richard Wynkeley both thought he had 12,000 mounted men; Villani, whose source may have been one of the Genoese, estimates the crossbowmen at 6,000. But both these figures are probably excessive. The army was in no very good order when it set out; and by the time it came up to the English army it was even more confused, straggling over some miles of countryside, just as the English forces would have done earlier in Normandy.

The first of this disordered mass came into sight of the English about mid afternoon. As soon as the English position was known, Philip sent a small party of trusted knights to go forward and reconnoitre. They included the royal standardbearer, Miles de Noyers, Jean de Beaumont, and Henri le Moine of Basle. Their report was unanimous: the English were well entrenched and the only possible course was to call a halt, and wait until the next morning, when the whole army could be arrayed in good order. But, by now, the first French troops were within a very short distance of the English. They were confident of victory, because the English had no great reputation as soldiers, while the knights of France were renowned as the finest in Christendom. The lack of order now became critical: the order was not to halt, but actually to retreat, and this the French knights refused to do. Philip watched impotently while the knights refused to be recalled, and then gave the order to attack. Such at least was the recollection of French leaders after the battle, as it reached the Flemish chronicler Jean Le Bel. It accords well with other similar episodes, notably at Poitiers; but one detail contradicts the picture of almost total confusion. The Genoese crossbowmen, disciplined and experienced troops who could have been expected to obey an order to retreat, attacked first. Other writers on the French side affirm that Philip, either out of sheer hate for the English, or persuaded by the more impetuous of his knights, eager for glory, ordered an attack before the main army was arrayed, directly against the advice of more experienced men.

The French army as a whole had had no experience in the field. Individual units had taken part in skirmishes, and there were war-hardened veterans among some of the contingents, as well as the Genoese; but it was a newly assembled force with no very clear organization or system of command. This is clear from the varying estimates of the number of corps into which the French were divided, ranging from one great body formed from three corps, to three separate, or even nine separate, corps. Philip probably attempted to arrange his forces in four units with the Genoese as vanguard, under Carlo Grimaldi and Otto Doria. Just behind them came king John of Bohemia and his son Charles, forming the first group of mounted troops. The second group was under Charles duc d'Alençon, the king's brother, and the third under the king himself, with the king of Majorca and other nobles. There were also a number of footsoldiers from the towns of northern France who seem to have been sent into battle with the crossbowmen.

Under whatever circumstances the first French onslaught was made, it was a confused and uncontrolled affair. The Genoese crossbowmen moved forward with a great noise of trumpets and drums, and as they did so, two great crows flew croaking over the battlefield, and a brief shower of rain fell from the overcast sky; in later legend these became a great flock of crows and a thunderstorm. As the Genoese opened fire, the Welsh archers replied: and in this first trial of strength between crossbowmen and archers it was soon clear that the archers had the advantage, firing three times as quickly as the crossbowmen, who had to wind back the windlasses that stretched their bowstrings by turning a handle, while the archer reloaded with one swift movement of his arm. The Genoese were also short of shields and quarrels (crossbow bolts), as these were on wagons at the rear of the army, while the English were well supplied with arrows. Furthermore, the Genoese came up on the right flank of the English army, and a number of them found themselves faced by the square of carts, underneath which were a handful of bombards, primitive stone-throwing cannon. These were being used in a major battle for the first time, and the psychological effect of the explosions and the hail of English arrows broke the Genoese attack. They turned to flee, but came face to face with the first French knights under the duc d'Alençon, who rode them down, both out of eagerness to get at the English and because they felt that the Genoese had betrayed them. Caught between the two armies, only a few of the crossbowmen escaped, either being cut down by the knives and spears of the Welsh or crushed to death under the charging French cavalry.[25]

The English vanguard now had to face the charge of the first French horsemen, broken not only by the obstacles dug by the English, but also by the encounter with the Genoese. This onslaught was easily beaten off, though one writer claims that the duc d'Alençon beat down the prince's standard, which he clasped as he was killed, but the second body of French cavalry also hurled themselves on the vanguard, and the fighting now became serious. The prince himself was in the thick of the fight, and at once distinguished himself by his skill and constant activity. Among this second division were the blind king John of Bohemia, who, according to the Czech chroniclers, had urged Philip to pursue the English rather than turn back when they had crossed the Somme. He was now told that some of the French had fled, and he was urged to take the same course. But he refused to do so, and ordered his attendants to take him into the thick of the battle. He was followed by a group of Bohemian nobles; and both he and many of his fellow-countrymen were killed. Even though many of the French had their horses killed under them by the English archers, the pressure on the prince and his men became so great that at one moment he was himself forced to his knees. He was rescued by his standardbearer, Sir Richard FitzSimon, who put down his banner and stood over it while he drew his sword to defend his master. A Flemish writer says that the prince was actually captured for a moment by the count of Hainault. Meanwhile, a messenger ran to the king, who sent twenty knights under the bishop of Durham to help the prince. By the time they reached him the enemy attack had waned, and the prince and his men were resting, leaning on their swords. Sir Richard FitzSimon, with the help of Sir Thomas Daniel, again raised the banner, fringed with silver and bearing the arms of France and England, and so they awaited the next enemy attack in the fading light.[26]

The battle continued until dark, each French charge meeting a similar fate: decimated by the crossfire of the English archers, and increasingly obstructed by the bodies of men and horses from previous attacks, only a handful of knights reached the prince's position on the hillside. The king's division and the rearguard had relatively little to do except to provide reinforcements for the prince's division, on whom the brunt of the fighting fell, mainly because the French attacked as they came up, and his men were nearest to their line of march. As each attack – an English writer claims there were fifteen in all – was beaten off, the survivors turned and fled, following the Genoese and the footsoldiers. Only a small group around Philip himself stood firm, including the communal levies from Orléans. Philip himself, who had certainly come under fire from the English archers, was said by the English to have been wounded in the face, and he was twice unhorsed. As the last attacks took place, he was either persuaded to leave the field or else he fled, accompanied by John of Hainault. He went to the near-by castle of Labroye, and thence in the following days to Doullens and Amiens.[27]

But even though the French king had withdrawn and the victory was clearly on the English side, the fighting continued. Edward III ordered his men to remain where they were and established a strong guard round the camp in case of surprise attacks. A Norman writer says that he filled a windmill on the battlefield with wood and set it alight, as a kind of beacon, which lit the camp all night. Skirmishes certainly continued through the night, mostly with small groups of French, some of whom betrayed themselves by shouting their password. The following day a large body of French troops, ignorant of the situation, came on to the battlefield, which was deep in mist. They were largely footsoldiers, summoned from Normandy and Picardy. The king sent the prince with Northampton and Warwick to deal with them. The French were not really prepared for battle, being more concerned with finding their own army, and were quickly put to flight and a number of prisoners taken.[28]

The English now set about discovering the extent of their victory. The dead nobles were identified and buried, and a count was made of the men-at-arms killed: 1,542 in all. The king is said to have asked the prince what he thought of going into battle and fighting, and whether he found it good sport. The prince, to his credit, 'said nothing and was ashamed'. The king himself is said to have been much grieved by the death of the king of Bohemia, 'because he was full of years and worthy and valiant in arms in his lifetime, and courteous enough to Englishmen captured in battle at the time'. Indeed, one of the English commanders, the earl of Suffolk, was reputed to have owed his life to the king of Bohemia's intervention: when the earl was captured by the French in Flanders in 1340, Philip threatened to behead him and only spared his life at king John's request. A solemn requiem mass was said for the dead king by the bishop of Durham, and in his honour the prince took his badge of ostrich feathers, as John Arderne, who may have been his doctor, recorded in a medical treatise at the time of the prince's death:

... Edward the eldest son of Edward the king of England bore a similar feather above his helmet, and he obtained the feather from the king of Bohemia, whom he killed at Cresse in France. And so he assumed the feather which is called 'ostrich fether' which that most noble king used to carry above his helmet.

In John Arderne's illustration (Plate 16) of the ostrich feather, the scroll is left blank; but in the prince's own use of the feathers as a badge, the motto *Ich dene* ('I serve') always appears. There is no evidence to associate it directly with the king of Bohemia, but a poem of 1352, *Winner and Waster*, has a vivid pen-portrait of the prince in which crest and badge seem to be associated:

> The king biddeth a baron by him that standeth,
> One foremost in fame, that failed him never; –
> 'Bethink, I dubbed thee knight with dints to deal,
> Wend quickly thy way my will to make known!
> Go, bid yon bold hosts of battle that on battlefield bide,
> That they never come nigh any nearer each other;
> For, strike they one stroke, to stint think they never.'
> 'I serve, lord,' said that liege, 'while my life shall endure.'*
> He doth him down on the bank, and dwelleth a time,
> Till he busk'd was and bound in the bravest array.
> He lapped his legs in iron to the lower bones;
> With pisane and with pauncer, polish'd full bright;
> With braces of burnish'd steel, closely braided with rings;
> With plates buckled behind, the body to ward;
> With a well-fitting jupon, joined at the sides;
> A broad scutcheon at the back; the breast had another;
> Three wings within, truly wrought after kind,
> Engirt with gold wire. When that warrior I knew,
> Lo, he was youngest of years and yarest of wit
> That any wight in this world wist of his age.[29]

The spelling of the motto *ich dene* is said to be Low Countries dialect, but on the prince's tomb it is given as *ich diene*, the normal German form. The prince probably spelled it in the most familiar way, which would be that of the Low Countries, but this does not necessarily tell us where the motto came from. It has more than an echo of the Pope's title, *servus servorum Dei* ('servant of the servants of God'). We can only speculate about when and why the prince adopted it, but it is worth noting that three rings of pearls 'with the prince's motto' were apparently bought on 24 June 1346, that is, before the expedition set out.[30]

The victory at Crécy was spectacular, and it established the prince's reputation as a soldier immediately, as the author of *Winner and Waster* confirms. Even allowing for the fact that much of our information probably derives from men in the prince of Wales's division, his part in the battle was crucial. The strategy was

* The reading, 'I serve, lord', is an alteration by the editor; the MS. reads, 'Yes, lord.'

decided in advance by the king and his advisers, and their preparations were the main reason for the English victory. However, the
battle hinged in the last resort on the ability of the prince's knights
to resist the French charges, and this they did, despite fierce hand-
to-hand fighting over relatively long periods. The prince himself
showed that he had inherited his forebears' great physical strength.
His great-grandfather had lifted a knight bodily from his horse at
Chalons in 1279; Edward II, despite his lack of success in battle, was
no mean fighter; and his father had a great reputation in both
tournaments and war. All the Plantagenets were tall and muscular,
and this sheer physical strength stood the prince in good stead.[31]

The king's successful strategy, using his archers and a well-
prepared defensive position to break up the French cavalry charges,
owed much to English experience in Scotland. But it came as an
overwhelming surprise to the French, who were said to have shared
out the important English prisoners in advance. The French were
regarded as the finest soldiers in Europe, though on relatively little
evidence in the field: while the English were not considered to be
particularly effective. A French army had never previously been
defeated in a pitched battle by the English; and this was to contribute greatly both to the demoralization of the French nobles in
general and to the confidence of the close-knit group of English
commanders.[32]

The battle of Crécy founded the prince's reputation; it also
formed the basis of his military experience, and its lessons stood him
in good stead in later years. Why was it such a triumph for the
English? We have already looked at the superiority of the English
archers, but there are other factors. The most important is that the
English were a relatively well-disciplined force, under experienced
commanders, fighting from a planned and prepared defensive
position. Their communications during the battle were good –
witness the carefully judged response to the request for aid for the
prince. The king was able to detail off a contingent suited to the
needs of the moment, in sharp contrast to the French commanders'
inability to coordinate even the main strategy of their attacks.

The French army relied to a large extent on non-French contingents from relatively recent allies: control was evidently hampered by communications difficulties between knights from as far
afield as Bohemia, Spain and Lorraine, and there was also a body of
mercenaries in the shape of the Genoese crossbowmen. In contrast
to this, the English army had very few foreigners in it: one

chronicler mentions six German archers, but the only non-English-speaking contingent of any size were the Welsh archers, and they were carefully organized in small groups under English-speaking leaders. Hence the English were able to act as a single force, while the French attack was, in effect, the work of a number of un-coordinated groups. Only one instance of indiscipline is reported from the English side: Aimery Rokesley is said to have been killed, 'hurling himself impetuously into the battle-line'. Most of the French onslaughts were little more than groups of knights doing exactly this.[33]

The character of the commanders on both sides was equally contrasting. Edward and the leaders of his army had all had con-siderable experience in the field, either in the merciless fighting in Scotland, under difficult conditions, or in Brittany and Flanders. Warwick, Arundel, Oxford and Suffolk had all served in Scotland, Flanders (where there was little actual fighting) and Brittany in the period 1333-45; Northampton had served in Flanders and Brittany between 1338 and 1345, and had held off a vastly superior French army at Morlaix in 1342, using dismounted men-at-arms and a defensive position – tactics similar to those adopted at Crécy. The last-named, Warwick and Arundel, had all been at Sluys in 1340. The king's own experience was more formidable still, beginning with his victory over the Scots at Halidon Hill thirteen years earlier.

Against this array of talent and experience, the French could only offer men of great individual courage but little tactical skill. The one exception was John of Bohemia, one of the great warriors of the day. He had campaigned in Lithuania (in 1328-9, 1337 and 1345) and in Italy (1330-31), as well as on his own frontiers, with considerable success. But he was now advanced in years and blind, and although he brought with him a seasoned band of Bohemian and German knights, his contribution to the tactics of the French side was minimal; indeed, one Bohemian chronicle represents him as attack-ing as a forlorn hope after a general retreat had been ordered, rather than withdrawing in the face of the enemy. Philip himself had had some experience in the field; indeed, his first campaign had ended with a spectacular victory at Cassel in 1328 over the Flemish com-munal forces. This was one of the last occasions when an orthodox cavalry attack decided a battle, and it may have given Philip unwarranted confidence in such tactics. Certainly the Flemish cam-paign of 1338 onwards would have taught him nothing about full-scale battles. The conflicting accounts of the chroniclers, even on

the French side, make it clear that any tactical decisions Philip may
have taken were valueless once the Genoese crossbowmen had
moved forward. Indeed, the only correct tactical decision was
precisely the one that Philip seemed to reject: to hold back his troops
and attack on the following day. There is some slight evidence that
he tried to do this but was prevented by an undisciplined advance
by his own men. But the majority of the French chroniclers depict
him as full of hate for the English and eager to attack.[34]

The minor elements in the battle were relatively evenly balanced:
both armies were in less than good physical shape, the English from
the effects of their earlier marches, the French from that day's march.
The numerical advantage was if anything on the French side, though
one recent French historian has tried to argue that the French army
was definitely smaller. The English army contained the best soldiers
available, while many of the seasoned French troops were in
Gascony, at the siege of Aiguillon, held by the earl of Derby with
an Anglo-Gascon garrison. The presence of cannon may have produced surprise and terror among the French army, 'making such a
shaking of the earth and noise that it seemed as though God was
thundering', but had little effect on the result of the battle.[35]

To sum up: the English relied on prosaic details like organization
and tactics, and had the advantage of superior armament. The
French fought as though they believed wholeheartedly in the
attitudes purveyed by knightly romances, in which individual
prowess was exalted above everything else; they showed no interest
in discipline, and almost a contempt for their own supporting
infantry. Yet the paradox is that, today, the young prince Edward
at Crécy is remembered for his individual prowess, exactly the
reputation that the French knights sought to achieve.

The king's way was now clear to move north to join his Flemish
allies and to re-establish contact with England. He was urgently in
need of supplies, but, unable to press his men too hard, he made his
way north in stages of ten miles a day, keeping along the coast in
the hope of making contact with and receiving support from his
fleet. The army none the less continued to ravage and burn, and an
unsuccessful attack was made on Montreuil-sur-Mer. The army
halted twice for a day, once near Neufchâtel on 1 September and
again near Wissant (which was burnt) on 3 September. He may
have considered besieging Boulogne before coming up to Calais
on 4 September. On his arrival there, the king at once wrote to

England, giving news of the victory of Crécy and announcing his decision to besiege Calais. He added an urgent appeal for supplies; the letter was received at Windsor by 6 September, and circulated throughout the country. His plea was echoed in Michael Northburgh's long letter describing the campaign since Poissy:

> From what I have heard, he [the king] intends to besiege Calais. And for this reason the king has sent to you for supplies to be sent as quickly as you can; because since we left Caen we have lived off the country, with great difficulty and much harm to our men, but, thanks be to God, we have had no losses. But we are now in such a plight that we must rely on fresh supplies of food.

On 8 September, notification was sent to parliament of the prince's knighting at La Hogue, with a request for the feudal aid due on the knighting of the king's eldest son, amounting to 40s. on each knight's fee. The knighting had been planned as a way of financing the campaign, and both the king and the prince had already anticipated this source of revenue.[36]

Meanwhile, the English fleet, which had attacked Boulogne on 4 September but had been driven off, had made contact with the king and had presumably supplied his immediate needs. The king also needed new supplies of equipment and reinforcements, because he was now embarking on a very different kind of undertaking. Calais was a strongly fortified town, surrounded by a double wall and two rings of water-filled moats, and all the skills of siegecraft were required: miners, engineers, carpenters were now more important than knights. There were three possible methods of taking the town: by scaling the walls, by breaching the walls and attacking through the breach, or by starving out the defenders. All three methods might be used at once, but the strength of the defences was such that scaling or destruction of the walls was almost impossible. The height of the walls – believed to have been built by Julius Caesar – was such that the king was said to be unwilling to risk his men in such an attempt; and the marshy ground made it impossible either to undermine the walls or to erect siege engines to batter them down with stones, because there was no firm ground beneath. Furthermore, the exposed points of the walls had been covered by the defenders with matting and sacks of brushwood to break the impact of missiles. So the king's strategy was to attempt to starve out the defenders. This, too, was a difficult task, as Calais had an excellent harbour and a sea-blockade was therefore necessary. Within a few days of the king's arrival, Sir John Montgomery arrived with the English fleet and put this into effect. Another arrival, about Michaelmas, was queen Philippa; as winter approached, the English camp, built in a defensive position between two rivers which drained the marshes, became a town of huts and more permanent buildings nicknamed 'Villeneuve-le-Hardie', or 'English Calais'.[37]

The French were not long in rallying their forces, and as early as 3 October the king had word of an army being gathered at Compiègne with a view to raising the siege. Further troops were hurriedly summoned from England; the king asked specifically for 368 men-at-arms and nearly 750 archers, but also asked eight lords to come with as many men as they could muster. The prince also sought reinforcements, asking for 200 Welsh archers from Flint, and ordering the justice 'not to be so negligent or tardy as he was in the last array'. The threatened French appearance had still not materialized by early November, but nor had adequate reinforcements, and another round of summonses went out in the middle of that month. Despite raids by the Flemish army, an attempt to take Saint-Omer and an attack by Northampton on the near-by town of Thérouanne, the monotony of the siege, after the activity of the summer's campaigns, was leading to a number of desertions, and sickness in the shape of a kind of camp fever was also taking its toll. The prince himself may have suffered from this, as his physician, William Blackwater, was paid 100s. advance on his wages, 'that he may quickly come to the prince, as ordered', on 6 March. And this was another urgent reason for seeking new troops. Towards the end of November, the king evidently had plans for an assault because ladders and hurdles were requisitioned from Dover and twenty fishing boats were ordered for an attack on the port.[38]

The weather now turned very cold, and the marsh dykes were frozen over until the ice would bear a man's weight. The earl of Warwick took advantage of this to attack the castle of Hammes, about three miles from Calais, crossing its moat on the ice. The castle was captured and burnt. The garrison of Calais, anxious about their fast-diminishing supplies, expelled 500 old and young townspeople who were unable to help with the defence. Their fate is variously recorded: Jean Le Bel praises Edward's generosity in feeding them and sending them on their way with a gift of 4s. apiece, while Henry Knighton says that they perished miserably in the no-man's-land between the armies. Most of the action during the winter was at sea: despite energetic attempts by the French to find sailors able and willing to break the blockade, no supplies reached the town after the very early stages of the siege. In April an attempt to relieve the town by bringing flat-bottomed barges up through the shallow water just offshore, where the English ships could not sail, was prevented by a detachment under the earl of Northampton, who built a palisade out from the shore. A great tower was built at the entrance of Calais harbour as well, and these measures effectively blocked the port. When another attempt was made on 25 June with forty-four ships of various sizes, word of this reached the English, and the earls of Northampton and Pembroke went on board the English fleet with a large number of archers to lie in wait for the French squadron. The enemy came into sight that evening, and a brief skirmish followed. The Genoese galleys acting as escorts rowed off to seaward and abandoned the cargo ships to their fate: some escaped by dumping their cargoes in the sea, while others were so closely pursued that they ran ashore and were abandoned by their crews.[39]

When news of this disaster reached Calais, the garrison decided to try to get a message through to Philip; and the following day two small boats left the harbour. They were seen by two English sailors, William Roke and Stephen Hickman, and the English gave chase. One escaped back into the town; the other was captured, and with it the master of the Genoese troops at Calais and a number of letters. One letter, however, was thrown overboard tied to an axe just before the boat was captured. The English found it at low tide, and it proved to contain a graphic appeal for help from the captain of Calais, describing the plight of the besieged:

> For know that there is nothing in the town which has not been eaten, both dogs and cats and horses, so that there is nothing else to live off in the town unless we eat human flesh. Earlier on you wrote to say that I was to hold the town as long as there was food. We are now at the point where we have nothing to live off. So we have agreed that if we do not soon have help, we will make a sortie out of the town into the fields, to fight for life or death. For we would rather die honourably in the field than eat one another.[40]

However, there must have been some exaggeration in the captain's report, because at the end of July the town was still holding out. By this time Philip had raised a new army, and on 27 July he reached Calais and encamped 'on the other side of the marsh, on a hill', facing the English besiegers. Edward had long been expecting his arrival, and the reinforcements which he had first summoned in February and March had reached him by this time. In May he and the prince also summoned a number of knights and barons who had returned to England during the winter. The prince's list included the earl of Pembroke, Sir Bartholomew Burghersh the younger, Sir Richard Stafford, Sir Thomas Daniel, Sir Stephen Cosington and others, so his retinue must have been considerably diminished in the interval. Part of the reason was that many knights seemed to have been engaged the previous spring to serve for one year, though none of the original indentures survive. New indentures were certainly drawn up between March and May between the prince and knights who had already served in the campaign, all for the term of six months or a year. The king, for his part, sent summons to the earl of Oxford and Sir John Verdoun, and others who had been fighting in Gascony, among them Sir Walter Mauny. The leader of this contingent was Henry, earl of Lancaster, who had been responsible for the recent successes in Aquitaine. Mauny's journey home had been hazardous: he had obtained a safe-conduct from the French king to cross France and join the prince at Calais, but had been treacherously arrested and imprisoned in Paris. In retaliation, the prince ordered that the chamberlain of Tancarville, captured at Caen, and now enjoying considerable freedom as the prince's prisoner, was to be put in close custody at Wallingford Castle. Whether because of this, or because the French nobles were so horrified at the king's behaviour that they obtained his release, Mauny was soon set free.[41]

Just after Philip's arrival, a large body of Flemish reinforcements under the marquis of Juliers reached the English camp. All these additions to the English army were welcome, because the camp fever of the winter had continued, and many men were lost in an outbreak of dysentery. The wooden buildings, too, were a hazard, and the king lost most of the wardrobe in a fire.[42]

Understandably, Philip was cautious about mounting an attack. A few English knights engaged in a skirmish as the army arrived, and took some prisoners. Philip's first move was to send two cardinals down to the end of the causeway across the marsh with letters addressed to Lancaster and the English commanders, requesting a parley. Lancaster and Northampton went across, and the cardinals asked them to open peace negotiations, assuring them that the French would offer appropriate terms. This was agreed, and two tents were pitched in the no-man's-land between the armies. The English delegation consisted of Lancaster, Northampton, Bartholomew Burghersh the elder (one of the most experienced English diplomats), Reginald Cobham and Walter Mauny. The French sent the dukes of Bourbon and Athènes, the sire d'Offemont and Geoffrey de Charny. But the talks opened badly, as the French insisted that the siege must be lifted before the peace negotiations proper began. The English said that they had no authority to do this, but were commissioned only to negotiate general peace terms. Eventually, and with great reluctance, the French made an offer of Aquitaine, as it had been held by Edward I, together with the county of Ponthieu: but this was rejected by the English as too small an offer set against the loss of Calais. The talks dragged on until 31 July, the French continually reverting to the question of the town. On the Tuesday evening, the French decided to try another course; a number of their lords and knights appeared at the conference tents with an offer from Philip to fight the English on open ground, the site to be chosen by four knights from each side. This was accepted by the king, and he issued a safe-conduct for the four French knights to come over to the English army and go with their opposite numbers to find a suitable site. The French, however, tried to revert to the question of raising the siege first, and nothing happened on the Wednesday, 1 August. Before dawn on 2 August, Philip struck camp, burning tents and equipment in what was evidently a hurried departure. Lancaster's troops harassed the French rearguard as they withdrew southwards. The rest of France was shocked and alarmed at this apparent cowardice on the French king's part: but Philip would have had considerable difficulty in mounting an attack on the English camp, and it is hardly surprising that he was reluctant to meet them in the open field with the experience of Crécy fresh in his mind. The expedition was evidently mounted in the hope that the English force had been reduced by the winter's campaigning and was in poor shape. The delays over the negotiations may have been intended to allow Philip to get a better idea of the English forces and their condition, and when he discovered that they were as large, or larger, than his own besides being well-equipped, he withdrew.[43]

The proceedings outside the town had been watched with mounting anxiety by the besieged. On the night of Philip's arrival, according to Baker, they flew all their flags and lit a great fire, making a great noise with drums and trumpets; the following night there was a similar, but less jubilant, display; while on the third night, they lit only a small fire, which they allowed to fall in the moat, and hauled down the flags, as if to signal that they could hold out no longer and were about to surrender. On Saturday, 4 August, two days after Philip's retreat, the gates were opened, and John de Vienne, the captain of Calais, rode out on a little hack, because he was unable to walk from sickness, with a rope round his neck; the other knights and chief citizens, also with ropes round their necks, followed on foot. He offered up his naked sword and the keys of the town, and the sword of peace which symbolized his authority over the town. Edward accepted these, and agreed that the townspeople should go free; John de Vienne and the leading citizens were taken as prisoners to England. Flemish writers claimed that they were only saved by the intercession of the queen, since the king was ready to hang them all. Most of the townspeople were expelled after being given food, and some died from over-eating after the long weeks of hunger. Calais became an English possession: the Flemish were said to be eager to demolish it, but Edward repopulated it with English settlers, recruiting them by a general proclamation throughout England (though maintaining its previous laws and customs). After 1363, when the wool staple was established there, Calais became not only the main strategic base for English military operations in northern France, but also an important commercial centre.[44]

Philip and his army still remained a threat, however, and on 20 August the English king ordered a general recall of all those who had been given leave to go back to England, both from his own and the prince's retinue. These orders were repeated on 8 September, but by the end of that month both sides were ready to negotiate, and on 25 September the earls of Lancaster and Huntingdon and four other lords were given the necessary commission. The negotiations were brief, and a truce was signed on the evening of 28 September. It was to run until 8 July 1348, and was binding on all the allies of both parties.[45]

The king spent a further six weeks at Calais; he and the prince returned to England in early November. Over a year had passed since the triumph of Crécy, and they brought no great train of prisoners or booty, most of these having preceded them. It was a quiet and unspectacular homecoming after a campaign which had been dramatic in the extreme. The prince had had experience of all the major types of warfare: raids, a pitched battle and a siege – and was now acknowledged as a fully fledged soldier, even if his glory was overshadowed by both that of his father and of the earl of Lancaster, whose successes in Gascony in the same period had been very considerable.

The Order of the Garter
and the Years of Truce

4

The king left Calais on about 12 October, accompanied by the queen and the prince and many of the army. The crossing was a stormy one, and a number of ships were lost; the king is said to have exclaimed that the weather was fair whenever he crossed to France, but foul when he tried to return to England. They landed at London on 14 October. The profits of the campaign had not been particularly great as far as the king was concerned: individual soldiers might have made their fortunes, but the ransoms and booty which fell to the king's share were no more than a contribution to the costs of the war, particularly when the cost of operations in Gascony was taken into account. The prince was paid £22,302 for his wages and other war debts for the expedition in the course of the next four and a half years: and there may have been other untraced amounts, since one payment of £13,000 was described as wages for three months for the prince and the lords accompanying him to Calais. As the siege alone had lasted nearly a year – albeit with variations in the size of the prince's revenue – a total bill of over £50,000 would be implied. The prince was certainly expected to bear a proportion of the costs himself, because when further war subsidies were granted, his lands were exempted on the grounds that he had already made substantial contributions. Even so, he had to have recourse to new means of raising funds. One source of revenue which he enjoyed, as administrator of justice in his lands, was the revenue from fines, and as campaigns made increasing demands on his finances, so commissions of justice were sent out more and more frequently. Sir William Shareshull, one of the prince's council and an experienced royal judge, went with a number of other justices to Wales and Chester in 1347; and at Cardigan the following year the town granted £740 to the prince as a blanket payment for the great sessions, though it is not clear whether they were buying off the judges' visit or making a lump-sum payment for fines already meted out.[1]

The truce by no means put an end to this heavy war expenditure. Gascony, once a source of profit to the crown, cost an average of over £6,000 a year in payments to the constable of Bordeaux between 1348 and 1361. Calais in the same period cost an average of over £10,000 a year. This meant renewed appeals to parliament for money, and endless delays in making payments out of the exchequer. The king managed to make up a small surplus by 1355, but the strain of late payments on the finances of many lords was acute, and we shall see the effect on the prince's own lands.

Activity on the diplomatic front was redoubled as soon as the truce came into force. The king's chief interest was in Flanders and Spain, where new possibilities for marriage alliances had offered themselves. The situation in Flanders had been completely altered by the death at Crécy of Louis de Nevers, killed fighting for the French. His son, Louis de Mâle, was still under age, and in March 1347 the Flemish townsmen coerced him into agreeing to a marriage with Edward's eldest daughter, Isabella, now fifteen. But Louis had been brought up at the French court, and was more anxious to revenge himself on the English for his father's death than to enter into an alliance with them. Despite the eagerness of the towns to be reconciled with their duke, the English alliance was too important commercially to be abandoned; so Louis de Mâle resolved the matter by fleeing to France a few weeks later. Once safely at the French court he rejected the proposed alliance; in July, he married the daughter of the duke of Brabant instead, whose allegiance was firmly with the French. This was a double blow because the English had for some time been planning a match between the prince and the heiress of Brabant themselves: in 1345 Sir Nigel Loring and Michael Northburgh had been sent to the papal court to obtain the necessary dispensation, and it was still rumoured to be a possibility in February 1347. Worse was to follow, because the count's party soon gained the upper hand in the Flemish towns, only Ghent holding out for the English alliance by September 1348.

However, Louis de Mâle had begun to realize that his pro-French policy had strong economic disadvantages, and a truce between him and the towns, coupled with a new English alliance, was arranged during the autumn. In fact, Flanders was now neither an English nor a French satellite, but an independent power; Louis de Mâle was to prove a skilful diplomat, using the Anglo-French conflict to his own best advantage, and Flemish troops never made any substantial contributions to subsequent English campaigns in northern France.[2]

Crécy had lost England another potential ally: in 1348, Charles of Bohemia, who had fought beside his father, the blind king John, became emperor. Edward's alliance with the old emperor, Louis IV, had not contributed greatly to English campaigns in France, and his appointment as vicar-general, celebrated with great pomp in 1338, had scarcely taken effect before it was withdrawn and Louis became an ally of the French. But Louis's attitude had been open; with Charles there was no question of an English alliance, and Edward was actually approached by various dissident princes who opposed Charles's election to become emperor himself. This he wisely declined, on the grounds that he was fully occupied in France.[3]

In Spain and Portugal Edward's diplomatic efforts were initially successful, but ultimately came to nothing. While the king and prince were at Calais, messengers had come from Portugal, repeating Alfonso IV's request that the prince should marry his youngest daughter Leonor. The king sent messengers back to Portugal to conclude the match; they were empowered to deal with all the necessary details, but because of delays in communications, Leonor was married to Pere III, king of Aragón, by the time they arrived. A marriage alliance with Alfonso of Castile was in fact concluded the following year, between the king's eldest son Pedro and Edward's daughter Joan. The negotiations had begun at the same time as those for the Portuguese match. There was a close connection between the two, as the queen of Castile was the elder sister of Leonor of Portugal: in 1345 the former had been asked to use her influence to secure both matches. Edward, acting on information from the earl of Derby, who had just returned from Spain, also wrote to Leonor de Guzman, the king's mistress, offering a place in the prince's retinue to any of her sons whom she cared to send to England, in order to secure her goodwill. A further link was that the dowry of Leonor of Portugal was to have been used to provide Joan's dowry. The English envoys who set out with

Joan in the spring of 1348 were therefore instructed to make the necessary excuses and provide sureties: but Joan died of the plague at Bordeaux that summer, and all Edward's efforts came to nothing, as Alfonso soon returned to his traditional alliance with France.[4]

Meanwhile the truce agreed in the autumn of 1347 had expired, but a series of negotiations over prolongations of the truce, and, rather half-heartedly, over a permanent peace, continued. A renewal for ten months was agreed on 13 November. The king and the prince returned to Calais at the end of November 1348: though they did not take part in the negotiations, they directed the English ambassadors, who were now negotiating with Louis de Mâle. A treaty was signed with the latter on 4 December, though its provisions never came into effect.

This seems to have been one of the few official occasions, apart from two parliaments in January and March, in a year given up to pleasures. The most memorable event of the year is also one of the most obscure. It is now generally accepted that the Order of the Garter was founded in this year, but there is still much debate as to how, when and why. The nearest to a contemporary account of its foundation that we possess comes from Geoffrey Baker's chronicle, and even he is far from entirely accurate. First, he dates the foundation to 1350, while both royal accounts and the foundation of the chapel at Windsor point to an earlier date. Secondly, he enters two knights (Sir Walter Mauny and Sir William Fitzwarin) as founders, whereas they did not receive the garter until later in the reign. But his version must be our starting point:

> This year, on St George's Day, the king held a great feast at Windsor Castle, where he instituted a chantry with twelve priests and founded an almshouse in which impoverished knights, for whom their own means did not suffice, might have adequate sustenance in the service of the Lord from the perpetual alms of the founders. Others beside the king were fellow-sureties for the foundation of this almshouse, namely the king's eldest son, the earl of Northampton, the earl of Warwick, the earl of Suffolk, the earl of Salisbury and other barons; and ordinary knights namely Roger Mortimer, now earl of March, Sir Walter Mauny, Sir William fitzWarin, John Mohun, John Beauchamp, Walter Paveley, Thomas Wale and Hugh Wrottesley, whose tried worth associated them with the most noble earls. They were all clothed like the king in cloaks of russet powdered with garters, dark

blue in colour, and also had similar garters on their right legs, with bluet mantles bearing shields of the arms of St George. Dressed like this, they heard Mass bare-headed, celebrated by the bishops of Canterbury, Winchester and Exeter, and similarly they sat at table together in honour of the holy martyr, from whom they especially took the title of this most noble brotherhood, calling the company of these men 'of St George de la gartiere'.[5]

If Baker is correct in naming the three bishops who celebrated mass, the ceremony could not have taken place in 1349, as Thomas Bradwardine was only consecrated as archbishop of Canterbury on 19 July of that year, John Stratford having died in August of the previous year. Against this, the surviving fifteenth-century copies of the statutes open with the words: 'To the honour of Almighty God, Saint Mary the glorious Virgin and St George the Martyr, Edward the third, king of England, in the 23rd year of his reign [1349] ordered, established and founded a certain fellowship or military order at his castle of Windsor, in this fashion.' This is clearly not the original foundation deed, but an abstract of it, and therefore carries little weight.[6]

The best evidence as to the date of foundation comes from royal accounts, and points to a date of 1348. On 18 December the prince's wardrobe keeper bought twenty-four garters specially made for the prince, and these were – at an unspecified date – given to the knights of the companionship of the Garter. A series of entries in a list of liveries provided between January 1347 and January 1349 by the keeper of the king's wardrobe includes a large number of items with the garter embroidered on them: a bed of blue taffeta 'powdered with blue garters', a great streamer for a ship with the image of St Lawrence and the arms of England and France quartered, 'powdered with garters', and various items of clothing, including the mantle and surcoat mentioned by Baker, as well as three harnesses for the king's horses. The motto is given for the first time in these same accounts: *Honi soit qui mal y pense*. Because the entries cover a two-year period, they are not conclusive evidence that 1348 was the foundation date: but as the entries represent payments made before the end of January 1349, and there was often a delay in making such payments, it is unlikely that they are preparations for a feast to be held in the April following the end of the account. The entry in the prince's accounts, although copied into them in 1352, clearly indicates an existing fellowship.[7]

Additional evidence is provided by letters patent of 6 August 1348, which give details of the plans for completion of the chapel at Windsor, the addition of the Virgin and St George to the dedication (previously to Edward the Confessor), and the arrangements for the twenty-four knights and chaplains. This reads like the official document completing a promise already made, and would therefore follow the foundation ceremony rather than precede it. So the weight of evidence clearly favours 23 April 1348 as the date of the first Garter feast, at which the details of the order and its statutes were agreed.[8]

The reasons for the Order's foundation, and for the adoption of the garter as a symbol, are equally obscure. The early statutes give no clue; even Froissart, who confuses the foundation of the order with the Round Table proceedings of 1344, gives no story to account for the choice of the Garter. It was only in 1534 that an explanation appeared in print, in the *Historia Anglica* of Polydore Vergil. Vergil was Italian by birth, but had become a naturalized Englishman in 1510. He was a sceptical, methodical scholar, who aroused much fury by his dismissal of the stories about King Arthur as fiction. In the case of the Order of the Garter, however, it was he who gave a possible myth its first airing. This is what he had to say:

But the reason for founding the order is utterly uncertain; popular tradition nowadays declares that Edward at some time picked up from the ground a garter from the stocking of his queen or mistress, which had become unloosed by some chance, and had fallen. As some of the knights began to laugh and jeer on seeing this, he is reputed to have said that in a very little while the same garter would be held by them in the highest honour. And not long after, he is said to have founded this order and given it the title by which he showed those knights who had laughed at him how to judge his actions. Such is popular tradition. English writers have been modestly superstitious, perhaps fearing to commit lèse-majesté, if they made known such unworthy things; and they have preferred to remain silent about them, whereas matters should really be seen otherwise: something that rises from a petty or sordid origin increases all the more in dignity.[9]

Vergil places this story almost on a par with the stories about Arthur: here it is *fama vulgus*, popular tradition, in Arthur's case

vulgus mirandis fert ad coelum laudibus Arthurum, ordinary people
praise Arthur to the skies. For his attitude to the fables of Geoffrey
of Monmouth, Vergil was vigorously attacked by John Leland; but
English antiquaries recognized a good story when they heard it,
and Vergil became the authority on the foundation of the Garter.
His version reappears in Camden and Selden at the end of the
sixteenth and beginning of the seventeenth century; Camden is
equally cautious about it, but adds his own invention to the story
by turning the king's mistress into Joan, countess of Salisbury. The
tradition was undoubtedly genuine, for Vergil was not given to
invention: and it has been claimed that he drew on popular tradition
going back to the early fourteenth century: the same authority
cites the Garter story as evidence that Vergil 'knew when to admit
that a popular legend contained a true tradition'. There is also a
hint of such a tradition in a treatise of 1463 on the Garter, by
another Italian, Mondonus Belvaleti, who says that 'many assert
that this order took its beginning from the feminine sex, from a
lewd and forbidden affection', but the passage is an obscure one,
and when he comes to discuss the Order's motto, he does so in
conventional rhetorical terms. But, as the seventeenth-century
historian of the Order, Ashmole, pointed out, there are similar
tales attached to the foundation of the Order of the Golden Fleece
in Burgundy and the rather more obscure Order of the Collar in
Savoy, both of which are equally without documentary support.
In the case of the Golden Fleece, the insignia was probably chosen
to represent the wealth of Burgundy, derived from the Flemish
weaving towns: the Collar is uncertain, but seems to have been
religious; while the Garter was very probably political, and
Ashmole's suggestion that the motto *Honi soit qui mal y pense* refers
to Edward III's claim to the French throne is still the most plausible
explanation. Blue and gold were the French colours, and the motto
could be seen as a retort to the propaganda produced abroad to
discredit Edward and his French ambitions: 'Shame on him who
thinks ill of it'. Two examples of this propaganda are the poem
known as *The Vows of the Heron*, a bitter and subtle satire of about
1340 implying that the war had been begun by Robert of Artois's
machinations, and the alleged rape of the countess of Salisbury by
Edward III as told by Jean Le Bel. If the Order's motto was perhaps
Edward's reply to these shameful stories, might not the story of
foundation retold by Vergil also be from a hostile source?[10]

There is further slight evidence which weighs against the story of the countess of Salisbury in the early fourteenth century. The word 'garter' is extremely rare, and indeed only appears once before the foundation of the Order, in either English or French (in Walter of Bibbesworth's Glossary, about 1325); here it is applied to an item of apparel worn by fashionable squires to keep up their hose. At the end of the century, another writer claims that the fashion was started by the Order itself: 'From those men of the garters comes the use of garters.' I have found only one piece of evidence of ladies wearing garters before the fifteenth century: in 1389, the prostitutes of Toulouse were to wear a badge of a garter by royal decree – once again, there is a suggestion of political mockery and propaganda. The form of the garter, as shown in the earliest known representation (Plate 1), is also unusual: it is a miniature belt, with buckle and perforated tongue, hardly a purely practical item of clothing. Later garters were usually a strip of cloth or silk, tied in a knot. I would tentatively suggest that the design is connected with the knight's belt, one of the insignia used in the ceremony of knighthood.[11]

Whatever the immediate cause for the choice of motto and badge, there is the wider question of why Edward should choose to create such a novel institution as a secular order of knighthood. For the Order of the Garter is the earliest well-attested foundation of this kind, despite the claims of nationalist antiquarians in the seventeenth century, who made most such orders go back deep into the mists of time. It was not, however, an entirely new idea, and just after Edward had been mooting the idea of an Order of the Round Table, John duke of Normandy and Odo duke of Burgundy obtained six Bulls from Pope Clement VI, dated 5 June 1344, giving permission for the building of a collegiate church, with twenty-four resident canons and a fellowship of 200 knights, under the patronage of the Virgin and St George. The knights were to assemble on the patron saints' festivals, 'not for jousting or tournaments or any other deeds of arms', but to worship. It is possible that this was a direct imitation of Edward's project: but there is also a possible common source for both. According to the official chronicles of Castile, Alfonso XI founded an Order in 1332 whose members wore white surcoats with a vermilion sash

as broad as a man's hand worn over cloaks and other garments from the left shoulder to the waist [? diagonally]: and they were called the knights of the Sash (de la Banda) and had statutes among themselves on many good matters, all of which were knightly deeds. And when a knight was given the sash, he was made to swear and promise to keep all the things that were written in that book of statues. And the king did this so that men wishing to have that sash would have reason to do knightly deeds. And it happened afterwards that if a knight or squire did some feat of arms against the king's enemies, or tried to perform such a feat, the king gave him a sash and did him high honour, so that all the others wished to do good knightly deeds to gain that honour and the goodwill of the king, like those who already had it.[12]

A sixteenth-century copy of the statutes for the Order of the Sash survives, from which it becomes clear that this was to be a chivalric as much as a military order. Behaviour is the subject of the first eight headings: four deal with criminal acts, one specifies that the knights shall all serve in the same squadron in the royal army on campaigns, and the rest cover ceremonials and tournaments, the latter evidently playing a large part in the Order's affairs. But as the preamble to the statutes says, the Order was 'founded on two principles, chivalry and loyalty . . .'; and loyalty in the shifting sands of Spanish politics was vital to the king. Alfonso seems to have tried

to create a corps of gentlemen who would distinguish themselves by knightly deeds and who would prepare for war by constant physical exercise: and to group round himself and his successors an elite body whose members, bound by a special oath of loyalty and entirely devoted to the sovereign's person, would be a solid support for royal authority at a time when it was weak and ill-established.[13]

Such corps were by no means unknown in Spain: the military religious Orders of Santiago and Calatrava had formed the backbone of the Spanish armies of the Reconquista, and had become very much secularized. The knights of Santiago could marry, and the king had a large say in the elections to the mastership in both Orders. They were vital to the king's interests, but he could only influence their conduct indirectly, and this may have been one impetus for the founding of the Order of the Sash: to have a corps similar to the military orders which was directly under royal control. There were no similar institutions in either France or

England, and though it is impossible to prove, particularly in the absence of any contemporary Castilian documents relating to the Banda, I believe that the Banda may well have inspired the French and English projects of 1344 and the Order of the Garter. Relations between both France and England and Castile were much closer between 1330 and 1344 than they had been for decades as a result of rivalry for diplomatic alliances. We have already seen how an Anglo-Castilian marriage alliance was almost achieved in 1348. In the course of preparations for this match, the earls of Derby and Salisbury had gone to Castile in 1343, and had taken part in the siege of Algeciras, where they would have met the knights of the Banda. Among Spanish dignitaries to whom Edward wrote seeking support for the alliance, four out of the dozen or so names can be tentatively identified as members of the Order, apart from members of the royal family. Two of these offered to come to Edward's aid when he was planning his campaign in France in 1345. Derby was at the height of his fame and influence when the Order of the Garter was founded, and it is quite likely that his knowledge of the Order of the Sash helped to shape Edward's decision. Although the statutes of the Garter say nothing about tournaments, and have a much stronger element of religious confraternity, the size of the two Orders and in particular their adoption as a badge of a piece of clothing which could be worn over armour without difficulty, point to some degree of common origin.[14]

One other Order of this period should also be mentioned, the Order of St Catherine, founded in the Dauphiné at an uncertain date, probably in the 1330s. This was created to foster 'the good love, good faith and good affection' between the lord of the Dauphiné and his knights, and besides its religious functions on St Catherine's day, was also designed to provide a kind of military corps: members were to have horses and armour always at the ready, and they were to help each other in all possible ways in questions of war. Members of the Order are also obliged to lend steeds and equipment to each other at jousts if need be. If the dating is correct, this is another possible model for the Order of the Garter.[15]

The original twenty-six members of the Order of the Garter formed a very close-knit group. They were the chief commanders of the English armies in the Crécy campaign, and although some knights were almost as young as the prince himself, they had all seen active service. The king, the prince and the earl of Derby, now earl of Lancaster, headed the list; there were two other earls

(Warwick and Stafford), while William Montacute and Roger Mortimer became earls in 1349 and 1354 respectively. Sixteen English knights and three foreigners made up the total: Sir John Lisle, Sir John Beauchamp, Sir Hugh Courtney, Sir John Grey, Sir Miles Stapleton, Sir Hugh Wrottesley, Sir John Chandos, Sir Otto Holland, Sir Bartholomew Burghersh, Sir John Mohun, Sir Thomas Holland, Sir Richard FitzSimon, Sir Thomas Wale, Sir Nigel Loring, Sir James Audley* and Sir Walter Paveley. The three foreigners were the captal de Buch, Sir Sanchet d'Abrechicourt and Sir Henry Eam.

How was this group of knights chosen, and what common interest and backgrounds did they share? First, they represent the chief commanders of the English forces in France: the king, Lancaster, Warwick and Stafford. Over half of the first members of the order had served in the prince's retinue at Crécy and Calais: though the prince himself was the youngest knight, Montacute, Mortimer, Bartholomew Burghersh the younger, Thomas and Otto Holland, Sir John Mohun and Henry Eam were all in their early twenties; Walter Paveley was twenty-seven. Thomas Wale, in his mid forties, was the oldest of the knights, while James Audley, Hugh Wrottesley and John Chandos were all over thirty: they had also served in the prince's retinue, but had already acquired distinguished war records before then. Richard FitzSimon, the prince's standard-bearer, was the other member of this group.

Of the remaining knights, John Beauchamp had been the king's standardbearer at Crécy. Sir Miles Stapleton had been in the king's retinue on the same campaign. Nigel Loring had been knighted for his bravery at Sluys. John Lisle and John Grey had held commands in Brittany and Scotland. Jean de Grailly, captal de Buch (whose name is wrongly recorded as Piers in the early records), was the leader of the pro-English nobles in Gascony, while Sir Sanchet d'Abrechicourt was a member of a prominent family in Picardy who had helped the king during his exile in France in 1326, and were leaders of the English party in that region.[16]

It is difficult to say precisely how the founder-members of the Order were chosen: a number of knights of equal distinction at the time had to wait until vacancies occurred before becoming members, while yet others, such as the earl of Oxford, who had a long military career in close association with the prince, never became

---

* Not to be confused with his contemporary James Lord Audley of Heighley (d.1386), one of the prince's Cheshire tenants.

members. But two points are clear: the Order was meant to be exclusive, and it was intended primarily for the rising generation of commanders and knights. The king himself, at thirty-six, was the second or third oldest of the members.

The actual function of the Order, if the earliest copies of the statutes do in fact reflect the content of the original foundation documents, was almost exclusively religious. The only three secular provisions are that knights of the Garter shall not leave England without permission; that they shall not fight on opposite sides, nor engage in the retinue of any lord who is fighting another lord who has already retained one member of the Order; and that no member of the Order is to be seen in public without his Garter. The celebration of mass for dead knights and the maintenance of the college of canons at Windsor were also emphasized. No knight was to pass through Windsor without hearing mass at the chapel. The religious element centred on the annual St George's day feast, at which all members were to be present. If they were unavoidably absent by the king's leave, they were to celebrate the feast themselves as they would have done at Windsor. There is no mention of jousting or of everyday behaviour, as with the Order of the Sash, nor of rash oaths such as the vow never to retreat in battle taken by members of the French Order of the Star, founded in 1351. It was precisely this serious and solemn approach that gave the Order its dignity and enduring quality: and it reflects a facet of the characters of both Edward and his son that is not often emphasized.[17]

The Order made a considerable impression, despite the lack of attention paid to it in the chronicles. A year or two later, the anonymous author of the political satire, *Winner and Waster*, made it the central theme of his description of the king: the sides of his tent are adorned

> With English bezants full bright, beaten from gold,
> And each one gaily encircled with garters of blue
> And every garter with gold worked full richly
> Then were these words worked into the weaving
> Painted in pale blue, with stops in between,
> That were formed full fair on freshly-drawn letters,
> And it all was one saying, in the English tongue:
> 'Hethyng have the hathell that any harme thinkes'.*

---

* The alliterative line neatly translates *Honi soit qui mal y pense*, but it is impossible to modernize: hethyng=scorn, hathell=man.

The king, 'one of the handsomest lords you have ever seen', sits on a silken bench outside, with crown and sceptre, his apparel

> Berry-brown as his beard, embroidered with wildfowl,
> Falcons in fine gold, fluttering their wings,
> And each one bore a badge, blue as I thought
> A great garter of indigo . . .[18]

On his belt were ducks and drakes, cowering in fear from the falcons embroidered above. The poet goes on to describe the prince, in the passage already quoted (page 69). What is interesting is that within a very few years of the Order's foundation, the Garter should already be taken as the symbol of the king and his court.

The serious element in the Garter ceremonies did not mean that the king and prince had abandoned lighter amusements. Tournaments, hunting, fine clothes and jewels continued to be their chief pleasures. The years following their return from Calais saw some of the most splendid and luxurious tournaments of the reign, enthusiastically supported by the nobles. Henry earl of Lancaster had even found time to hold a tournament at Lincoln in April 1347, between his return from Gascony in January and his departure for Calais in May. The king was at tournaments at Bury, Reading, Windsor, Lichfield, Eltham and Canterbury during this period, and spent considerable sums on special badges and costumes. The Windsor jousts on 24 June 1348 were to celebrate the queen's churching after the birth of her sixth son, William, to whom the prince stood godfather, presenting the child's nurse with a silver cup and ewer and the three girls 'who guard his cradle' with a cup each. At the tournament, he also gave the queen a horse called Bauzan de Burgh. The various French nobles held captive in England, Charles de Blois, the count of Eu and the chamberlain of Tancarville, were given permission to take part, and 'the favour of the field was awarded to the count of Eu' as the best jouster. King David of Scotland also took part, and the clothing provided was suitably rich: the king wore a long green robe embroidered with pheasants' feathers, his third son, Lionel, now ten years old, was given a sea-green and azure doublet. The prince himself was accompanied by a sizeable retinue, for whom he provided robes and trimmings. Then the royal party and the prisoners went off for some weeks to hunt at Clarendon and other royal forests.[19]

Many tournaments seem to have had a theme or special motto:

indeed, the Order of the Garter itself may possibly stem from such a motto, since in 1348, for a tournament at Eltham at an unknown date, twelve blue garters embroidered in gold with the motto *Honi soit qui mal y pense* were made. At the tournament at Lichfield in April 1348, the king wore the arms of one of the prince's knights, Sir Thomas Bradeston. The prince was certainly present, but there is no record of whether he was of the same party. Again at Canterbury in 1348 eight 'harnesses' with the arms of Sir Stephen Cosington, also one of the prince's knights, were provided, as if the knight in question had been invited to provide a team for the occasion. At Canterbury the eight knights were from the same close-knit group as before: the earls of Lancaster and Suffolk, John Grey, John Beauchamp, Robert Maule, John Chandos and Roger Beauchamp. At a tournament at Bury St Edmunds, the prince gave a war-horse called Morel de Burghersh to one of the minstrels, and there are frequent entries for gifts to the prince's own minstrels, including four silver-gilt and enamelled pipes bought from the count of Eu at the Windsor tournament.[20]

Far more lavish even than the expenditure on tournaments was that on jewellery. A list of the prince's New Year's gifts for 1347 or 1348 has survived. The king was given an enamelled gold cup, the queen a brooch set with three rubies and an emerald, while the prince's sisters Isabella and Joan received elaborate clasps: that for Joan was 'set with a great Lady, one balasse ruby above, with three diamonds round it, two pearls on two pinnacles and two emeralds at the sides of the ouch, one balasse ruby at the bottom, and six pearls in three clusters (each cluster having a great emerald in the middle) near the said ruby'. Members of the prince's household also received jewels: his master, Bartholomew Burghersh, received a ruby and sapphire brooch; Richard de la Bere a clasp with a rose and crown; other clasps went to John Chandos, Bartholomew Burghersh the younger and Walter Paveley. The prince's physician, John Gaddesden (who received £10 a year as his fee), was given a rose of gold, in allusion to his famous treatise, *Rosa Medicinae*, written forty years earlier.[21]

The prince's other entertainments were also far from frugal. We have no full records of his expenditure on horses, falcons and hounds, but to judge by the accounts for the royal kennels, these must have been a major item. There were certainly three 'yeomen of the falconers' in the prince's household in 1352, implying a considerable number of lesser servants in the mews. There are frequent entries for cash given to the prince for gambling, culminating in the spectacular amount of £105 for a session with the king at Sandwich on 23 December 1348.[22]

Such high living did not go without comment; the monastic chroniclers had a good deal to say both about extravagance and loose living. In 1344, John of Reading expostulated about the way the English had imitated the fashions of Hainault, ever since a number of Hainaulters had come over with queen Philippa, changing their style each year, and forsaking the long, ample robes of the old days. They wore instead 'short clothes with narrow waists, with pointed fringes and slashed, trimmed with lace and stiffened with bone, with buttons everywhere, the sleeves of surcoats and tippets of hoods hanging right down, looking more like devils and torturers in their clothes and shoes than ordinary men'. The chronicler of the monastery of Meaux, taking up the perennial outcry of the Church against tournaments, had this to say about the celebrations of 1348:

> The lords and knights of England . . . held tournaments and jousts in different cities and towns of the kingdom, to which they summoned ladies, matrons and other noblewomen. There was hardly a lady or matron there assigned to her own husband; they were with other men, by whom they were debauched as the lust took them.

Henry Knighton, writing later in the century, embroiders on this theme:

> At that time there were many rumours and a great outcry among the people, because almost wherever tournaments were held, a troop of women were present, almost as if they were taking part in the sport; they were dressed in various and amazing men's clothes, and numbered about forty or fifty of the wealthier and more beautiful (but not the best) women of the kingdom. They wore parti-coloured tunics, half one colour and half another colour, with short hoods whose long points were wound round their heads like ropes, belts studded with silver or gold, and they also had knives called 'daggers' in pouches slung over their stomachs; and they made their way to the scene of the jousts mounted on choice destriers or other well-found horses; and so they spent and wasted their goods, and inflicted wanton and foolish lusts on their bodies, according to popular rumour. Nor

did they fear God or blush at the stories people told, as they threw off the bonds of marriage.

He adds, however, that heavy thunderstorms and rain effectively put a stop to their activities.[23]

Whatever the truth of the accusations – and Edward's court was not particularly strait-laced – some such criticisms were made with hindsight in later years, and made a cause for the visitation that followed. A particularly virulent type of plague, the so-called Black Death, had begun to make its appearance in Europe in 1347, reaching Sicily early in October that year. It spread rapidly through Italy and France; in the great towns as many as half the population died. By June 1348, the epidemic had reached Paris, and in August princess Joan died of the plague at Bordeaux on her way to Spain. (Early in the autumn another member of the royal family, the prince's godson William, died, though almost certainly not of the plague; he was buried at Windsor on 5 September.) The plague reached England at about the end of June 1348, probably by way of a ship which put into Melcombe Regis in Dorset; it certainly spread first across the West Country before moving towards London at the beginning of 1349. Medieval doctors knew nothing of the complex causes of the disease, which, confusingly, seems to have taken three different forms (bubonic, septicaemic and pneumonic), and preventive measures were mostly misguided. It was, however, generally believed that it was dangerous to have much contact with victims of the plague, and the first notice of its arrival in London was the king's prorogation of the parliament summoned for January 1349 on the grounds that plague had broken out, and anyone coming to London would be in danger. The king and his court dispersed to the country, and, probably because they lived in airier and more hygienic surroundings than either the citizens or the peasants, fewer of them died of the plague. Indeed, none of the knights of the Garter died of it, which is remarkable when the mortality rate among the clergy was as high as 45 per cent in some dioceses, and even the average for the knights' contemporaries, those within the age-group twenty-one to thirty-five, was about one in four. So although the Black Death and its attendant horrors of the unburied dead, abandoned houses and land lying waste must have impressed the prince as much as anyone who had lived through it, the disease spared his close companions.[24]

The king and prince spent most of the summer in the royal

manors in the west and south, where the pestilence had begun to run its course, while the normal work of government continued at Westminster: there is no break in the series of official records, though their contents increasingly reflect the havoc wrought by the pestilence. When the plague had passed, much of the work of the prince's council was taken up with its consequences. Like every other landowner in England, the prince's revenues suffered severely, if temporarily. In 1350–51, his receipts from Cornwall were only three fifths of the 1347 figure, and he and his council were prepared to forgo rents rather than find that the tenant abandoned his holding. It is tempting to look at this action and claim 'that his estates were often governed with a degree of benevolence that far exceeded the feudal obligations of a lord to his tenants . . . The magnanimity with which the Prince conducted his affairs is all the more laudable in view of the desperate impecunity that dogged him for most of his life.' The prince and his advisers were far from charitable; they were, however, practical enough to know that their tenants had small resources. Lenience was in order in the wake of a disaster like the Black Death, if only because harsh enforcement might ruin the tenant, and replacements for such holdings were hard to come by. A directive to the steward, auditor and receiver of Cornwall late in 1351 starts by instructions to enforce the prince's rights and to let empty holdings at the old going rate 'without any decrease'; only then is it provided that poor tin-miners who have failed to pay coinage on their tin are to be allowed to pay fines rather than forfeit the tin, 'having regard to the present bad times'. Likewise, the 'oppressions and extortions' of the archdeacon of Cornwall are condemned because the prince's council fear that they may lose revenue into the archdeacon's pocket. On occasions, the prince could be genuinely charitable; but in the face of this over-whelming disaster there was little scope for doing more than striking a balance between the interests of lord and tenant.[25]

In the autumn, both the king and the prince were at Hereford for the translation on 25 October of the relics of St Thomas Cantilupe to a new and elaborate shrine. Although the bishop had recently forbidden plays and interludes to be acted in the city churches, for fear that such gatherings would spread the plague, there was no attempt to restrict the audience at the translation, and a large crowd was present at the ceremony. A great feast was held at the expense of the saint's kinsman, Nicholas Cantilupe.[26]

The Black Death had brought about an almost complete cessation

of military activity in France, and the truce had been renewed for a
further year. However, at the end of 1349 Calais was threatened by
a plot to betray it to the French. Aimeric of Pavia, a Genoese
mercenary, had been in Calais during the siege in the pay of the
French: but when the siege ended, he changed to the service of
Edward III, and was appointed master of the royal galleys and
crossbowmen on 24 April 1348. In the autumn of 1349 he was again
at Calais, this time as part of the English garrison. He was
approached by a leading French commander, Geoffrey de Charny,
with the suggestion that, for a suitable reward, he would betray the
town to a small force under Charny's command. Aimeric encouraged Charny's overtures, and a price, said to be 40,000 florins,
was agreed. The French were to be admitted to the town at the
end of the year. At this point Aimeric either decided to play a
double game depending on how the operation went, so that he
could emerge with equal credit as either an English or French
partisan, or genuinely regretted what he had done. He therefore
wrote to England, telling the king of the details of the plot, and the
news reached the king while he was at Hereford.[27]

The king and the prince set off in some haste, accompanied only
by Roger Mortimer and a few other knights, and reached Calais
shortly before the betrayal was due to take place. They decided to
lay an ambush for the French, and knights were stationed around
the portcullis and doors of the main entrance to the castle behind a
carefully constructed dry wall, made to look as though it was part
of the original masonry. The main timbers of the drawbridge
were partly sawn through, so that an armed knight could ride over
it, yet it could be quickly broken by throwing down a large stone
specially positioned in the tower above, behind another false wall.
A knight was posted by the stone with orders to hurl it down once
enough French had entered. The presence of the king and prince
was kept a closely guarded secret.

The day before that agreed for the surrender of the town, fifteen
French scouts were let in to the castle by Aimeric, and he was paid
the greater part of his fee. The French searched the castle thoroughly,
and found no signs of treachery. The next day they raised the
French standard and those of Geoffrey de Charny and other lords
on the towers as a sign of their success. The townsmen, who were
largely English settlers, hastened to attack the French; but by now
the gates had been opened. In the general confusion, one of the
garrison of Calais, Sir Thomas Kingeston, who was not in the plot,

was captured; and those of the garrison who did know about it had some difficulty in restraining the townsmen, who threatened to spoil the plan by driving out the attackers. At the appropriate moment, before too many of the French had gained entry, the stone was thrown down and the drawbridge shattered. The knights around the entrance, who had been in their hiding places, 'like hermits, unconcerned by the long wait of three days', now burst out and attacked the French, who were overwhelmed after a brief but fierce fight.[28]

Outside the walls, the remaining French troops, seeing that they had been tricked, took to flight. The king and some thirty knights, with a handful of archers, rashly set off in pursuit, and did some damage to the French before the latter realized how few their opponents were. They halted, and the king found himself faced by perhaps 800 armed men. He and his force were now in the marshes around Calais, and he quickly dispersed his archers on dry knolls of land in the marsh, where the heavily armed French knights could not reach them without sinking into the morass. He encouraged them by telling them that he was Edward of Windsor, and prepared for a bitter fight. The French were on the causeway out of the town, and could only line up twenty abreast, making an excellent target for the archers. The prince, seeing his father's plight, had sallied out of the seaward gate of Calais, and as he came up with reinforcements he saw the French attack and heard his father's war-cry of, 'Ah! Edward! Ah! St George!' He reached the king just as the French were beginning to press him, and quickly turned them to flight. Charny, his son and some thirty knights were captured. Guy Bryan, the king's standardbearer, was given 100 marks per annum as a reward for his courage in 'keeping the king's standard raised' during the fight. Aimeric of Pavia was rewarded by a pension of £160 a year, a very substantial amount; but he was captured by the French a year or two later, tortured horribly, hanged, beheaded and quartered. Froissart says that Charny himself was responsible for capturing him.[29]

During the spring and summer, the French continued to observe the truce. The king and prince returned to England shortly after the Calais episode and no very concrete plans for military action were made, though the war in Brittany continued, and an attack on northern France was projected. In the late spring, a threat appeared from a new quarter. The death of princess Joan in 1348 had meant that plans for an Anglo-Castilian alliance were laid aside. This would not have been serious in itself, but in the winter of 1349, under the terms of a Franco-Castilian alliance signed in 1345, the Castilians formed a large fleet with the object of marauding along the English coast and generally intercepting communications between England and the English forces in Gascony and Brittany. Relations between the Castilian and Gascon seamen had always been poor, and the French request for aid offered an opportunity for revenge. The king probably learnt in detail of the Castilian fleet from the earl of Lancaster, who returned from Gascony early in May, although naval preparations began on 1 May with the impressment of crews for the king's own ships. It was only at the end of July that serious preparations were put in hand. Sir Robert Morley, an experienced sailor, was put in charge of the northern fleet again on 22 July, and on the 23rd a general summons for the fleet to gather at Sandwich was issued. On 10 August the king wrote to the archbishops of Canterbury and York, explaining that the Castilians had raided English shipping and were now threatening to invade the country, and that he was preparing to attack them; prayers and processions for victory were requested.[30]

The Spaniards, who had attacked the Gascon wine-fleet on its way to England earlier in the summer, taking or sinking ten ships, were now at Sluys. Their admiral, Carlos de la Cerda, was intending to return home before the winter storms in the Bay of Biscay, and knew that the English were preparing to attack him, but none the less laid his course close to the English coast, possibly hoping to make a profitable raid on one of the ports. The latter were evidently well informed as to the Castilian fleet's movements, as the king arrived at Winchelsea, where the English fleet had gathered, in mid August, but only boarded his flagship, the *Cog Thomas*, the day before the Castilians appeared, sailing out to meet them. The heavily laden ships contained most of the great lords of England: the prince of Wales, the earls of Lancaster, Northampton, Warwick, Salisbury, Arundel, Huntingdon and Gloucester; and there were most of the best of England's knights as well. Naval warfare was little different from land warfare: a preliminary loosing-off of arrows, followed by a charge – in this case attempts to ram or otherwise disable the enemy – and a fierce hand-to-hand mêlée. The manoeuvrability of the ships was slight, and even in the open sea the fight would become an almost static one between drifting pairs of ships grappled to each other. The two fleets engaged between five and six in the evening on 29 August. The numbers of the two fleets were roughly equal: forty-four Spanish ships to fifty or so English vessels. The great Spanish 'busses' towered over the English ships and brigs, so that the Spanish were able to bombard the English from above; but the Spanish crossbowmen were worsted by the English archers, who forced the Spanish to take cover; and the hail of stones and spears diminished as the enemy sought refuge behind the rails. Any Spaniard who stood up to hurl a stone was at once picked off by the archers. Yet the superior size and height of the Spanish ships was still a formidable obstacle to the boarding parties, and when the English ships grappled themselves to the Spaniards, rocks dropped blindly over the side by the crouching enemy did considerable damage. Froissart claims that both the king and the prince had to fight their way aboard the Spanish ships because their ships were sinking. By nightfall, about twenty-four of the forty-seven Spanish ships were in English hands, and the remainder escaped under cover of darkness. The English fleet anchored off the coast for the night, and prepared for a renewal of the battle on the following day; but when reveille was sounded, there was no sign of the enemy. The English fleet returned in triumph to Winchelsea, though much the worse for wear. The chroniclers agree that it was a particularly savage battle, though only one knight is named as killed; the Spaniards are said to have refused to give themselves up for ransom, preferring to die. It was by no means a total victory: on 8 September the king wrote to the citizens of Bayonne, the southernmost city of Gascony and old rivals of the Castilian seamen, warning them of the imminent arrival of the Castilian fleet and ordering them to arm themselves against the enemy; and the annual wine convoy from Bordeaux in October was provided with an escort of warships. There seem to have been few substantial rewards in the wake of the victory: pardons were issued to men in the retinues of the prince, the earl of Lancaster and Warwick, Sir John Lisle, and Sir Reginald Cobham. Sir Stephen Cosington, whom we have met earlier in connection with the Canterbury tournament of 1348, was given a grant of 100 marks per annum for his services to the prince, the only such reward made by the prince. The king and the prince probably realized that the victory had not been a decisive one; but they made as much capital out of it as they could. In parliament, early the following year, the king was given the title 'King of the Sea', while popular ballads rejoiced that the Spaniards 'feed many fishes, for all their great pride'. On the other hand, Flemish chroniclers were uncertain as to whether the English had even won the battle, because such conflicting reports were circulating.[31]

The newly won prestige of the English king was underlined in the following month, when two knights who had served in Sicily arrived in London to submit a quarrel to Edward. Giovanni Visconti, a Cypriot, had accused Thomas de la Marche, said to be the illegitimate son of Philip of Valois, of treacherously failing to reveal a plot to seize the king of Sicily, of which he had learnt during the siege of Catania in 1347. The matter was to be settled by a judicial duel, which was duly held at Westminster on 4 October in the presence of the king and the prince. The combatants were fully armed, except for visors; and this decided the issue, because after they had fought on horseback and on foot, they ended by wrestling, and Thomas used the sharp edges of the armour protecting his fingers to lacerate his opponent's face. His opponent, wearing a different kind of gauntlet, was unable to retaliate, and 'cried out horribly', at which the king stopped the fight. Thomas presented his prisoner to the prince, who gave him his freedom and presented Thomas with two silver basins enamelled with his arms. On 6 December, the prince was at a more peaceful kind of contest, a tournament at Norwich; with him were the queen and Robert Ufford, and they were entertained at the city's expense.[32]

Despite the sea-battle with the Castilians, who were allies of the French, the truce with France continued. It was due to run until 1 August 1351, provided that peace talks were opened in Avignon by 1 November. The French were not inclined to break the truce, because Philip VI had died on 22 August and the new king, John II, was in process of taking over power. The change of king made little difference to Edward's attitude to the French; where Philip had been mediocre and vacillating, John was obstinate and temperamental, and open to influence by his favourites. Philip had been well served by royal officials; John all too often ignored the advice of experienced administrators and preferred to listen to his nobles. He was a lover of chivalry, and his generosity and benevolence earned him the name of John the Good – good in the sense of good-tempered rather than in moral terms.

The diplomatic manoeuvres relating to the truce were in fact in the hands of royal officials, and neither Edward nor John interfered to any extent in the detail of the negotiations, which had become virtually a standing conference under Guy de Boulogne, which met in tents pitched near Calais. The complexities of the renewals of the truce and the search for a permanent peace need not concern us here. They were nominally led by the earl of Lancaster, newly created duke; and only for a few months in 1354 did it seem that a peace treaty might emerge, by which Edward would have gained Aquitaine, Ponthieu, Poitou, Anjou, Maine, Touraine and lands around Calais, in full sovereignty, in return for his abandoning his claim to the French throne. The conduct of the talks was largely influenced by the relative success or failure of English diplomatic initiatives elsewhere: there were plans for a closer alliance with Flanders, based on a marriage between John of Gaunt and the count's infant daughter; for an alliance with the captive Charles of Blois, claimant to the duchy of Brittany; and for another alliance with Charles, king of Navarre, son-in-law of king John and himself a claimant to the French throne. Each of these failed in turn, but the truces continued until the spring of 1355. Views on the advisability of renewing the war were mixed: in 1354, parliament had acclaimed the idea of perpetual peace with shouts of 'Yes, yes!', but propagandists in favour of the war were circulating poems attacking the truce:

> O king, waging a fine war, you now seek a truce:
> Fighting, you will win; make a truce, you will be tricked.

Many of the English knights, and probably the prince himself, would have agreed.[33]

The truces were far from being universally observed, and the outbreak of full-scale war was still expected. In 1350, Bartholomew Burghersh the elder obtained a two-year deferment of his vow to go on pilgrimage to the Holy Sepulchre, evidently because war was too much of a possibility; and in 1351 and 1352 general proclamations of an imminent French invasion were published and appropriate measures taken.[34]

During the years 1350-55, there was military action in Gascony, Brittany and Picardy. In Gascony, the French gradually regained towns in Saintonge and Poitou, though there were occasional English counter-attacks. The war was largely in the hands of licensed freebooters, such as a certain Pierre Morin, issued with letters-patent by the French in September 1346 by which he would receive a year's rent of any lands or towns he captured from the English. The English garrisons supported themselves by brigandage, and most warfare was on a small scale. The French made one major incursion, led by Guy de Nesle, in the spring of 1351, and a pitched battle was fought at Taillebourg, a few miles north-west of Saintes, scene of a battle between Henry III and Louis IX a century earlier. The French were defeated, but they none the less recovered Saint-Jean-d'Angély and Lusignan soon afterwards.[35]

A series of minor episodes centred on Calais, the most important being the capture of the neighbouring fortress of Guines in 1352 by an English adventurer, who sold it to the king. In the previous year, the duke of Lancaster and Sir Walter Mauny had led raids on separate occasions towards Boulogne, Étaples and Saint-Omer, but no serious fighting was done, and the duke's attempts to take Boulogne were repulsed.

In Brittany, something approaching a full-scale war continued, the English commanders being Sir Walter Bentley and Robert Knolles, culminating in the battle of Mauron in August 1352. The French were again led by Guy de Nesle, and were heavily defeated, Guy de Nesle and other nobles being killed. This was the first encounter in which the knights of king John's newly founded Order of the Star had fought; the Order's oath of admission was reputed to contain a clause that knights would never turn their backs on the enemy, and as a result 45 of the original 140 members were captured or killed.[36]

Three years of almost general peace followed, though this was due more to John's preoccupation with the intrigues of Charles of Navarre and the English king's efforts on the diplomatic front than to any military factors. The prince was not involved in any of this diplomacy, and even in later years showed little interest in foreign affairs unless they had some bearing on possibilities for war. This was by no means unusual for a prince, as kings only took a direct part in such matters when it came to the signature of a peace treaty or other ceremonial state occasion. The dukes of Lancaster, in the person of both Henry of Grosmont and John of Gaunt, acted as a kind of foreign minister while the prince was the king's deputy. Like all deputies, the prince often had little to do, and there was the ever-present possibility of tension between him and his father over the division of power. But the prince was still only twenty, and more interested in his own pleasures than in responsibilities. We learn relatively little of his activities between 1351 and 1354, most of the details coming from his household records. He seems to have lived apart from the king and queen at this time, and to have met them occasionally at great feasts or at state events. In February 1351 he was present at the parliament in which the earl of Lancaster was made a duke, and later in the year there were rumours of a possible expedition abroad. Ships were requisitioned in March, and an order for archers to be arrayed by 25 July was issued on 15 June; but plans were evidently in some confusion, because on 12 June, the prince allowed carthorses which had been requisitioned for the expedition to be released for the time being. He also dismissed two Cornish knights who had been retained, on the grounds that their conduct 'has been and still is so outrageous and offensive to us, our subjects, ministers, and tenants, as well as to your other neighbours in Cornwall, as to be improper and unsuitable for a man of your order, so that we are advised not to have any such man in our company'. This contrasts sharply with the practice of recruiting any available ruffians and gaolbirds for service among the footsoldiers; and it is interesting that the prince felt that a rebuke of this sort could bring a petty county tyrant to heel, who would probably have echoed Falstaff's sentiments on honour. But the fine words conceal a financial punishment – there would be no wages or booty either.[37]

The prince's main concern during the years of truce was with the administration of his estates, though the nature of the surviving records tends to give the impression of a more serious interest in estate management than was actually the case, because we have almost complete details for these years of the letters written in his name by his officials, and know very little of what the prince was actually doing. Early in 1351 he intended to go to Cheshire and North Wales, but at the end of March put off the journey, probably in view of military activity; in May, he expressed surprise that no one from his lands in Cheshire, Devon and Cornwall had come to do homage 'for a long time past', and said that he wished 'to become acquainted with them and receive their homage' before he next went abroad. This was less a personal gesture than part of a general effort to ensure that all the prince's holdings were properly documented and that homage and other duties were performed: in March, Robert Eleford had been appointed to inquire whether a large number of knight's fees belonging to the prince 'had been usurped . . . and concealed by divers means'. It is possible that these directives, and the new registers of letters begun in early 1351, are all connected with the prince's coming of age in June 1351 and changes in administrative procedure resulting from his increased personal involvement.[38]

The prince spent Christmas at Berkhamsted, a castle which was to be one of his favourite residences. It had been rebuilt by Richard of Cornwall in the 1250s, but the prince had inherited it in a ruinous state, and an inquiry in 1337 revealed that at least £750 needed to be spent on it: the great tower was split from top to bottom. Repairs were carried out in the early 1340s, and the prince used it occasionally during that time; but he now returned there regularly for Christmas, this being the first of three such visits in four years. In the spring of 1352 he was at Wallingford, and from June onwards he and John of Gaunt, now earl of Richmond, spent a considerable time at Byfleet in Surrey. John of Gaunt, now twelve, seems to have been attached to the prince's household from at least 1350 onwards; various entries refer to purchases made for both him and the prince, such as that in March 1351, when clothing was provided for Wulfard Gistels, his child of the chamber (and probably related to the Oliver Ghistels who had served with the prince on the Crécy campaign). At the same time, coats, hats and cloaks were provided for ' "Sigo and Nakok", the Saracen children'. In July 1352, the prince made arrangements to pay his saddler, Lambekyn of Cologne, the large sum of £110, for saddles provided for himself and John of Gaunt between March 1350 and July 1352. Again, between March 1353 and May 1355, the prince spent a further £119 in the same way. At Christmas 1353, the prince was at his manor of Sonning, on the Thames near Reading, but he went over to Eltham for a tournament on 31 December, accompanied by Sir John Chandos and Sir James Audley: the latter were provided with 'plates' (breastplate and backplate) covered in black velvet, while the prince wore plates covered with red velvet. Soon after this tournament, the prince, evidently dissatisfied with his harness, ordered four bits 'which the prince has devised' to be made for the next jousts, 'in accordance with the instructions of Roger, the prince's smith'. Tournaments seem to have been relatively rare events during this period, the only other being at Woodstock in February 1355. Indeed, tournaments were actually banned in Yorkshire, London, Hereford and Huntingdon in July 1354, a measure which had been frequent in the troubled days of Edward II, but is difficult to explain in the early 1350s. At some time during the winter the prince went on pilgrimage to Cirencester.[39]

In the summer of 1353 the prince decided that affairs in Cheshire, which had concerned him two years previously, now required his presence. A bailiff of the prince's, Hugh Hamson of Northwich, had recently been killed 'on the prince's service', and feuds such as that 'between the relatives of Trafforths and Radclyffes at Liverpool' were frequent in the area. It was clear that a display of judicial authority was needed, and in such a turbulent area this would have to be supported by a show of authority. In June, he instructed his chamberlain at Chester, John Burnham, to 'supervise the buying of provisions for his visit', and 'to make clean and prepare the prince's houses of Shotwick, where the prince intends to stay with his privy household to have his sport in the park'. A fuller notice of his impending visit gave as the reason that 'too often grievous clamours and complaints have reached him of wrongs, excesses and misdeeds . . . which cannot be fittingly redressed without his presence'. He announced that justices would hold an eyre while he was there, both of general pleas and pleas of the forest. As to the danger of riots arising from the holding of an eyre, he arranged that the duke of Lancaster, and the earls of Stafford and Warwick, should all be in the area at the time so that he might call on their assistance if need be, though they do not appear to have actually gone to Chester with him. Lancaster held the castle of Halton in Cheshire, while both Stafford's and Warwick's estates were within a day's journey. Recent writers have conjured up the vision of the prince marching into the county at the head of a large armed force, but there is no evidence for this, or for a 'rising' in Cheshire. There was a possibility of attacks on the justices, certainly, but not an open revolt: this is borne out by the fines levied, which reflect years of weak government and a huge backlog of cases involving the prince's rights.[40]

The prince set out for the north-east at the end of July, reaching Tamworth on 1 August and Chester on 4 August: the eyre was due to begin on the 19th, but the men of the county were sufficiently overawed by the prince's presence to be anxious not to be brought to book for their misdemeanours. For the very substantial sum of 5,000 marks they bought off the threatened eyre, and on 18 August the justices were instructed to supersede its business, referring back outstanding cases to the ordinary courts. The following day, the pleas of the forest were likewise abandoned. On the day appointed for the eyre, the men of the county appeared before the justices and 'alleged that that eyre, if carried on, would be harmful to the laws and customs of that county, because no such eyre had ever been held before'. A debate followed on this, and the agreed fine was formally offered and accepted, without prejudice to either side. A series of lesser concessions were also made 'for the said fine': renewal of the traditional laws and customs and minor exemptions

from customary charges. But the prince and his advisers were not
going to allow the individual lawbreakers to escape entirely, and a
circuit of trailbaston was instituted instead, aimed specifically at
felons and trespassers. The prince himself spent much time hearing
petitions from the tenants and on 15 August, the feast of the
Assumption, he held a dinner at Chester for local nobles. On
12 August, he hunted at Shotwick, and ordered that the local reeve
should be allowed 4s. 8d. on the next account because his horses had
trampled down part of a field of oats. The next month was
occupied with administrative business and with the trailbaston
hearings. Among lesser items, the traditional alms given to the
various friaries and hospitals of the city were reorganized and confirmed, the payments being made out of the profits of the session of
trailbaston. The profits of the prince's visit were considerable: the
Cheshire revenues, which had been about £1,500, were raised for
this year to nearly £4,000, and in following years instalments of the
fine for abandonment of the eyre kept them in the region of £2,500.
When the eyre of the forest was next held, in 1358–9, the total the
following year was again high, at nearly £3,500; so it is unfair to
see the prince's journey as a purely financial exercise, designed to
raise extraordinary revenue. The profits of justice were a normal
source of finance; all that the prince and his advisers desired was to
see that justice, and the resultant income, were dealt with on a
regular basis and not allowed to go by default, though if the
Cheshire men's plea before the justices was true, there may have
been an element of novelty in the eyre.[41]

On 24 October the prince was at Westminster, to witness William
Montacute's homage to the king for the county of Denbigh,
which was technically part of his principality, but was granted to
Montacute with his assent. After spending Christmas at Berkhamsted, he went to Sonning in March; on 28 April, he attended
parliament at Westminster. The evident success of his journey to
Cheshire now led to plans for a visit to Cornwall, and in May
repairs to the prince's houses there were ordered. He intended to
set out about 8 July; but in fact, as in the previous year, the prince
set out in late July, reaching Gloucester at the end of the month,
Chudleigh in Devon by 11 August, and arriving at Launceston by
18 August. At 'Poulston Bridge' he was met by John Kellygrey,
who held his lands on condition that he escorted the duke for forty
days whenever he visited Cornwall, wearing a grey cloak and
probably acting as guide through the remoter parts. For Cornwall

was a more difficult country than even Cheshire: the prince frequently had to invoke the full might of the king's justice against lawbreakers who hunted in his parks, raided his ships as they lay at anchor in the harbours or evaded duty on tin. It was a relatively poor country, most of the revenue coming from the tin mines or stannaries rather than from agriculture, with some income from harbour dues. The stannaries were 'farmed' for over £2,000 per annum to the Hanse merchant Tideman of Lymberg in 1347–9; the average manorial profits were between £400 and £600 a year for the period 1340–66. There was no question of a substantial revenue from profits of justice, and the prince was mainly concerned with such matters as homage and settlement of outstanding disputes. There had also been a recent difficulty with the receiver of Cornwall, John Kendale, which had caused the prince to relieve him of his office for the time being.[42]

The prince stayed much of the time at Restormel Castle, rebuilt by Edmund of Cornwall in the late thirteenth century and described in 1337 as

> a castle well walled round. And there are within the walls of the said castle a hall, three chambers, and as many cellars, a chapel . . . [with] an image of the Blessed Mary made of alabaster and valuable . . . a stable for six horses, three chambers over the gateway poorly roofed with lead: and the leaves of the gate of the said castle are weak and insufficient. And there are outside the gateway of the said castle a great hall with two cellars and a chapel in good order.

The other buildings – kitchen, bakehouse and stables – were in poor repair, as was the water-conduit 'by means of which water is brought into the castle into every domestic office'. Some of the necessary repairs, such as those to the water-conduit, were not yet done in 1354, and had to be hurriedly put in hand. Today the great hall outside the walls has completely disappeared, but the impressive circular outer wall is intact, and the rooms within lack only roofs and interior floors (Plate 21).[43]

At Restormel he received the homage of a number of his tenants-in-chief: there was no great business in hand as there had been in Cheshire the previous year, but there were problems with the prince's officials in the county. John Kendale was restored to his officer of receiver, but John Dabernoun, sheriff since 1350, resigned, and was replaced by Sir John Sully. However, Sully was unable to take up the office, and Robert Eleford was given the post on 18 August. Dabernoun had also been keeper of the fees for Devon and Cornwall; in charge of the feudal affairs of the counties. This office was now separated from that of sheriff, and given to John Skirbek. Dabernoun himself was ordered to collect the debts still outstanding for his time as sheriff.[44]

The prince returned home in early September, stopping for some days at Exeter (where he stayed at the bishop's palace) to deal with his affairs in Devonshire. During the autumn he went on pilgrimage to Walsingham, returning to spend Christmas at Berkhamstead again, where his grandmother, queen Isabella, visited him. In February he was at Woodstock, for a tournament to celebrate the queen's 'churching' after the birth of Thomas, her youngest son. More serious matters were now in view, however, and for the following months the prince was in London, at his town house of Pulteney's Inn.[45]

The series of truces and peace negotiations that had continued since 1347 broke down very early in 1355. At that point Edward's envoys saw hopes of alliances both with Charles of Navarre and with the emperor Charles IV of Germany, and the projected peace treaty of 1353 had been finally abandoned. It therefore seemed a good moment to renew hostilities, and when the prince arrived in London, plans were put in hand for action that summer. In view of the impending campaign, the prince went on pilgrimage again, accompanied by his father, to various holy places in England.[46]

Aquitaine: the First Period

◆━━━▶

5

Gascony was in many ways the central problem of the Anglo-French quarrel. Edward's claims extended to the crown and kingdom of France itself, if put in their highest and most extreme form. At the other end of the scale, the absolute minimum for which he was prepared to settle was the restitution of Gascony, with its independence from French interference guaranteed so that there could be no question of its being seized again. Between these two extremes lay the various settlements agreed at different times during his reign. It is therefore not surprising that Gascony had been the scene of the most protracted warfare since the war began there in 1337, even though only one battle of any importance had been fought there, that of Auberoche in 1345.

The lands claimed by Edward, called variously Gascony, Guyenne and Aquitaine – though each of these names had a slightly different meaning, Aquitaine being the widest, and Gascony the smallest, area* – were originally brought to the English crown by Eleanor, duchess of Aquitaine in her own right, when she married Henry II in 1152. Their individual culture and language, that of the *langue d'oc* as opposed to the *langue d'oil* of the north, as well as the fierce independence of their lords, meant that the ties between Gascony and France were by no means close: and two centuries of inter-

---

* Guyenne, derived from the word Aquitaine itself, first appears in 1259, applied specifically to the English domains in the area; but I have preferred to use the other terms as being more familiar.

mittent English rule had made this into a clear division. For this period we must forget the map of modern France and think instead of two 'bands' of common culture and social patterns, one running across northern France into Flanders and down into Burgundy with England and Brittany on its fringes, the other stretching from northern Spain, up to Bordeaux and through Provence into northern Italy. The world of the Gascons was therefore strange to English and French alike. However, the Gascons themselves, and particularly the citizens of Bordeaux, preferred English rule to that of the French king. They preferred the looser control exercised by the English, who were content to leave Gascon affairs to run themselves provided that revenue was forthcoming and there was no threat of interference from France; and in a world where tradition counted for much, the English king was their 'natural lord' as duke of Aquitaine. England, too, was the main market for the Bordeaux wine trade, on which much of the region's economy was based. Bayonne, the other bulwark of English rule in the area, looked for English support in the running battle between her seamen and those of Castile and Normandy.[1]

The early part of the war, between 1337 and 1340, had seen an initial fierce assault on the hinterland of Bordeaux. La Réole, Bourg and Blaye were taken, and a long attempt was made to blockade Bordeaux, finally abandoned in 1340. Bordeaux suffered severely, none the less, because many vineyards were destroyed, and the French spent the next four years consolidating their successes by granting lands to anyone willing to change sides. In March 1344, as a countermeasure to Edward's claim to the French crown, Philip created his eldest son John duke of Guyenne, and in the summer of that year John received the homage of many nobles of the region.[2]

Edward, preoccupied by his attempts to wage war in Flanders, left the defence of the duchy to his officials there. By tradition the senior officials were English, though the bulk of the administration was staffed by Gascons. However, in July 1338 a joint command was set up, divided between Sir Oliver Ingham, the seneschal of Aquitaine, and Bernard-Ezy II, lord of Albret. The lords of Albret had long been staunch supporters of the English; under Edward I, Amanieu VII of Albret had been entrusted with negotiating an Anglo-Castilian alliance. Bernard-Ezy II continued his predecessor's policy despite approaches made to him by the king of Bohemia on behalf of Philip of France, promising him large sums of money if he would change allegiance. Bernard-Ezy II was reappointed in

1340, and in 1344 led the army which went to recapture Saint-Jean-d'Angély from the French. The lordship of Albret, consisting of lands along the coastal strip south of Bordeaux stretching as far inland as Bazas, was only rivalled in extent by the territory of the captals of Buch, which extended from the Médoc, west of Bordeaux, to Castillon-sur-Dordogne to the east, and included the remaining seigneurial rights in the city of Bordeaux and its suburbs. They, like other lords of the region, had town houses in Bordeaux, and were therefore open to the anglophile influence of its citizens. Jean de Grailly III, who succeeded to the title in 1343, was to be the leader of the English party in Gascony during the prince's lifetime: his great-great grandfather had served Henry III. The lesser lords of the Bordeaux area were equally pro-English, Pommiers, Lesparre, Langoiran among many others. But English supporters from further afield were rare, and only one important lord from the area round Agen was allied to them, Arnaud, lord of Durfort.[3]

By means of considerable subsidies, the local lords were persuaded to work actively for the English cause, and not all the advantage during the four years following 1340 was on the French side. Sainte-Macaire and Blaye had been retaken, and the French advance was checked until the summer of 1344, when a new campaign was launched, which once more drove the English back into Bordeaux and the Médoc. The earl of Derby's counter-attack in 1345–6 radically altered the situation: the opposing French army under John duke of Normandy was largely ineffective. The Garonne valley, Périgord and Quercy came into English control after the battle of Auberoche in August 1345, where part of the French forces under the comte de l'Îsle were defeated; and a number of lords returned to their old allegiance. Late in 1345, Aiguillon surrendered on the approach of an English army, and in 1346 Derby made a raid deep into Saintonge and Poitou, establishing a strong chain of garrisons in central Saintonge supplied by sea from Rochefort. Derby's successes meant that the whole defence of Gascony had to be rethought: in place of infantry garrisons mobile corps of cavalry were needed to protect such a large area, but instead of being permanently retained, they were summoned (and paid) as and when required. These soldiers were to form the basis of the prince's army in 1355–6, but they were a heavy expense. Until now, Gascony had been more or less self-financing, sometimes providing surpluses for the English exchequer. For the next two decades, the story was to be a very different one.[4]

Despite the reorganization of the Gascon defences, the maintenance of the English position depended on the presence of an
active commander. The earl of Stafford, appointed to succeed
Derby in 1351, was no match for Jean, comte d'Armagnac,
appointed lieutenant-general in 1352. The lands of Armagnac were
nominally part of Aquitaine, lying to the extreme south-east, but
they had long been unruly vassals. It was a shrewd move of king
John to appoint a Gascon lord as his lieutenant, and he may have
learnt from his own experiences there in 1345–6. In September and
October 1353, he invaded the area around Agen; and in January
he attacked several places in southern Quercy, notably the hilltop
castles of Beauville and Frespech, before taking Port-Sainte-Marie
on the Garonne. In June he laid siege to Lusignan in southern
Poitou.[5]

Early in 1355, apparently about the time that negotiations at
Avignon finally petered out, the captal de Buch and the lords of
Lesparre and Mussidan came to England to discuss the situation in
Gascony with Edward and his council. The council realized that
military action was needed, and their first proposal was to send the
earl of Warwick to Gascony, orders for shipping for him being
made out on 10 March. The final shape of the strategy did not
emerge until after the duke of Lancaster's return from Avignon at
the end of March. The plan was almost a carbon copy of 1346. One
expedition was to go to Normandy, where support was expected
from Charles of Navarre, the other to Gascony. The leaders were
to be the prince and Lancaster: but, surprisingly, Lancaster was
to go to Normandy and the prince to Gascony, although Lancaster
knew Gascony well and the prince knew Normandy. Apparently
the captal de Buch had suggested that it would greatly encourage
the Gascons if the prince were sent there; and indeed the last
English king or prince to go to Gascony had been Edward I in
1286–9, some seventy years before. The prince himself was eager to
set out, and 'prayed the king to grant him leave to be the first to
pass beyond sea'. The king agreed to his request, and by mid April
plans for the double expedition were well in hand.[6]

The main burden of the preparations for the expedition fell
directly on the prince and the six magnates chosen to accompany
him, the king's part being largely concerned with arrangements for
shipping and supplies. Each of them had to provide a retinue of
knights, squires and archers, the prince's being the largest at 433
men-at-arms, 400 mounted archers and 300 archers on foot, and the

smallest being 59 men-at-arms and 40 mounted archers. In all, the total force was about 1,000 men-at-arms, 1,000 mounted archers and about 600 footsoldiers, of whom 300 to 400 were archers. Compared with the force raised for the Crécy campaign, of some 10,000 men, it was very small: but its function was somewhat different. The prince was supplying the central nucleus around which an army was to be organized from Gascony itself, and the absence of specialist troops does not imply that sieges were not anticipated, but merely that such men would be recruited on arrival. The army was comparable to, but slightly larger than, that sent under Lancaster in 1345, which totalled 2,000 men.[7]

The six magnates who accompanied the prince were all experienced soldiers and veterans of the Crécy campaign. Robert Ufford, earl of Suffolk, was the oldest of the group and titular head of the prince's council, with which he had been associated since 1337. Thomas Beauchamp, earl of Warwick, and John de Vere, earl of Oxford, who had been one of the commanders of the prince's division at Crécy, were contemporaries of the king, in their early forties. William Montacute, earl of Salisbury, was the prince's contemporary, and had been knighted with him at La Hogue. Sir Reginald Cobham, marshal of the army, and Sir John Lisle were the other two to bring retinues. Of these only Lisle had had experience in Gascony, in the early 1340s; but the prince's own retinue contained at least three knights who had fought there, Sir Nigel Loring, Sir James Audley and Sir Richard Stafford all having served under the earl of Derby. This group of men, together with the prince's other chief knights, Sir John Chandos, Sir Bartholomew Burghersh the younger and Sir John Wingfield, who was in charge of administration, constituted the informal council of war who directed the campaign: the opinions of Audley and Chandos carried particular weight, despite the greater experience of Oxford and Warwick, largely because they were close friends and companions of the prince. Of these twelve lords and knights, seven were knights of the Garter: Suffolk and Cobham became members of the Order later. As a whole, they were a close-knit and experienced group of men.[8]

As was customary with such expeditions, the prince was sent to Gascony as the king's lieutenant, and on 10 July a formal contract of service was drawn up. It is interesting to compare this with the indenture drawn up for Lancaster in exactly similar circumstances in 1345. The prince is to 'stay in the said parts as lieutenant during the king's pleasure'; Lancaster was appointed for six months, renewable at the king's demand for a further six months (he in fact stayed for fifteen months). In terms of authority, the prince is to be supreme, with power to make ordinances, to appoint or dismiss ministers, and to dispose of the finances of Aquitaine as he sees fit. Lancaster's powers were limited to cooperation with the constable and seneschal of Bordeaux, whom he could not dismiss, and he had no control over finance. Powers of pardon, seizures and grants of lands, making of truces and armistices are similar in both cases. Interestingly, the prince's rights in terms of prisoners are limited in one respect where Lancaster's were not: the 'head of the war', if captured, is to be the king's prize, though the prince is to have a suitable reward. If Lancaster found himself 'besieged or beset by so great a force that he cannot help himself, unless he be rescued by the king's power, the king shall be bound to rescue by some means or other, so that he shall be suitably rescued'. The prince is given more specific guarantees: 'the king will rescue him in one way or another; and the duke of Lancaster and the earls of Northampton, Arundel, March and Stafford [i.e. the leaders of the planned expedition to Normandy] have promised and pledged their faith to give without fail all the help and counsel they can in making such rescue'. The prince's expedition was therefore considerably wider in scope than Lancaster's, in that it included complete control of the Gascon administration, and it was also regarded implicitly as the main strategic action, in that Lancaster was to abandon his own objectives if the prince got into difficulties. This was supported by a patent appointing him to the lieutenancy in similar terms, the preamble of which laid stress on the recovery of lands from rebels against the king's authority, and stated that the appointment was made 'trusting in your faithfulness and cautious foresight': in other words, the prince was to listen to his advisers.[9]

The prince and the other leaders of the army worked with reasonable efficiency, and the bulk of the army were at Plymouth by mid July. The prince himself arrived at Plymouth on about 26 July, only to find that there were nothing like enough ships for the transport of his army, even though ships from Bayonne, which had been used to transport Charles of Navarre's troops from Spain to Normandy, had been sent to Plymouth. One of these, the *Saint-Esprit*, was repaired at Southampton for use as the prince's hall or flagship. As a result it was Lancaster who left England first, or at least attempted to do so. He left Sandwich on 15 August, but a

steady south-westerly wind for the next few weeks prevented him
from getting further than Portsmouth by early September, when
news came of a gathering of French troops in the area where Lancaster
was to have landed. It was decided on 7 September that Lancaster
should go to Brittany, and soon afterwards news came of Charles
of Navarre's reconciliation with king John on 10 September. The
English effort in the north was therefore greatly reduced; plans
for sending Lancaster to Brittany were indeed put in motion, but
came to nothing.[10]

Meanwhile the prince was at Plymouth, awaiting ships which,
like Lancaster's fleet, had been prevented from coming down
Channel by the prevailing south-westerly. The delay created
problems: the troops had to be supplied and paid, and the prince,
already hard pressed financially, had to raise yet more money, even
though he had already received over £8,000 from the king in wages
of war. His debts were already such that, in the event of his death in
France, his executors were now empowered to hold his lands for
three years, instead of surrendering them to the king, in order to
raise money to pay his creditors. This extended an arrangement
made in August 1350 when, because the prince had raised 'great
loans in divers places on account of his retinue of men at arms and
others for the king's service', his executors could hold his lands for
a year after his death. In 1359, before the French campaign of that
year, the period had to be extended to four years: even so, it is
unlikely that the profits thus derived from his estates would have
been sufficient to meet his liabilities at any time during the decade.
He was now reduced to getting his officers to borrow money for
him, but the odd £100 raised in Cheshire was little enough to set
against a bill for provisions while at Plymouth amounting to nearly
£1,100.[11]

The fleet was at last ready to sail on 9 September. The prince went
aboard the *Christopher* of Southampton, whose captain was the
mayor of Southampton; the *Saint-Esprit* had evidently not been
repaired in time. The voyage was without mishap, the weather
fine; and on 20 September the fleet reached Bordeaux in good order.
The following day, in the cathedral of Saint-André, the king's letters
patent were read aloud to the chief lords and citizens of Bordeaux
by the constable, Sir Thomas Roos. Then the prince swore on the
gospels that he would be 'a good and loyal lord', and observe the
rights of the people as his ancestors king Henry and king Edward
had done; the oath was taken in Gascon, as was the homage of the

citizens and lords present. The chief supporters of the English cause in Gascony were all assembled there: Bernard-Ezy II d'Albret, Pierre de Grailly, vicomte de Benauges, the captal de Buch, Guillaume Sans of Lesparre, Bertrand de Montferrand, Amanieu d'Albret of Langoiran, Guillaume-Sanchez of Pommiers, Augier de Montaut of Mussidan, Amanieu de Fossat of Madeillan and Arnaud-Garsie de Fossat.[12]

Thus far the official account: a chronicle which is well informed about some other Gascon affairs describes the reading of the letters patent and the ceremony of homage and continues:

> and he [the prince] also explained to them that he wished to claim the kingdom of France on behalf of his father by right and inheritance, and on these points he asked their advice. Several of them advised him to go to meet the king of France with an army. And the prince said to them to make matters plain that he could not do this without their help, both in arms and in money, adding that if they would aid him with a fifteenth of their goods as was the custom in England, he would willingly undertake it; and this was granted him without contradiction. And the prince gave a date for all those who wished to go with him to be ready and equipped; anyone who was not ready on that day he would never regard as his loyal friend.

An attempt to levy a fifteenth would certainly have been a radical step in terms of the administration of Gascony; if the suggestion was indeed made, nothing more is heard of it. Instead, the prince began to make substantial payments to local lords, as his predecessors had done, in order to secure their loyalty.[13]

The council of war held either at this meeting or shortly afterwards decided to carry the war into the enemy's own home territory; in other words, to mount a direct attack on the domains of Jean d'Armagnac himself rather than cross into French territory to the north or east. But if a campaign was to be mounted, it was essential to move quickly, because it was late in the year, the days were drawing in and the weather worsening. A fortnight of feverish preparations followed, and on Monday, 5 October, the army departed. The first week's marches were erratic, indicating that the army was still not entirely ready: a long march on the Tuesday, of twenty-five miles, led to a rest day on which the Welsh soldiery did considerable damage to the little town of Castets-en-Dorthe where the army had halted. The next day the

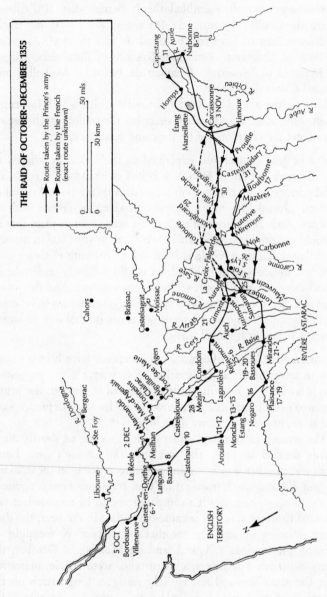

Map 3. The raid of 1355

army reached the ancient town of Bazas, and rested again, before leaving the area under English control two days later, having in the meantime marched thirty-six miles through the empty countryside of the Landes. Before crossing into French territory, the army was divided into three columns, exactly as had been done at La Hogue on the Normandy campaign. The vanguard was again led by the earl of Warwick, with Sir Reginald Cobham and others. The prince commanded the second column, keeping the earl of Oxford, Sir Bartholomew Burghersh and Sir John Lisle with him, as well as the captal de Buch, Bertrand de Montferrand and the constable of Bordeaux, Sir Thomas Roos. The rearguard was under the earl of Salisbury. As on the Crécy campaign, this division was necessary because the army would have to live off the land.[14]

The reorganization of the army took two days, during which the first minor forays into enemy territory were made. The lands of the comte d'Armagnac were what is now the *département* of the Gers; today it is a sparsely populated though fertile country, differing little in appearance from the prince's time in that the population has scarcely increased and the pattern of settlement has hardly changed. The many fourteenth-century castles which remain enhance this impression of an unchanging landscape, its rolling hills rising towards the Pyrenees.

On 13 October, the castle of Monclar fell to the English, and three towns were taken and burnt. It was an eventful day, because the prince, who had been lodging in the town of Monclar, was forced to leave it when fire broke out; and for the rest of the campaign he insisted on sleeping in tents pitched in the open countryside, both because of the risk of fire and because of possible surprise attacks. At Estang, one of the towns captured, Sir John Lisle, one of the founder members of the Order of the Garter, was wounded by a crossbow bolt and died the next day, a serious loss at the outset of a campaign. A number of new knights were made, including the prince's tailor, William Stratton. Two rest days followed, and on Friday the 16th, the army encamped outside Nogaro, which was not attacked, possibly because it had not yet recovered from a raid by the count of Foix three years previously. The next day they came to Plaisance, a *bastide*★ in the broad Adour valley, whose population had fled. The garrison under the comte

★ Bastides were new settlements founded by charter, usually fortified and built on a regular plan; the rival French and English foundations of this type were an important factor in the warfare in the region.

de Montlézun remained, however, and a party under the captal de Buch and Bertrand de Montferrand attacked and captured them. The Sunday was spent at Plaisance, but a raiding party took the near-by castle of Galiax. On Monday, Plaisance was burnt, and the army left the Adour valley, heading westward across hilly country divided by the tributaries of the Garonne: even today the roads are slow and winding, but a good march of nearly fifteen miles brought them almost to Bassoues, which belonged to the arch-bishops of Auch; it was unfortified then, the huge donjon which towers over the village today being built in the years immediately following the prince's raid. Here the prince's steward, Sir Richard Stafford, was made a banneret, and formally raised his banner for the first time. Because the town was church property, only some of the victualling officers were allowed to enter it. On Wednesday the 21st, the army crossed four rivers, leaving Montesquiou to the left, and reached Mirande, which was well garrisoned: the prince spent the night at the abbey of Berdoues, south of the town, which had been entirely deserted. Again, as church property, the abbey was spared; the prince spent the following day there.[15]

On Friday, 23 October, the prince and his army left Jean d'Armagnac's lands and crossed into the county of Astarac. Their first objective, to harry the Armagnac territories, had been achieved; their next aim seems to have been to draw out Jean d'Armagnac himself from Toulouse, where he was ensconced with a considerable army. The next four days' marches were through very difficult country, and progress was a bare eight miles a day until they reached Seissan on the 23rd, which, despite the prince's orders, was burnt. The three divisions of the army now fanned out across the countryside so that foraging would be easier: on the Saturday, they encamped at a monastery and two small towns about two miles apart, all deserted but well stocked with food, the prince being at Ville-franche. Another cross-country march took them to Samatan, 'as great a town as Norwich', with a Minorite convent; this was deserted, and the troops burnt it after lodging there for the night. An easy day's march on the 26th brought the prince and his men to Saint-Lys, within twenty miles of Toulouse itself, where they halted for the following day, probably in order to send out scouts to see whether Jean d'Armagnac had made any move.[16]

Jean d'Armagnac may have been inactive in face of the prince's invasion, but he had taken the necessary precautions long since; indeed, rumours of an incursion seem to have been current in

France long before any definite plans had been made in England. Early in the year orders had been given that the country people around Toulouse were to lay in good stocks of provisions and were to be ready to withdraw to fortified towns or castles. The nobles of the area had been summoned, and were instructed to make their troops wear a white cross badge, just as the English archers wore green and white. Genoese and Lombard crossbowmen were hired. Anything which might provide an opportunity for an enemy attack or prove detrimental to discipline, such as carnival masquerades and jousts, had been banned. All this points to a defensive strategy, very similar to that adopted by Philip in the first part of the campaign of 1346: the countryside was to be abandoned to the enemy, but the towns were to be defended. If a suitable opportunity offered, his retreat could be cut off. Jean d'Armagnac was probably also doubtful about the quality of his army: apart from the nobles from around Toulouse, he had only a small royal force under the constable of France, Jacques de Bourbon, and the marshal de Clermont, part of which was deployed at Montauban against a possible attack along the Garonne. Otherwise he had only mercenaries and an untrained local militia consisting of all able-bodied men over the age of fourteen. Because of the possibility of invasions in Normandy and Picardy, there was no hope of a relief force from the north.[17]

Faced with this *fainéant* strategy, which had prevented any great damage being done so far – despite the claims made in letters home of the capture and destruction of 'many walled towns' – the prince, who only learnt a few days later that Jean d'Armagnac was in Toulouse, now had three possibilities open to him. He could return by a different, more northerly, route, through countryside which had also been prepared against invasion; he could lay siege to Toulouse; or he could press on into an area which was believed secure against invasion, where much more damage could be done. The most prudent course would have been the first; but the army had only been on the warpath for just over a fortnight, of which six days had seen no action. Despite the lateness of the season, it was evidently too soon to think of turning back. The army was not equipped for a siege, so an attack on Toulouse was out of the question. If the raid was to continue, the only solution was a bold stroke: to bypass Toulouse and to press on into the heart of Languedoc, known to be rich territory and more likely to be open to plunder.

Once the decision to continue the raid was taken, the army continued its march east, coming to the Garonne about eight miles south of Toulouse, just above its confluence with the smaller Ariège. Both rivers were in spate with the autumn rains; the Garonne was rocky and 'marvellously terrible', the Ariège even more dangerous than the Garonne. Two such rivers and a ten-mile march were no mean feat for a day's work, particularly since all the bridges were broken and 'there was never a man in our army who knew the ford; yet by God's grace we found it'. The army encamped on the far bank of the Ariège at Falgarde, whose inhabitants fled in terror as the troops appeared: there had been a few casualties, but no attack by the enemy of any kind, even though an ambush could well have been laid at either crossing. The prince's movement had been swift and unexpected, with more than an echo of the passage of the Somme in 1346: indeed, one writer claims that it had carried him into lands where 'the fury of war had never been seen before'.[18]

Now the work of destruction was allowed full rein: 'hardly a day passed without our men taking towns, fortresses and castles by assault, plundering them and setting them on fire'. The army now headed almost directly for Carcassonne. On 29 October they reached Montgiscard, once a fief of Amanieu de Fossat, who was probably with the army, and whose advice, based on local knowledge, could have been crucial in deciding the prince's tactics at Toulouse. There was no question of keeping the town, and the place was burnt, together with twelve windmills just outside it. Here two spies were captured, from whom it was learnt that the comte d'Armagnac was in Toulouse and that the constable of France was at Montauban, believing that the prince might attempt to besiege Toulouse. From Montgiscard the prince moved up the valley of the Hers, along an old Roman road, following the course of the modern Canal du Midi. Avignonet, a royal town of some size, was reached on 30 October; this was taken by storm and the army encamped in the suburbs, burning twenty windmills before they left. Much damage was done the next day: a short march of ten miles to Castelnaudary, one of the larger towns in the area, was followed by an assault on the town, in which a church, two convents and a hospital were burnt. The near-by village of Mas-Saintes-Puelles was also burnt, together with a convent. Although Sunday, being All Saints' Day, was respected as a rest day, one detachment of the army attacked Pexiora, five miles south-east of

Castelnaudary, whose inhabitants reputedly ransomed the town for 10,000 florins, an indication of the wealth of the area. On the Monday the army entered the lordship of Carcassonne, the prince spending the night at the little village of Alzau.[19]

Carcassonne, like Toulouse, was well garrisoned and well fortified, even though the presence of a great number of refugees must have presented problems. The English were immensely impressed by it: 'its walls enclose a greater area than London'; 'greater, stronger and fairer than is York', they said. As in several French towns – Limoges and Périgueux being examples – the town and castle were separate, the castle or *cité* being the original site, the town a 'suburb' of the castle. The castle had a double curtain wall, and was separated from the town by the river Aude, over which there was a fine stone bridge. The inhabitants of the town, except for the friars, fled to the castle, and the army moved in, taking up scarcely three-quarters of the houses; there were abundant supplies of ordinary victuals as well as delicacies, and muscat wine as well. A display of strength was organized, the army being drawn up outside the town, and a number of knights were made, including the sons of Bernard-Ezy II d'Albret and Ralph lord Basset, who became bannerets, and Roland Daneis, the prince's usher of the chamber, who had served him since his first journey abroad in 1345. Two days' rest followed, while negotiations went on with the citizens. The citizens offered 25,000 gold crowns for the town to be spared from the flames, but seem to have refused to renounce their allegiance to the king of France. The prince could not accept such a refusal, however great the bribe offered, as his first commission was to bring back rebellious subjects to their true allegiance, to his father: even though he knew that such allegiance would be quickly thrown over, the formal acknowledgement of his father's right had to be made. The order was therefore given for the town to be burnt, sparing only religious houses. No attempt was made to attack the *cité*, which appeared impregnable without a prolonged siege: what the prince did not know was that the wells in the *cité* were almost dry, because the summer had been dry, and there was not enough water for the extra influx of people. If he had prolonged the siege, it would certainly have surrendered.[20]

The next obvious target was Narbonne, still a considerable trading port, as it had been since Roman times. The prince seems to have hoped that a town might yet be taken by surprise, but defensive measures were being taken as far afield as Montpellier and Nîmes on the strength of rumours that they were his intended targets. A difficult march of two days, away from Roman roads and over marshy and rocky terrain, brought the army across the river Orbieu through hilly country to encamp outside Narbonne. Like Carcassonne, Narbonne was divided into town and castle, joined by three bridges, two of stone and one of timber. The town was taken without much difficulty, but when the army moved in, the garrison, under the viscount of Narbonne, began to bombard the town with missiles from the castle. This went on throughout the night and the following day, and a number of the English troops were killed or wounded. On Tuesday, 10 November, the town was set on fire by blazing arrows fired from the castle, and the prince withdrew his men to attack the castle, but their assaults were repelled. This was the first serious fighting of the campaign, and it became clear that resistance was likely to increase rather than diminish if the English pressed on north-eastwards along the Mediterranean shore: scouts sent to Béziers reported that the city was strongly defended. Furthermore, news had come that the comte d'Armagnac had left Toulouse, and was intent on pursuing the prince. Rejecting offers of mediation from the Pope, on the grounds that he believed that his father had just crossed to France, and envoys should therefore go to him, the prince turned back to meet Jean d'Armagnac.[21]

A bad day's journey north brought the army to Capestang; there was a shortage of water, and even the horses had to be given wine to drink. The next day marked the furthest point of the expedition: another usher of the prince's chamber, Theodoric van Dale, was knighted, probably in expectation of a battle: the prince wrote later that he 'thought to have battle in the three days next following'. But Armagnac eluded him: they learnt that his officers had been at Ouveillan the night before they arrived there, and at Azille they were told that the French had intended to spend the night there until they appeared. But these accounts are from the English side only; it may be that the prince was in fact taking evasive action, and Armagnac was in pursuit. However, on the 15th, the prince was evidently sure that Armagnac was not going to attack, and as, because of bad conditions, he had certainly not outmarched him, it is reasonable to assume that he had retreated. On that day the army divided into separate corps again, having kept close order in view of the possibility of a battle. The prince himself went to the great house of the Dominicans at Prouille, an establishment of 100 men and 140 women in separate cloisters: here he was admitted to the spiritual confraternity, and a substantial offering of £32 was made. The other two corps of the army burnt the near-by town of Fanjeaux, together with twenty-one windmills and villages in the neighbourhood, before regrouping at Villasavary, north of Prouille. At some time during these two days, a separate column had attacked the large town of Limoux, fifteen miles south of the route taken by the main army, an unusually wide-ranging move in a campaign where the devastation had mostly been limited to a narrow swathe of territory.[22]

The prince was clearly anxious at this stage to stay clear of the enemy base at Toulouse, and instead of taking the Roman road to Castelnaudary and Montgiscard, he now kept well south of the city. One reason was that it was impractical to retrace his steps exactly, because an area that had been plundered less than three weeks earlier would not be able to support an army passing through it again, and little further damage could be done. However, the southern route brought him to the border of the county of Foix, which was virtually an independent principality, and whose ruler, Gaston III, nicknamed 'Phoebus' from his ruddy complexion, was the sworn enemy of Jean d'Armagnac. He had just emerged from two years' imprisonment in Paris, and was a potential ally for the Anglo-Gascon cause. The prince was careful to avoid any damage to his lands, and on the morning of 17 November the two men joined forces at the monastery of Boulbonne. They rode together along the border of the count's lands, but although several French strongholds lay on their route nothing was burnt 'out of respect for the count and his neighbours'.

The army now faced the problem of recrossing the Ariège and the Garonne. Even the little river Hers, crossed on the Tuesday, had been something of an obstacle. The Ariège was crossed without too much delay, and the army headed to Montaut, belonging to the count of Foix, hoping to find the ferryboats which were normally kept there.* But these had been removed by men from Noé on the other bank, and the army rode across in single file, to the amazement of the local inhabitants: a day later the river was in full spate and the crossing would have been impossible. Not content with this feat, the rearguard took Noé, while the prince's men recrossed the river and took Marquefare before rejoining the vanguard at Carbonne. After a day of such exertions – a march of

* There is still a ferry there today.

fifteen miles and three river crossings for the prince's division – the army rested for a day, 'in calm and delightful weather'. However, this gave the French an opportunity to catch up with the prince again. Armagnac appears to have retreated to Toulouse, and then to have made a new foray, in the hope of harassing the prince's rearguard. At midnight on 19 November, word came to the prince that the French army were within six miles of the rearguard. The next day, the prince and his advisers ordered that the English army should be drawn up in battle order outside the town; as this was done, a hare got up, and some of the soldiers started to halloo at it. This attracted the attention of the French, and a group of about forty knights appeared; but seeing that the army was prepared for battle, they rode off hastily, and the French army decamped without further ado, having no intention of engaging in a pitched battle. Sir Bartholomew Burghersh, Sir John Chandos and Sir James Audley pursued them with eighty knights, and took a number of prisoners, including thirty-two knights and squires.

The tactics of the next few days are obscure, largely because we have no French version of what was happening. The English writers, including the prince, claim that the enemy fled or 'hasted sore afraid to their quarters'; but if this was the case, they would have retired to Toulouse. Instead, the French succeeded in getting to the west of the prince's army; that night they encamped at Lombez and Sauveterre, breaking the bridges to prevent a surprise attack. The rains which had swollen the Garonne had also made the river Save difficult to cross, and the prince had to turn north-east along the bank. Bad roads and pouring rain meant that the army only made some ten miles on the Saturday. On the Sunday, the river was bridged and the army once again headed westward, only to find its way barred that evening by the French, who held the town of Gimont, on a hilltop astride the highway from Auch to Toulouse. Late though it was, the prince's division marched five miles south to Aurimont, which had been cleared of French troops by a hastily dispatched advance party. The vanguard remained near Gimont. The next day, the army was once more drawn up in battle order before dawn, leaving the carts and victualling officers at Aurimont. The French once more declined battle; a detachment remained at Gimont, which was not attacked for this reason, but the remainder retreated towards Toulouse.

The prince's main enemy was now the weather and lack of supplies. The French manoeuvres had succeeded in delaying the march and causing difficulties in foraging. The following day, despite the recent rain, there was a lack of water when the army encamped in open country at the end of a long march and horses were given wine to drink; on the Wednesday morning, many were still the worse for drink and were lost because they could not keep their footing. On 25 November, the army fanned out to cross the Gers south of Fleurance, hoping to meet enemy forces. The prince's division stormed Réjaumont, which 'for that reason' was later burnt. On the following day, the army rested, probably to regroup. A stray man-at-arms was captured, who reported that the constable of France, Jacques de Bourbon, had quarrelled with Jean d'Armagnac because he had failed to engage the English army in battle.

The army was now almost at the border of English territory; the last two rivers, the Baise and the Osse, were crossed south of Condom, in rather disorderly fashion. This area had been ravaged by Lancaster six years earlier, and no further attempts at destruction were made after leaving Réjaumont. On 28 November the first troops were dismissed, many of the Gascons and all the men from Béarn being paid off. The standards were furled, and the campaign formally brought to an end. Four days later, on 2 December, the prince reached La Réole, where he held a council of war. Orders were given that the leaders of the expedition should take up winter quarters along the borders with French-held territory, and should take every opportunity to raid French territories.[23]

The raid was judged a success by the English: Sir John Wingfield, himself an experienced administrator, looked at it in terms of economic damage to French resources:

The land and good towns which have been destroyed in this raid provided the king of France with more money each year for the war than did half his kingdom (apart from the profits of coinage and the profits and customs of Poitou) as I could show you from the records which were found in the receivers' houses in different towns. For Carcassonne and Limoux, and two other towns near Carcassonne provide the king of France each year with wages for a thousand men at arms and, over and above that, 100,000 old crowns towards the expenses of war. And according to the papers we found, the towns near Toulouse which we destroyed, and the towns near Carcassonne, Narbonne and the towns near it, provided, in addition to the sum above 400,000 old crowns . . .

The figures are exaggerated, but Wingfield's point is a good one: the vital economic base of the French war effort in the south-west had been seriously weakened. Revenue was essential to military success, and he went on to lament that if only the prince had enough money, he could win back many areas now in French hands, because enemy morale was very low.[24]

In retrospect, it was the decision to continue the raid beyond Toulouse that made the expedition a success. A raid as far as Toulouse had been made by Lancaster in 1349; to have turned back at that point would have left little economic damage and would have made little impression. The serious damage was done in the area between Toulouse and Narbonne, as Wingfield makes clear; this was also the area where an English raid was least expected, and therefore made the greatest impact. Once the prince was at Carcassonne, nothing seemed impossible: he was expected to appear before Montpellier and even Nîmes. It also made the prudent tactics of Jean d'Armagnac seem like feebleness: in the field, honours were more or less even, but the propaganda victory was almost entirely the prince's. Almost, but not entirely: for one of the purposes of such raids was to terrify the inhabitants into changing allegiance, on the practical ground that the English were more likely to harm them than the French. This underlines the prince's rejection of the attempt by the townsmen of Carcassonne to buy him off: his purpose was to show that he was more powerful than the French king, but they still feared French revenge at a later date more than they feared the enemy at their gates. In effect, he had failed to make his point at Carcassonne. As part of a larger English tactical plan, however, the prince's efforts had been largely in vain. The Normandy campaign had been called off before he set out, and Lancaster had been unable to achieve anything in Brittany. Edward himself had come over to Calais, but had to hurry back to England after news reached him, when he had barely begun his campaign, of the Scottish capture of Berwick.[25]

The end of the raid, however, did not mark the end of military activity. The lords had been engaged in most cases for half a year; and the prince and his advisers, in deciding to disperse them along the borders, were aiming to continue the warfare without the problems of maintaining and supplying a large force in one place during wintertime. In the next two months much was done: writing on 22 January to Sir Richard Stafford, who had returned to England, Sir John Wingfield described a raid down the Garonne valley, a

1. Badge showing the prince adoring the Trinity, within the Garter, c. 1350-76

2. *Frontispiece to Chandos Herald's*
Life of Edward Prince of Wales and Aquitaine,
c. 1385, showing the prince worshipping the Trinity

3. *Illumination to a copy of a deed
granting Aquitaine to the prince,
showing the prince doing homage to his father*

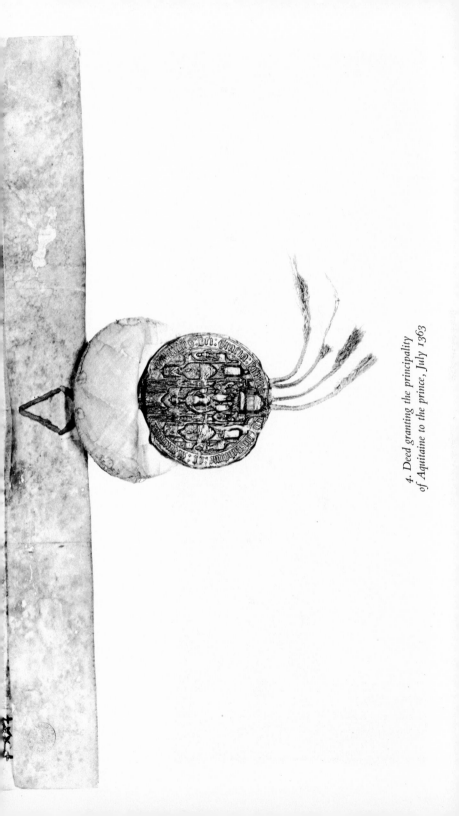

*4. Deed granting the principality
of Aquitaine to the prince, July 1363*

5. Painting of the Trinity on the tester above the prince's tomb in Canterbury Cathedral (reconstructed by Professor E. W. Tristram)

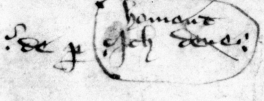

6. *The prince's signature 'Houmout ich dene' on a letter*

7. *State seal as prince of Aquitaine, 1368*

8. Small seal, as earl of Chester,

9. Large seal, as prince of Wales,

10. Large seal, as prince of W
Note the feathers

11. Royal d'or or pavilion, 83 grams
(Bordeaux, La Réole, Limoges, Poitiers, Tarbes), 1364

12. Hardi d'or, 61 grams (Bordeaux, La Réole, Limoges), 1366-7

13. Guiennois, 56 grams (Bordeaux), c. 1363

14. Leopard, 53 grams (mint uncertain), c. 1363

15. Chaise, 51 grams (Bordeaux), 1364

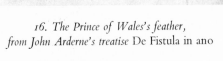

*16. The Prince of Wales's feather,
from John Arderne's treatise* De Fistula in ano

17. Effigy of Edward III in Westminster Abbey

18. *John II, from the portrait in the Louvre*

19. *Charles V, from the portrait in the Louvre*

20. *Pedro the Cruel*

21. Restormel

22. Effigy of the prince in Canterbury Cathedral

raid into Saintonge and a raid along the Dordogne towards Rocamadour. Along the Garonne, Chandos, Audley, Botetourt and Cobham took Port-Sainte-Marie, followed by Castelsagrat and Brassac in the hills above Moissac, which Chandos and Audley made their base, raiding the countryside around Agen. This was held until at least March, despite the presence of a French force under Boucicaut at Moissac, some five miles away. Nearer to La Réole, the earl of Warwick took Tonneins and Clairac on the Lot. Apparently he and Chandos's group had made their way down via Casteljaloux to the confluence of the Lot and Garonne near Aiguillon. Warwick then turned north, while Chandos continued westwards. The French still held the area around Marmande, and Warwick ravaged this in mid January, going on to take Le Mas d'Agenais and a town called Mirabeau in Quercy. The corps in Saintonge, under Bartholomew Burghersh, the captal de Buch and Bertrand de Montferrand were based on Cognac, and on Taillebourg, Tonnay-Boutonne and Rochefort, and were planning an expedition into Poitou. The earls of Suffolk, Oxford and Salisbury were, with the lord of Mussidan, somewhere in the direction of Rocamadour, but Wingfield had no news of them. It is possible that they joined forces later in the spring with the corps in Saintonge to attack Périgueux, because the town was actually captured by the captal de Buch's men, but the lord of Mussidan was paid for its garrisoning in March. Attempts to take the town had been in prospect since early February, because the count of Périgord had offered, via the mediation of his brother, the cardinal of Périgord, and the Pope, to pay a ransom for the town, but the prince had rejected this in terms very similar to his reply to the inhabitants of Carcassonne, saying

> that his lord and father, the king of England, was, by God's grace, rich enough, and had supplied him with enough gold and silver for his needs, nor would he take gold and silver for such an arrangement; but he would do what he came to do, to chastise, discipline and make war on all inhabitants of the duchy who were in rebellion against his father and recall them to their former allegiance, by force of arms.[26]

While operations continued on a considerable scale – there was probably as much activity during this period as on the raid of October and November – the prince himself returned to Bordeaux, arriving there about 9 December, and staying at the archbishop's palace. Christmas does not seem to have been celebrated in particularly high style, despite the usual entries in the accounts for spices, 3,000 lb of candles and 100 lb of sugar of various kinds, the latter costing nearly £15. There are a few entries for gaming, but only for modest sums, and for items such as the purchase of two nakers or drums for Hankin the minstrel. There are also payments to heralds and messengers, as the various commanders made their reports. With such far-flung operations, communications were often difficult: on 22 January, nothing had been heard from the earl of Suffolk for twelve days. There was activity on other fronts as well; messengers continued to come and go between the prince and the count of Foix, and there were also contacts with Pere IV of Aragón in June.[27]

On about 17 January, the prince moved to Libourne on the Dordogne, a *bastide* founded by one of the English seneschals of Gascony in the previous century. This was his base until mid March; his staff officers were with him, as were Bernard-Ezy II d'Albret and Jean de Pommiers. The prince was evidently waiting for news from England before planning his strategy for the summer; the war of attrition being waged so energetically would not bring any major rewards, though it was doing much to bring recalcitrant lords into the English fold. The lord of Limeuil on the Dordogne, Jean de Galard, and three lords from the leading families of the region near Agen, Gaillard and Bertrand de Durfort and the lord of Caumont, came over to the prince's side in April in the wake of Chandos and Audley's operations in the area. Other lords were won over by promises of land or gifts of money: for example, the lord of Chalais, on the borders of Saintonge, was given £16 on 14 April.[28]

At the end of March, the prince was back in Bordeaux, where he spent Easter. By this time he must have had news of the preparations in England. Reinforcements were to be sent to himself and to Lancaster in Brittany. The king seems to have been planning to repeat his invasion of Picardy, so that the overall strategy was to be the same as that of the previous year, but the prince's own movements would have to be in a different direction. First of all, however, the reinforcements had to be raised and conveyed to Gascony. On 15 March, 300 archers were allotted to the prince; ten days later the king increased this to 600, 500 of them to come from Cheshire. Ships were summoned to Plymouth, supplies were obtained in East Anglia, and the fletchers of Cheshire were ordered to work overtime, the prince offering 'such sums . . . as will serve to encourage them in their work' because there were no arrows to be had anywhere in England, as the king had requisitioned them for his own needs. The original summons had required the archers to be at Plymouth by 17 April; but, as always, there were delays, and despite the efforts of Robert Brampton, the clerk in charge of shipping, it was only in early June that Sir Richard Stafford and his men sailed for Gascony, reaching Bordeaux on 19 June.[29]

The prince was still at Bordeaux when Stafford arrived. He had whiled away the time by a pilgrimage to Notre-Dame-de-la-Fin-des-Terres at Soulac on the mouth of the Gironde, where he had offered 50s. This was the landing place for many pilgrims coming to Compostela from England, where they gave thanks for a safe crossing, and the prince may have had Stafford's impending arrival in mind. Even with the arrival of reinforcements, there was still a considerable delay before preparations for the summer's campaign were complete. On 6 July the prince left Bordeaux for La Réole and Bergerac, where the army assembled towards the end of the month.[30]

The choice of Bergerac indicates that the prince's plans were left open until the last moment: Bergerac was in the centre of the area under English control, and from there a raid could equally well be mounted eastwards into Quercy or Berry, southwards to Toulouse, or north into Poitou. Much depended on the king's and Lancaster's plans, which in turn hinged on events in France. Charles of Navarre, whose machinations in 1355 had ended with a reconciliation with king John, was now suspected of plotting with the dauphin, the duke of Normandy, to depose John and put the dauphin in his place. He may also have been plotting with the English as well. John was right to be suspicious of Charles (whose nickname 'the Bad' was fully justified in terms of duplicity rather than simple wickedness). On 5 April, John, who was by nature straightforward, brave, but unsubtle, chose to take direct action, seizing Charles while he was at dinner with the dauphin, and personally supervising the execution of some of the chief nobles who supported him, having them beheaded that night without trial. This display of *force majeure* instantly aroused all the disaffected lords on whose sympathies Charles had relied, and drove the relations of the victims straight into the arms of the English. Godfrey d'Harcourt, the Norman lord who had helped Edward so greatly on the Crécy campaign, but who had subsequently been reconciled to the French king, led a rebellion in

Normandy, together with Charles's brother Philip. A mission was sent to England to seek Edward's aid, and at once Lancaster's planned landing in Brittany was diverted to Normandy. On 28 May, d'Harcourt and Philip openly repudiated their allegiance to king John. There is some evidence that plans for a landing in Normandy, to be supported by Charles of Navarre, had already been made; if so, John's action merely ensured that Lancaster landed on 18 June to find the country almost entirely in support of the English. During the next fortnight, Lancaster followed the same general route as the opening stages of the Crécy campaign, reaching Conches near Évreux on 3 July. The effect of this was to disrupt John's preparations for an attack on the prince's army. John had left Paris on 1 June, and was at Chartres on the 9th, when news of the landing of Lancaster's advance guard reached him. He therefore had to change direction and march into Normandy to cover Lancaster's movements. Lancaster, with a relatively small army, was unwilling to risk a conflict, and when John came close enough to send two heralds to propose a battle, he refused, and made three forced marches on 9, 10 and 12 July to regain the Cotentin peninsula. John returned to Chartres, having wasted a month, while Lancaster had made a good impression by his show of strength, and a number of Norman lords came over to the English.[31]

The prince probably knew the outcome of Lancaster's manoeuvres when his army left Bergerac on 4 August. His tactics at this point have been much discussed, but there is no real reason to doubt the prince's statement after the campaign that he headed for Bourges in the hope of finding the comte de Poitiers there, and that he was expecting to hear that his father had landed in France. In other words, the prince was to take on the comte de Poitiers, who had been gathering an army since mid May, while Edward drew off John and his army by a feint or real invasion in the north. The prince's army was substantial and newly reinforced, and he may well have been actively seeking a battle with the comte de Poitiers, who had with him Jean de Clermont, marshal of France, Boucicaut, and the French seneschals of Poitou, Saintonge and Toulouse. Furthermore, the two sides were far from ill-informed about each other's movements: the prince's intentions had been betrayed to Jean d'Armagnac, who had at first feared another attack on the area round Toulouse when the prince moved to La Réole. The prince himself knew the position of the comte de Poitiers's forces.[32]

The first three days' marches brought the army to Périgueux,

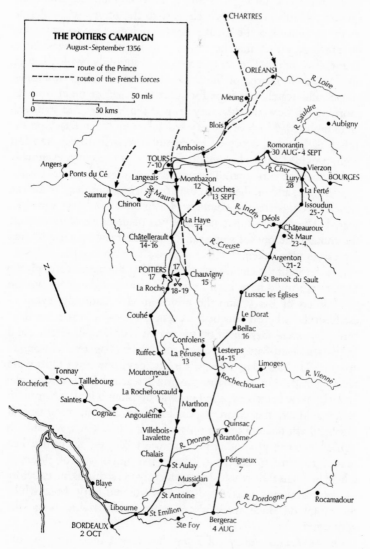

CHARTRES

ORLÉANS

R. Loire

Meung

Blois   Aubigny

Amboise   Romorantin
           30 AUG–4 SEPT

Angers   TOURS   Vierzon
        7–10   R. Cher   BOURGES
Ponts du Cé   Langeais   Montbazon   Lury
                 12   Loches   28   La Ferté
Saumur   St Maure   13 SEPT   Issoudun
    Chinon   13   R. Indre   25–7
                     Déols
           La Haye   Châteauroux
            14   St Maur
Châtellerault   23–4
   14–16   R. Creuse   Argenton
                        21–2
N

POITIERS   17   Chauvigny
  17   15   St Benoît du Sault
La Roche   18–19
                   Lussac les Églises

Couhé   Le Dorat

       Confolens   Bellac
Ruffec   La Péruse   16
         13   Lesterps
Tonnay   14–15   Limoges
   Moutonneau   R. Vienne
Rochefort   Taillebourg   Rochechouart
    Saintes   La Rochefoucauld
              Marthon
   Cognac
    Angoulême   Quinsac
        Villebois-   Brantôme
       Lavalette   R. Dronne
    Chalais   Périgueux
       St Aulay   7
Blaye   Mussidan
               R. Dordogne   Rocamadour
   St Antoine
Libourne   St Emilion   Bergerac
BORDEAUX   Ste Foy   4 AUG
2 OCT

Map 4. The Poitiers campaign

where an edict against looting was published by the bishop, but without much effect. The prince and his men avoided the main road and went through wooded, hilly country to Brantôme, Quinsac, Marthon and Rochechouart to the priory of La Péruse, on the south bank of the Vienne near Confolens, which they reached on 13 August after marches of varying length, the longest being twenty-five miles. The army proceeded cautiously, with Chandos and Audley in charge of the scouts, for fear of enemy ambushes; and careful watch was kept for surprise attacks at night. On the morning of the 14th, the army crossed the Vienne, and standards were unfurled. Much of the day was taken up by an attack on the abbey of Lesterps, occupied by enemy forces; its tower, 120 feet high, provided an ideal stronghold, but the prince's men eventually forced them to surrender. The next day, as a feast day, was treated as a rest day; and on the 16th a long march brought them to Bellac, which belonged to the countess of Pembroke and was therefore spared. The day after that an attack was made on Le Dorat, where the church held out for some time, but both it and two neighbouring castles were taken.[33]

Contact with the enemy, expected during the march through the Limousin, should have been imminent now that the army was on the borders of Berry, and the prince moved cautiously trying to establish the whereabouts of the enemy. Thursday was a rest day; three days were then spent on the march via Lussac-les-Églises and Saint-Benoit-du-Sault to Argenton, which was reached on 21 August. The next day was again a rest day; one corps captured a near-by castle. On 23 August the prince reached Châteauroux, the army by now being organized in three divisions with the rearguard at Saint-Maur, the centre at Châteauroux and the vanguard at Déols, all within about three miles of each other. There was still no sign of the enemy: another rest day was taken, and the prince then moved forward to Issoudun, twenty-five miles west of Bourges, where he spent two whole days, evidently in reconnaissance, before moving cautiously northwards to La Ferté and Lury. Meanwhile, the captal de Buch made a raid northwards, laying waste the country.[34]

On 28 August, north of Lury, he crossed the Cher, the old boundary of the duchy of Aquitaine, into French royal territory, spending the night at Vierzon. Contact was at last made with the enemy: Chandos and Audley, having taken and burnt Aubigny, came up with a French commander, Philippe de Chambly (known as Grismouton) with some eighty men-at-arms, of whom they captured eighteen and killed many more. At this point the prince learnt the whereabouts of the main French army: king John was at Orléans, and the royal army was intending to advance towards him, French scouts having already discovered the prince's whereabouts. But the comte de Poitiers had still not joined up with king John, and English scouts were sent out to locate him in the hope that this part of the French forces could be dealt with in isolation. At the same time, the possibility of crossing the Loire to join the duke of Lancaster somewhere in Anjou was to be explored, and the scouts were to discover whether the bridges were still intact. Meanwhile the advance guard of the French army under Boucicaut and Amaury de Craon found the outriders of the English army near Villefranche-sur-Cher. The English captured eight prisoners in the first skirmish; the French tried to lay an ambush, but the arrival of the main English army prevented them, and they were forced to flee to Romorantin, where the leaders and a hundred or so companions shut themselves in the castle. The prince decided to invest the castle, a decision which seems remarkable when his most urgent need was to cross the Loire. But the prince did not yet know either that the Loire was impassable, or that John's army was on the move. The resistance of the French knights was stiffer than expected: on the first day of the siege little progress was made, but on the second day, 31 August, the town was captured and the defenders driven into the keep. On the third day three siege-towers were built by the retinues of Burghersh, Suffolk and a Gascon lord, and after two more days the prince's men at last succeeded in setting the keep on fire by hurling flaming debris at it, at which the French force surrendered. The fourth of September was taken as a rest day, the troops being ordered to prepare their equipment.[35]

News now seems to have reached the prince that the comte de Poitiers was at Tours and that the bridges over the Loire to the north had all been broken, and he therefore headed westwards, averaging ten miles a day and reaching the outskirts of Tours on 7 September. The prince seems to have hoped to draw out the comte de Poitiers and the marshal de Clermont from Tours, defeat them and cross the Loire there to join up with Lancaster, whom he was expecting to appear on the north bank; at one point the English army thought they saw Lancaster's camp-fires. But when the prince encamped at Montlouis, near Tours, the weather changed for the worse: the fine calm spell was broken by three days of thunderstorms so that Burghersh and his men, sent to fire the suburbs of Tours, were unable to do any damage: the town itself had been newly refortified. The comte de Poitiers refused to be drawn, and the prince now attempted to join Lancaster. Lancaster had moved south with Robert Knolles and two Navarrese captains, and was in the neighbourhood of Angers, sixty miles away.[36]

By 11 September, the prince was unable to wait any longer for Lancaster's arrival, because the main French army, under king John, had left Orléans on 8 September, when the king was at Meung-sur-Loire, seventy miles away. His men crossed wherever they could, to avoid congestion at the bridges, and on the day that the prince turned southward much of the French army was south of the river, though there was still some distance between them and the English. On 13 September John halted at Loches to regroup his forces, and to allow the troops from Tours to join him. The prince had meanwhile crossed the Indre, with some difficulty, and had reached Monbazon on Monday the 12th, when cardinal Talleyrand de Périgord came to try to obtain a truce or a peace between the two armies; the prince later wrote that he refused to treat for peace on the grounds that he had no powers to do so. In fact a commission for this purpose had been issued to him on 1 August, though it could scarcely have reached him before he set out. As to a truce, he felt that this was not advisable at that point. The talks, however, meant that only twelve miles were covered that day, and the following night, despite a march by the English of twenty-five miles to La Haye-Descartes, the armies were only twenty miles apart.[37]

The next three days formed the critical moment of the campaign. On the 14th, the prince moved twelve miles south to Châtellerault, while John reached La Haye-Descartes. At this point, John, well informed as to his enemy's movements, decided to try to march round the prince and cut off his line of retreat. The prince did not expect this move, and his scouts failed to discover the French plans. It seems unlikely that the scouts had lost contact with the French army; rather, they were unable to interpret John's manoeuvres on the far bank of the Creuse correctly, possibly believing that they were a prelude to a formal challenge to battle or even a retreat. The prince therefore spent two whole days at Châtellerault, 'waiting to know more certainly about him', with the result that John achieved exactly the result he had hoped for. On 15 June the French king was at Chauvigny; but there was one weakness in his tactics.

To cover thirty miles in one day he had taken only the best-mounted men of his army. The rest had to catch up as best they could.[38]

The prince learnt of John's arrival at Chauvigny late on Friday the 16th, and at once ordered the carts accompanying the army to be moved across the Vienne during the night so that a rapid start could be made the next day towards Chauvigny. By taking his whole army at a brisk pace towards Chauvigny, and then cutting across country, the prince not only succeeded in getting ahead of John once again, but also gained the advantage that the French troops were now widely dispersed. John himself had ridden ahead with a small force to Poitiers, but did not have enough men to send out scouts. As a result, he lost contact with the prince, and the rest of his army were no better informed until part of the rearguard came across a detachment of the English in the woods near a farm called La Chabotrie, four miles from Poitiers. The English, outnumbered, beat a hasty retreat towards the main army; the French followed eagerly, only to find themselves faced by vastly superior forces. The counts of Auxerre and Joigny were captured in the pursuit, which took the English as far as Chauvigny. As a result the prince had to encamp in the woods where the skirmish had taken place so as to collect the stragglers. This enforced halt meant that the army were short of water.[39]

On Sunday, 18 September, the prince gave orders for the army to set out early in the morning, but his scouts now found the French army drawn up in battle order just outside Poitiers, John having succeeded in reassembling a large portion of his forces on the previous day. He had also re-established contact with the prince now that he could send out scouts once more, and the French army was blocking the prince's road southward to Angoulême and Bordeaux. The prince turned aside in search of a suitable defensive position, and was met by cardinal Talleyrand de Périgord, who once more urged a truce. The prince replied that he had better be brief: this was not the time for sermons, but rather for fighting. None the less, as the prince's men began to take up their positions five miles outside Poitiers, on the edge of the 'high wood, belonging to the abbey of Nouaillé, called Borneau', the cardinal succeeded in obtaining time to attempt to make a truce. In retrospect, both sides thought that the other was behind this delay: the English said that the French used it to bring up reinforcements, while the French complained that it had allowed the English to entrench themselves. Both were in fact done, but without the cardinal's complicity. One

English chronicler believed that 1,500 men-at-arms and many foot-soldiers reached the French army on the Sunday, and groups of up to 500 on the Monday. Allowing for the usual exaggeration of numbers, it is very likely that such groups did arrive, probably either belated arrivals from the main army or local militia. The English meanwhile made defensive screens for their archers and took up positions just inside the edge of the wood.[40]

What exactly transpired during the negotiations is difficult to discover, because most reports are either very brief or clearly invented speeches, representing what the chroniclers thought should have been said. A truce of one day was certainly agreed early on Sunday, and the cardinal even seems to have hoped that real peace negotiations might take place. Eleven nobles, six from the French side and five from the English, were chosen as negotiators. The French included Clermont, Geoffrey de Charny and the archbishop of Sens, while the English representatives were the five chief commanders apart from the prince: Warwick, Suffolk, Burghersh, Chandos and Audley. Froissart reported later that members of the cardinal's entourage said the prince had offered considerable concessions: the surrender of everything he had taken during the expedition, towns and castles, and the release of all prisoners, and his personal oath not to take up arms against the French for seven years. King John, however, demanded a complete surrender. At the end of the day no agreement had been reached, and as a possible solution Charny proposed a duel between a hundred of the best knights on both sides, an echo of the famous Combat of the Thirty in Brittany in 1351, but Warwick rejected this, and negotiations were broken off, the truce being due to expire at daybreak.[41]

Early on the morning of Monday, 19 September, the cardinal reappeared in the English camp. The English army had passed an uneasy night, and were short of water and provisions. The prince once again offered a truce, but the French would not hear of it, and the cardinal withdrew. Throughout these negotiations, king John had been advised by the two marshals of his army, Audrehem and Clermont, and Sir William Douglas, a Scottish knight with experience of English tactics in the northern wars. Douglas's advice had already led to a decision to fight on foot, in the hope of avoiding the disastrous toll taken by the English archers on the French horses at Crécy. Retaining only a small body of cavalry, it was intended to open the battle by riding down the English archers. This spearhead was to be led by Clermont and Audrehem. The three main battles, which were to follow on foot, were led in turn by the dauphin Charles, the duc d'Orléans, brother to the king, and by the king himself. The total strength of the army was probably considerably greater than that of the English, but precise figures are, as usual, impossible to arrive at. Following Dr Hewitt's estimates, 'it may have included 8,000 men-at-arms, 2,000 arbalesters and a considerable number of lightly armed and imperfectly trained other men'. The latter were probably those who had joined the army in the previous two days; the army as a whole had been in the field for eighteen days, and had never, so far, acted in concert. The French army seems to have been drawn up on a ridge overlooking the little river Miosson, to the north-west of the English army, resuming a position which they had taken up the previous day. They were in relatively open country, and could only just see the English positions about 500 yards away.[42]

The English, so far as can be judged from the often conflicting details of the chroniclers, were grouped round the north-west corner and down the western edge of Nouaillé wood. Between them and the French were vines, hedges and a narrow lane with a hedge on either side. To the left of the English, the land fell away steeply to the valley of the Miosson, with two fords at the bottom and an equally steep slope on the far side. There were about 6,000 to 8,000 men in the army, about half of them men-at-arms, the rest being archers and infantry. All the archers were English or Welsh, the men-at-arms being partly Gascon and partly English. They had been working together for over six weeks, during which time they had seen some, though not very much, fighting. Their commanders were all experienced men, most of them veterans of Crécy. Those who had not been at Crécy were Gascon lords who had fought on Lancaster's campaigns in Aquitaine. The army was organized into three divisions: Warwick and Oxford were in command of the vanguard, which contained many Gascons, including the captal de Buch. The prince and his advisers, Burghersh, Audley, Chandos and Cobham, were in the centre. The rearguard was led by Salisbury and Suffolk. The preceding campaign had not been a particularly fatiguing one, and the men and horses were generally in good condition, though they had not been able to forage properly during the previous two days, and had been short of supplies and water.[43]

It was the prince who made the first move, at about eight o'clock. He and his advisers had decided on this movement the previous

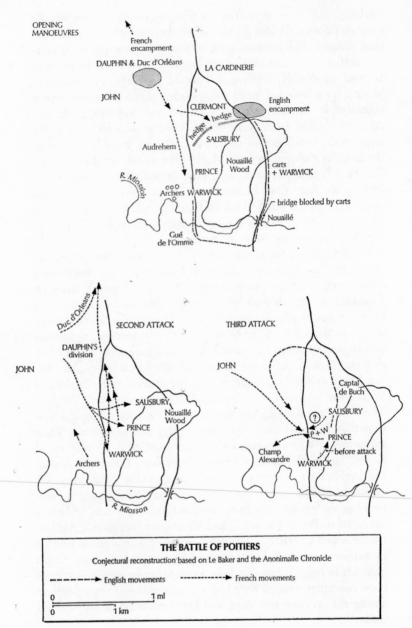

OPENING MANOEUVRES

French encampment

DAUPHIN & Duc d'Orléans

JOHN

LA CARDINERIE

CLERMONT

hedge

English encampment

hedge

SALISBURY

Audrehem

Nouaillé Wood

carts + WARWICK

PRINCE

R. Miosson

Archers WARWICK

bridge blocked by carts

Nouaillé

Gué de l'Omme

SECOND ATTACK

Duc d'Orléans

DAUPHIN'S division

JOHN

SALISBURY

Nouaillé Wood

PRINCE

WARWICK

Archers

R. Miosson

THIRD ATTACK

JOHN

Captal de Buch

SALISBURY

(?)

P + W   PRINCE

Champ Alexandre

before attack

WARWICK

THE BATTLE OF POITIERS
Conjectural reconstruction based on Le Baker and the Anonimalle Chronicle

- - - ➤ English movements   ------ ➤ French movements

0   1 ml
0   1 km

Map 5. The battle of Poitiers

night, and both its purpose and direction are controversial. The vanguard, under the earl of Warwick, who seem to have been on the left of the army, moved with the baggage train away from the battlefield, and crossed the Miosson in the village of Nouaillé itself, behind the wood where the rest of the army was stationed. The exact details are far from clear, chiefly because none of the writers who describe the movement actually knew what Warwick was doing, or were familiar with the territory. Most of the information that we have about the battle probably comes from men who were in the prince's entourage, towards the top of the hill, clerks and other members of his staff, and who would only have heard what happened. As to the purpose of the manoeuvre, the prince himself later wrote that 'it was agreed that we should take our way, flanking them, in such manner that, if they wished for battle or to draw towards us, in a place that was not very much to our disadvantage, we would take them on; and so forthwith it was done'. As the prince was, on the evidence of the French scouts, well entrenched in his positions at the top of the hill, the curious phrasing can only mean that he was attempting a cautious retreat. If it had been a feint, designed to provoke a French attack on ground which would be better suited for defence, there was no reason to move the baggage. The prince knew that most of the French were dismounted when they drew up for battle on the previous day, and he and his advisers may have hoped to make good their escape before the French army could mount and pursue them, fighting a covering rearguard action against the small mounted corps. Such an escape was by no means impossible: Lancaster had carried out a very similar manoeuvre in Normandy the previous year, at Thubeuf.[44]

Meanwhile a small scouting party under Sir Eustace d'Abrechicourt was sent out, but they were captured. Just as the French could not see the prince's positions clearly, so the prince was unsure of the exact whereabouts of the French. At the top of the hill were arable fields, beyond this vines and the lane, and he believed the French army to be somewhere there. The French scouts, however, discovered and reported the English movement towards the Miosson, and the two marshals in charge of the cavalry at once assumed that the retreat had begun. After a brief argument, during which Clermont was insulted by Audrehem for advising caution, they therefore moved forward separately. Audrehem attacked the vanguard, who were now returning by way of the Gué de l'Omme to report that the causeway at Nouaillé was blocked by carts.

Clermont rode off to the other end of the English line, and attacked the rearguard under the earl of Salisbury. This was a fatal and decisive move. The commanders of the cavalry had been assigned a very precise function in the French tactics: to act as a single spearhead which would crash through the obstacles between them and the English archers and break up the formation of the latter, leaving them open to attacks on foot. They had abandoned this task and had left the centre of the English army intact. This was bad enough; but to make matters worse, they failed even to defeat the two wings. In the case of Warwick and his men, the French charge came straight at them, and the archers found that the horses had been armed in front, so that their volleys had little effect. However, a detachment stationed in a defensive position on the river bank was moved forward and, by shooting at the hindquarters of the horses, made them rear up and unseat their riders. Clermont tried to take Salisbury's men in the flank by using a gap in the hedge, but Salisbury saw his manoeuvre in time and posted archers by the hedge, who picked off the horsemen as they came through: as a result this attack fared even worse than Audrehem's, and Clermont himself and many others were killed.[45]

King John was still some distance away, and unable to see the effect of Audrehem's and Clermont's attacks. The essence of his strategy was that once the English archers had been thrown into disorder, the dismounted knights should follow up almost immediately to take advantage of the confusion. The first line of the main French force, commanded by the dauphin Charles and consisting of 2,000 or so men-at-arms, about half the total English force, therefore moved forward without waiting to discover whether the first onslaught had in fact succeeded. Both sides shouted their respective war-cries, 'St George!', 'Saint-Denis!', as the mass of armed men moved steadily forward. The archers made some impression on them, but caused nothing like the havoc that they had wreaked on the cavalry, because only a direct hit or a fortunate shot between jointed plates would penetrate full armour: glancing blows slid off, even though special armour-piercing arrows may have been used. Most of the French troops reached the English line; but they had lost their impetus, while the English army was fresh and outnumbered its attackers. Warwick's men had moved up during the pause after the first onslaught, and were now grouped with the prince's battalion, in a position where they were protected by the ditches, hedges and man-made obstacles, such as barricades of stakes and trenches. All accounts agree that such defences were a prominent feature of the English defence; but their exact location is impossible to reconstruct. It may be that archaeology could trace the remains of entrenchments that were said to be still visible in the nineteenth century. The prince's preparations on the Sunday were probably designed to break up any attack by channelling it through a number of small gaps in hedges or paths through vineyards; almost all the chroniclers refer to such features, but try to reduce the number to one or two points where all the action took place. A more probable picture is of as many as a hundred little groups of men locked in a fierce hand-to-hand struggle along a line to the west of Nouaillé wood. The entire English army, except for a reserve of some 400 horse, were engaged. The prince, in the centre of the line, had his war-council around him, as well as a bodyguard. His standard, carried by Sir Walter Woodland and a small guard, marked his position, and he was defended by a bodyguard of trusted followers: his chamberlain, Sir Nigel Loring, Sir William Trussell, Sir Alan Cheyne and others. The knights who advised him, besides Chandos, Audley and Burghersh, seem to have been the earl of Oxford, Sir Baldwin Botetourt, Sir Edmund Wauncy, and others of his immediate household. As the French found that they were unable to breach the English line, they broke off gradually and made their way back to the main body of the army, much depleted in numbers, and without their standardbearer. The English did not pursue them, knowing that there was much more fighting to be done; only Sir Maurice Berkeley broke ranks, and was promptly captured.[46]

The first battle rejoined the main army without its leader. The knights entrusted with the safety of the dauphin and his brothers, either on the king's express orders or on their own initiative, rode off with them in the direction of Chauvigny. As the attack had been made on foot, they must have gone back past the rest of the army to fetch their horses. To remove the dauphin was doubtless a wise precaution; but it was a severe blow to French morale. The second battle, instead of attacking, did not even await the order to dismount, but, led by the duc d'Orléans, retreated, 'seized by an inexplicable panic'. The evidence on this extraordinary move is very obscure. After the battle, it was put about that the duc d'Orléans too had been ordered to withdraw by the king, but only the official chronicler of Saint-Denis believed it. One late chronicle hints at a faintly plausible reason: 'then the king dismounted, and everyone in his battle; when the rest of the French force saw this, they thought the king was killed and began to flee'. Apart from this, which in itself may well be a conjecture, there is only guess-work: a reluctance to fight on foot, a pure lack of liaison in circumstances where communications were certainly very difficult.[47]

King John and his men now moved forward to attack. The failure of the duc d'Orléans to attack meant that the English had time to rest and regroup, to retrieve arrows and to bring up their horses. The sight of the new host advancing towards them was enough to make them lose heart, particularly as their own ranks had been considerably diminished during the first two onslaughts. The advantage of numbers, however, was slightly in their favour; and the prince and his advisers decided on a bold stroke. Instead of continuing to fight a defensive battle, they would counter the enemy advance on foot by a cavalry charge, which would not only give a physical advantage but would improve English morale. Combined with this, the captal de Buch, with 60 knights and 100 archers, would encircle the French army and take them in the rear, unfurling the St George's Cross as a signal that he was in position.[48]

As soon as the captal had completed his manoeuvre, a wide sweep to the north-east, the English trumpets sounded and the prince's men charged, led by Sir James Audley, halting the French advance on the high ground to the west of Nouaillé wood. A long and bitter fight ensued, and the French were driven down towards the river, if we are to believe the later tradition which pinpoints the site of the end of the battle as the champ Alexandre, a field lying between the Miosson and the hamlet of Les Bordes. Here, in the afternoon, the king's bodyguard made a last stand before being overwhelmed. Geoffrey de Charny, the bearer of the French standard, the *oriflamme*, was killed here, defending the king. The king himself surrendered either to Denys de Morbecque, a knight from Artois, or to Bernard de Troy, a Gascon knight in the retinue of the Sieur de Tartas: in the confusion it seems that Morbecque lost his prisoner, who was then retaken by Bernard de Troy. The lawsuit over their rival claims was never settled, and both were rewarded by Edward with a yearly pension. The king's young son Philip, aged only fourteen, and numerous other nobles were also among the captives.[49]

Those of the French army who escaped were pursued as far as the gates of Poitiers, while on the battlefield the search for the wounded and for dead nobles began. Audley, who had been unhorsed in the final charge, was found in a serious condition, and was brought in while the prince was at supper with king John: the prince insisted on leaving the king and seeing that the wounded man was properly looked after, raising his spirits with the news of the king's capture. The English losses were certainly lighter than the French, though they were certainly more than the 'sixty men, of whom four were men at arms' claimed by Sir Bartholomew Burghersh in a letter to Sir John Beauchamp, or the forty men claimed by the prince, writing to the prior of Winchester. Sir Robert Bradeston, a member of the prince's entourage since 1344, was killed at the same time as Sir Maurice Berkeley was captured, but otherwise there are no details of English losses.[50]

Turning to the French side, the list of dead is a long one. About eighty nobles and knights and forty squires were buried at the Dominican convent in Poitiers after the battle. Heading the list were the duc d'Athènes, who was constable of France, the duc de Bourbon, Jean de Clermont, marshal of France, and several viscounts, as well as Geoffrey de Charny, whose body was later transferred to Paris. A number of local lords were among the slain, including the vicomte de Rochechouart, the lord of Rochefoucauld, Renaud de Pons and the lord of Landas. The prince claimed that 2,446 men-at-arms in all were killed, but this means nothing more than 'a great number'. The captives were put at an equally high figure, 1,974 in all, including thirteen counts, five viscounts, twenty-one bannerets and leading knights. Among them were the seneschals of Saintonge, Touraine and Poitou; with these and other local lords either dead or captured, the basis of French power in the lands claimed by the English was seriously weakened. Guichard d'Angle, the seneschal of Saintonge, was to become one of the prince's most active supporters in later years.[51]

How had this overwhelming defeat been inflicted on a well-equipped, larger army by a force who were genuinely ready to accept a truce the previous day? The answers for Poitiers are broadly the same as for Crécy. The French cavalry, used to decades of unchallenged superiority in battle, had no sense of discipline and could not believe that the English archers were more than a match for them: hence the foolhardy attack by Clermont and Audrehem, who underestimated their opponents. This indiscipline, like that of the first battle of French cavalry at Crécy, was almost decisive in itself, disrupting the tactical plan of king John and costing the French two of their commanders in the opening stages of the battle. Again, as at Crécy, communication between the divisions of the attacking force was very poor: it was lack of clear communication and a different kind of indiscipline that led to the flight of the division of the duc d'Orléans. The first onslaught on foot was the one moment when the French plan worked perfectly; but a more astute commander might have realized the flaw in king John's scheme. If the cavalry attack failed, the attack on foot was likely to fail as well, but there could be no interval between the two, or the English would regroup. John therefore had to assume that his first move would work, and send in the dismounted knights regardless. The last part of the battle was undoubtedly decided by the English cavalry charge; but this, in turn, was only made possible by the strict discipline of the English, who, with their horses near at hand, had refrained from pursuing the departing enemy, and late in a hard-fought day carried out the remounting in good order. At the core of the English success was the good working relationship between the prince, his chief officers and their men, a relationship which, as at Crécy, had evolved during the previous weeks of campaigning, but which hinged on the presence around the prince of a group of tried and trusted knights. To them, as a group, belongs credit for the victory; to the prince belongs credit as *primus inter pares*.

A greater prize than anyone had dreamt of had fallen to the English army. That prize had now to be conveyed to safe-keeping. The French were uncertain whether their king was still alive: rumours that he was dead were rife in Hennebont in Brittany on 8 October: it was said that one of the Navarrese captains had killed the king, showing that Lancaster was believed to have joined the prince. The dauphin probably had more accurate information within a day or two of the battle, from the burial parties sent out from Poitiers to collect the bodies of the French nobles: neither he nor the duc d'Orléans were in a position to rescue the king. The morale of the French army had been shattered, and murmurings of discontent were beginning to grow, directed at the nobles who were believed to have betrayed the king. An anonymous cleric in Paris wrote a *Complainte sur la bataille de Poitiers*, in which, mingled with the usual clerical attack on the pride and luxury of the nobles, he also makes accusations of treachery, collusion with the English to prolong the war, and even conspiracy to cheat the marshals of the army by assuming different identities in order to draw extra wages. The hero of the poem is king John, but the dauphin is not regarded as one of the traitors: the writer hopes that 'our duke will make such an alliance of trusty honest men that he will take vengeance on our enemies'. A more sophisticated attack was written by François de Monte-Belluna in 1357; his work is interesting as evidence of the growth of national feeling and the idea of a distinction between France as *patria*, and foreign parts, *alienus*. More to our immediate purpose is his attack on the nobles, who pay such homage to Bacchus that the enemy can move his camp quicker than they can get up from the table:

> Now indeed, you degenerate French soldiery, we have been made the laughing stock of everyone, and they sing about us every day. For who would not laugh at the people of France who used to be so fierce, mocking everyone because peace had lasted so long, and who have now stooped so low that almost in the middle of the kingdom they let their king be captured, fighting bravely for the peace and liberty of his kingdom? Who would not mock the French, who allow their king to be led away through the midst of his kingdom by a small handful of enemies to captivity beyond the edge of the world itself?[52]

On the night after the battle, the English army had remained near the battlefield, feasting on the French army's provisions and adding to their booty by ransacking the French camp, where they found a considerable quantity of jewels and other valuables; the prince subsequently acquired a silver ship or nef, designed as a centrepiece for king John's table, as well as his crown and his insignia of the Order of the Star.

On the day following the battle, the prince moved his camp to the village of Roches-Prémarié-Andillé, three miles south-west of the battlefield; here the army was reorganized for the march, the booty piled into carts and guards allocated to the prisoners. Messengers were sent on ahead to take the news to London; Thomas Rede went to the duke of Lancaster, while Geoffrey Hamelyn, one of the prince's attendants, was sent to London with king John's tunic and helmet as convincing proof that the news was genuine. The first to arrive with the news was John le Cok of Cherbourg who received 25 marks for his pains. On 22 September the army began its march to Bordeaux, moving in steady marches of twenty miles or so a day, first down the road to Angoulême to Couhé and Ruffec, crossing the Charente at Vertheuil on 24 September and skirting Angoulême by way of Mouton and La Rochefoucauld. On 26 September the army almost crossed its outward route, near Marthon, but continued south-west to Villebois-Lavalette, Sainte-Aulaye and Saint-Antoine-sur-l'Îsle, reaching Saint-Émilion on the 30th. The main army reached Bordeaux on 2 October, while the prince and king John stayed in Libourne until suitable accommodation had been arranged for them in the city. When, about a fortnight later, they made their solemn entry into the city, they were met by a procession of the clergy, and crowds came to see the prince and his captive. At about the same time, the English king was writing to the English clergy to make the news known, describing how John of Valois, 'unjustly occupying the French throne', had fallen into the prince's hands and asking for prayers and 'other works of piety' to celebrate the divine favour shown to his just cause.[53]

The Making of Peace

6

The prince and king John spent the winter in Bordeaux, in the archbishop's palace. Of the lighter side of that winter's business, the feasts and general rejoicing at the victory, we have only general reports; the troops doubtless dispersed much of their booty while waiting to return home. No further military action was planned, and the most intense activity was on the diplomatic front. The prince's powers to make peace, issued from London just before he had set out in August, were repeated in December, perhaps because the first letters had never reached him. No limitations were placed on the prince's actions, but it is clear that the document was intended to give authority to his signature on a truce or peace rather than to entrust the whole matter to his judgement, unless communication was impossible. Messengers went to and fro between Bordeaux and London throughout the winter, while proposals for a truce or a permanent peace were considered. There were considerable problems to overcome, such as the status of the French king, who was, after all, only the *de facto* ruler of France in English eyes. There was also the difficulty that the negotiator sent by the pope was again cardinal Talleyrand de Périgord, who had been compromised in the eyes of both French and English by his attempts to make a truce before the battle. The English now had a more serious charge to make against him, because some of his men were said to have stayed behind after his departure from the battlefield in order to fight on the side of the French. However, he succeeded in obtaining an interview with the prince, who accepted his protestations of innocence. A later story told how he alone of the cardinals at Avignon had rejoiced at the news of the English victory; although apocryphal, it shows that his standing with the English was completely restored.[1]

Once the negotiations began, the prince took no part in proceedings. Two experienced officials were entrusted with the talks: in October, William Lynne, dean of Chichester, was sent from London to talk to the papal envoys, even before it was known for certain whether they would take part in the Bordeaux negotiations. John Stretelee, the constable of Bordeaux, a civil servant of long standing and a graduate of the law school at Oxford, was the other official, while the remainder of the English representatives were members of the prince's war council: Warwick, Suffolk, Cobham, Burghersh, Stafford, Chandos and Loring. There were also three Gascon lords closely associated with the English cause: the captal de Buch, Guillaume Sans, lord of Pommiers and Bertrand de Montferrand. The French negotiators were the cardinal of Rouen and the archbishop of Sens, and seven of the captives – Jacques de Bourbon, Jean and Charles d'Artois, the counts of Tancarville and Ventadour, Audrehem and Boucicaut – with two envoys from the dauphin. The negotiations proper opened a fortnight after Christmas, in Saintonge, the French staying at Mirambeau and the English at Blaye. The papal mediators hoped that this would develop as a peace conference, but neither the English nor the French negotiators were really in a position to treat for peace. The English side, despite the messengers to and from London, clearly felt uncertain about their position; the arrival of news of king John's capture had been startling enough to keep the king's council at Westminster in session for an extra two days, and only William Lynne had had an opportunity of discussing the implications of the situation with the king and his council. The prince was certainly empowered to release king John on ransom, or to make any other such arrangement that he wished; but he and his advisers, although experienced in war, were less at home in diplomacy. Suffolk was the only member of his council with much knowledge of this sphere, his diplomatic activities stretching back some twenty years, including the negotiations at Calais in 1347 and 1350. On the French side, the complication was that the dauphin's position as *lieutenant du roi* and the extent of his real power in France were still very much in question; by the end of the year he was reasonably well established, despite differences with the États-Généraux that autumn, and he had secured the friendship of Charles IV of Germany at the Diet of Metz in December 1356, a meeting at which the two papal legates had also been present. It was hoped that the Emperor would use his influence to secure the release of king John. French chroniclers believed there had been a draft peace, which Edward had rejected, but with so many imponderables, the only possible outcome was a truce, which was signed after two months of negotiations on 22 March. It was to last until Easter, and thereafter for two years, until Easter 1359, and was to apply to all the armies and allies of both sides, the clauses being similar to those of the truces of 1347–55. The only problem was the siege of Rennes being conducted by the duke of Lancaster: the prince was to write to him commanding him to raise the siege, but it was clear that the negotiators expected difficulties, because provisions were made for Lancaster to occupy the town until Edward himself commanded him to surrender it, and a final clause covered the eventuality of his disobeying the royal order. Lancaster did not in fact raise the siege until July, saying that he was acting for John de Montfort, claimant to the duchy of Brittany. One suspects that, having seen a copy of the truce, with its elaborate provisions, he took these to be a broad hint on the part of the English negotiators that he was to secure the town before acknowledging the truce.[2]

The truce also covered the question of the prisoners. The leading nobles who were being held to ransom were bought from their captors by the prince; they, and all other prisoners held by Englishmen, were to go to England, unless they had reason to dispute the justice of their capture. The same provision was to apply in reverse to English prisoners held by the French, implying that there were such captives. The most important prisoner of all was, of course, the king himself; by the terms of the prince's appointment at the outset of the campaign, the 'head of the war' was the king's property if captured. Le Bel and Froissart report that there was a dispute over the proposed removal of John to England; the Gascon lords who had helped to capture him claimed that they could keep him secure against any rescue attempts, and were anxious to retain such a valuable bargaining counter under their control. Only on payment of 100,000 florins, says Froissart, would the Gascons allow the prince to take king John to England. There is, however, no record of this payment, and Froissart is, as usual, making a good story out of a rather more mundane affair. If there was a dispute, the Gascon lords were hardly on strong ground, as the rights in such a prisoner had been specifically reserved to Edward; and the payments made were probably the usual end-of-campaign rewards to a successful army which Froissart has treated as a single item rather than sums paid to individuals.³

On 20 March, before the truce had been completed, Edward issued instructions to the sheriff of Devon to make arrangements for the prince's arrival. A mere three weeks later, on 11 April, the prince and king John sailed from Bordeaux, reaching Plymouth early in May after a difficult voyage. The journey to London was made at a leisurely pace, probably because of the large number of nobles in the king's and prince's entourage. The prince spent a few days at Salisbury and Sherborne; from Salisbury he ordered the keeper of his great wardrobe to provide 26 lb of sweetmeat 'with all speed', sending a messenger to London to fetch it. On 19 May the company left Salisbury for Winchester, reaching London on the 24th. Edward had sent various nobles to meet king John on the way, and one day had arranged a mock ambush of 500 men dressed in green, who appeared from the forest bordering the road in the guise of robbers armed with swords and bows. To the French king's inquiry as to what sort of people these were, the prince replied that they were foresters, living in the wild at their ease, and that it was their custom to appear like this every day. This piece of rustic play-acting, forerunner of many similar royal entertainments, was the prelude to a much more elaborate display in London, a formal 'entry' of a kind that was to continue on state occasions until the Restoration. Henry Picard, the mayor of London, together with the city aldermen, rode out to meet the prince, and he and his captive entered the city with them, preceded by members of the City guilds all dressed in one colour, amid scenes of great rejoicing. The conduits in the City were running with wine, the houses were hung with armour and bows and the inhabitants lined the streets to watch the procession. In Cheapside, two beautiful girls sat in a kind of birdcage suspended from the goldsmiths' shops, scattering gold and silver leaves on the heads of the cavalcade as it passed below. At St Paul's, the bishop of London and his clergy came in procession to meet them, and they then made their way down Ludgate and Fleet Street, arriving at Westminster that evening. Amidst all these festivities, king John himself struck a sombre note, dressed in a black robe trimmed with miniver, 'like an old chaplain'. King John was given the Savoy Palace as his lodging, its owner, the duke of Lancaster, being away in Brittany.[4]

The prince had already made many large gifts to his followers for their 'good service at the battle of Poitiers'. These now had to be enrolled on his central records, and where possible translated into an equivalent landholding: the grants were usually for annual payments in money until lands to the same annual value could be provided. The largest payment went to Sir James Audley, who was granted an annuity of £400 per annum, an immense sum considering the size of the prince's own annual income, which implies that his part in the battle may have been more crucial than the chronicles indicate. On the other hand, he had been seriously wounded, and he had continued to fight to the end rather than taking prisoners to ransom, and had therefore come out of the affair less profitably than Sir John Chandos: both received a grant of 600 gold crowns from the revenues of Marmande in Gascony, but Chandos's English annuity was only £40 per annum, together with the issues of Kirkton in Lincolnshire and Drakelow in Cheshire: the value of the latter is difficult to estimate. The prince's rewards were only to his own retinue: after Chandos and Audley come a group of knights from his household: Sir Nigel Loring, his chamberlain, received £83 6s. 8d. a year; Sir Richard Stafford, his former steward, a gift of 500 marks; Sir Baldwin Botetourt, 'master of the prince's great horses', the manor of Newport, £100 and an annuity of £40; Sir Edmund Wauncy, his steward, £20 a year. The members of his bodyguard on the day of the battle, and the standardbearer's attendant, William Shank, were likewise rewarded. A group of knights, many of them associated with the prince on the Crécy campaign, received gifts and annuities, including Sir Roger Cotesford, who had acted as a messenger between Bordeaux and London, Sir John Sully, whom the prince had retained for life in 1352, Sir Stephen Cosington, prominent as a diplomat and marshal of the prince's army in 1366-7, and Sir Thomas Felton, later steward and an important figure in Aquitaine. Four squires were rewarded; one of them, Theodoric van Dale, had been knighted on the expedition, while Richard Punchardoun seems to have transferred from Sir John Chandos's service to the prince's at about this time. Three German or Flemish knights were given annuities of 100 marks, as well as substantial gifts, and a squire from 'Almain' was also rewarded. Finally, members of the prince's household, such as William Blackwater, his physician, the friar Richard of Leominster,

Richard Doxeye, the prince's baker, and William Lenche, the prince's porter, were rewarded, the last-named receiving the ferry at Saltash near Plymouth because he had lost an eye at Poitiers.[5]

The Gascon lords were largely rewarded by grants of lands or revenue within Gascony, and relatively few records of such transactions survive. The army had contained a considerably smaller number of Gascons than of English, which further accounts for the disproportionately slight number of rewards. The captal of Buch had already received, in January 1356, the town and castle of Cognac; the lord of Pommiers, the lord of Lesparre and the lord of Tartas received gifts and pensions, and the prince bought some of their booty from them.[6]

The prince's own revenue from the expedition is much more difficult to trace. Technically, he was entitled to a share, usually half, of all ransoms collected by knights retained by him, and there were also his own prisoners, and those whom he had bought outright from their captors. The latter included Philip, king John's son, who, with the count of Sancerre and the lord of Craon, was sold to the king for £20,000. Other important prisoners were transferred to the king, among them the duke of Bourbon, the marshal d'Audrehem and the count of Joigny, because the prince had been unable to raise sufficient cash to pay for them, having agreed to buy them from their various captors. The duke of Bourbon had been bought from the captal de Buch and others for 25,000 crowns, and the prince had no such sum available in ready cash. The prince's generosity, both over the purchase price of the prisoners and in terms of ordinary rewards, may have meant that he was actually little better off when the business side of the expedition had been wound up, despite the considerable wealth that the campaign had realized.[7]

Besides king John and the French nobles, David Bruce and many Scottish lords were still held in England, having been captured in 1346. The presence of so many knights from overseas was the excuse for a magnificent series of tournaments during the following year. These began in the early autumn of 1357, at Smithfield, when all three kings were present, and continued shortly after Christmas, with a night-time tournament held at Bristol early in January. After a parliament at London in February, at which many of the French and Scottish captives were present, the next great gathering was for the Garter feast at Windsor on 23 April. A safe-conduct for three weeks was offered to all foreigners who wished to attend the gathering, and this attracted the dukes of Brabant and Luxemburg, while many of the prince's Gascon allies came, including the lord of Montferrand. The queen of Scotland, Joan, and many of her ladies were also present. The jousts after the ceremony were proclaimed by Roger Mortimer, earl of March, and were on the most lavish scale. The prince paid no less than £100 to the assembled heralds and minstrels, and distributed presents of armour and harness to his friends. King John watched all this extravagance and remarked wryly that he had never seen such a festival paid for without gold and silver by using tallies, knowing full well that most of the money would eventually come from his own ransom. The proceedings were marred only by an injury to the duke of Lancaster.[8]

The following year, in honour of John of Gaunt's marriage to Blanche, Lancaster's only daughter and heiress to his estates, jousts were held in London. John and his attendant knights are said to have jousted all the way from Reading to London, 'fighting in the fields and towns'. The jousts proper were held at Smithfield, the mayor and aldermen of London challenging all-comers to a three-day tournament from 27 to 29 May. These civic dignitaries proved to be the king, his four sons and nineteen other nobles in disguise, one of them Sir Batholomew Burghersh.[9]

The prince also spent some time travelling round his estates, chiefly in 1358. In April and May of that year, he and his household were at Peterborough Abbey for a month, perhaps in order to hunt in the bishop of Lincoln's warrens and parks, of which the prince had just been made keeper by the bishop. In August the prince visited Cheshire, where further problems with the administration of justice, and particularly of the forest laws, had arisen; two very large fines had been levied as a result of a survey by the justices in eyre in the previous autumn. The foresters of Wirral and Delamere had to pay £1,000 and £2,000 respectively in respect of encroachments on the prince's forest rights, some of the misdemeanours going back well into the previous century. The revenue from this visitation was £777 in the following year, and £698 the year after, and the prince's presence in the county may have been intended to ensure that there was no trouble in collecting the first payments. On his return journey, the prince visited Vale Royal abbey in Delamere forest, whose grandiose building plan had been initiated by Edward I in 1277. The prince had already granted the abbot 500 marks in 1353 out of the earlier fine on the men of Cheshire, because a shortage of funds had meant that the abbey church was still unroofed and the monastic buildings not yet begun. Now the prince gave another 500 marks, and in June 1359 a contract was drawn up with William Helpeston, by which the prince was to pay £860 for the building of the rest of the church, the foundations to be laid at the abbot's expense. The plan was a very ambitious one: Vale Royal was to be the largest Cistercian abbey church in the kingdom, ten feet longer than Fountains and the second largest in the entire Order. The work to be done by Helpeston was the building of an elaborate series of chapels round the east end, to a complex plan which seems to derive from Toledo Cathedral in Castile. These were duly finished in the following decade, but soon after Helpeston had begun work, a new disaster struck the long-delayed works. A great gale on 19 October 1360 blew down the columns of the nave, which were relatively insecure while they lacked the vaulting above. The church as a whole was never completed, and at the dissolution of the monasteries in 1539 was promptly demolished.[10]

While the prince was in Cheshire, he received news of his grandmother Isabella's death. She had spent the last twenty years of her life in retirement at her various manors, the chief being Castle Rising in Norfolk, and in her last years devoted herself to good works. She made several pilgrimages to Walsingham, and the prince may have visited her on his journeys there; she came to Berkhamsted when the prince was there in 1354 and 1355. Her death did mean that Castle Rising, and the manor of Cheylesmore in Warwickshire, with revenue of nearly £100 a year in Coventry and a quarter of the King's Lynn customs, came to the prince under a deed of reversion made twenty years earlier. Such an addition to his revenues was welcome, and orders for the taking over of her estates were made on 28 August, under a week after her death. The prince himself was at Cheylesmore and Coventry by 19 September, on his way back to London. On 27 November he attended Isabella's funeral in the new Franciscan church at Newgate.[11]

Meanwhile the attempts to reach a peace settlement had been continuing unabated. At the end of June 1357, the cardinals of Périgord and San Vitale had arrived separately in England, to pursue the talks broken off at Bordeaux in March. On 3 July they were met outside London by the prince and the archbishop of Canterbury, and escorted to their lodgings. A month later, a great feast was given in their honour at Westminster; but the negotiations dragged on, because Edward insisted on his claim to the French throne being discussed, even though the papal envoys offered restitution of 'all his ancestors' lands'. In the end, however, the agreement that emerged in the following May was concerned only with the terms of king John's release, the general settlement being left for future discussion. No formal record of the terms survives, but from a surviving draft and evidence in the chronicles, Edward demanded the restoration of the whole of the English domains in Aquitaine and Ponthieu, and a ransom of four million florins, of which 600,000 were to be paid before the king was released. It was a very considerable requirement, and the payment of the ransom would have been very difficult to fulfil, but on 8 May, shortly after the great St George's day feast at Windsor, king John formally agreed to its terms in the presence of the king, the prince and his leading councillors. But the dauphin and his council in Paris, although outwardly accepting the terms, and even putting the collection of the ransom in hand, deferred the actual ratification of the treaty month by month; and it appears that one of Edward's conditions had been that the terms must be precisely and punctually carried out. When the first instalment of the ransom, due on 1 November, had not been paid, no hostages given or the treaty itself ratified, Edward told the French that they must prepare for war.[12]

The French failure to comply with these terms is surprising; steep as Edward's price may have been, the dauphin and his council were in no position to quarrel with the English. Faced by peasant revolts, the appearance of the 'free companies' owing allegiance to no man, and the continuing intrigues of Charles of Navarre, who had escaped from prison late in 1356 and was now proclaiming his own title to the French crown, their authority was at best uncertain. In July 1358, there had been an attempt to betray Paris to Charles of Navarre by Étienne Marcel, the provost of the city, which had almost succeeded. The discovery of Marcel's plot, however, proved to be the turning point. Up to then, the dauphin's authority was barely sufficient to allow him to make arrangements to collect the ransom and to ratify the treaty; by November, when Edward declared war, the tide was running strongly in the dauphin's favour, and his council could begin to think in terms of resisting such an invasion. Such hopeful signs as there were remained unknown to king John, however; and watching the preparations for a new invasion, which began in December, he evidently felt that it was worth offering almost any concession to prevent the English army from departing. Without details of the negotiations, it is impossible to say how the next scheme for peace was arrived at: all we have are copies of a document dated 28 March which bear Edward III's privy seal, which implies that it was issued at John's request, listing 'the points and articles discussed and agreed at London'. There were certainly neither French nor papal envoys in England at this point, and the exorbitant and one-sided terms seem to have been Edward's price for agreeing to any kind of arrangement at all, and for prolonging the truce when he had an army ready. The terms were now that Edward should have Aquitaine and Ponthieu in full sovereignty, and the old Angevin territories of Touraine, Anjou and Normandy as well, also in full sovereignty. In effect, the rival claimants to the throne of France would partition the kingdom. Three quarters of the ransom of four million ecus was to be raised by 1 August. The truce agreed at Bordeaux, which expired on 9 April 1359, was moreover extended to 24 June.[13]

The document was taken to Paris by the archbishop of Sens, the counts of Tancarville and Dammartin and marshal Audrehem; they left after 11 May, and a fortnight later the États-Généraux, summoned by the dauphin, declared that the treaty was neither acceptable nor feasible. Edward must have been surprised by this reply, for his military preparations were far from complete, even though they had been in hand for six months; it was only in June that work on the expedition began in real earnest. As always there were delays, the more so because the initial expeditionary force was to be the largest single army ever sent abroad, of nearly 12,000 men; this number had been surpassed at Calais, but only after the initial army had been reinforced. The prince had originally, on 1 March, summoned 300 archers from Chester to assemble at Sandwich by 1 August; 50 archers from North Wales were summoned on 10 June, and 1,000 sheaves of arrows and 3,000 bowstrings were requisitioned. Later in June the numbers were changed to 400 Chester archers, 10 Welsh archers and 40 lances, and by the end of July, the date of assembly had been deferred to 1 September. In August, eight knights and seventeen squires were retained for a year, until 1 August 1360, and their fees for the first half-year were paid. The expedition of 1359 was exceptional in that it was financed entirely from the king's and magnates' own resources, without recourse to taxation. It is not surprising that the prince had recourse to massive loans, giving Sir John Wingfield a bond for 20,000 marks against sums he had borrowed for the prince, and raising £1,000 from London merchants and £2,000 from the wealthy earl of Arundel. At the same time the exchequer bought some of the remaining prisoners of the Poitiers campaign from him. As the day for departure approached, the prince made other preparations: he and Edward went on a series of pilgrimages, and when he arrived at Sandwich on about 16 September, his officials drew up a list of his debts and payments made on his personal authority, including the huge sums of £387 to his painter and £340 to his 'embroiderer'. The main fleet finally sailed on 27 October, the prince's final retinue consisting of seven bannerets, 136 knights, 443 squires and 900 horse archers. Chandos, Burghersh and Botetourt were all with him once again, and Audley joined him later in the campaign.[14]

Difficulties of transport meant that the expedition had had to cross the Channel piecemeal. Lancaster was sent as an advance guard on 1 October, with instructions to collect a large number of mercenaries under the marquis of Meissen, who had arrived at Calais in hope of employment, and who were wasting the stores for the main army because they had been there so long. With these forces and his own retinue, he made a preliminary raid to Arras, and thence to the Somme. He attempted to take Bray-sur-Somme in order to cross the river, but failed when the town resisted and he was attacked by a force commanded by the French lieutenant of Picardy. He then marched along the north bank of the Somme, crossing at Cérisy. Here he was recalled, and recrossing the Somme, he continued to Abbeville, and turned north near Crécy, returning to Calais by way of Montreuil. Roger Mortimer was the next to cross on about 22 October. He raided the Channel coast as far as Étaples, burning the latter town before joining forces with Lancaster as he marched back towards Calais. The preliminary raid had been of the usual kind, with much burning and pillaging; but on the instructions of the dauphin, supplies had been deliberately stored in towns or destroyed, and when Lancaster's army returned, they were 'in much want of bread and wine'.[15]

Edward's objective for the main campaign had been announced long before: the army was to march on Rheims, where he was to make good his claim to France by being crowned in the cathedral and anointed with the holy oil of Saint-Rémy, with which French kings had been consecrated since the sixth century. He had taken no pains to conceal his intentions from the French, assuming that there was little they could do to prevent him. As early as 10 July, measures had been taken by the dauphin to strengthen Rheims, and late in the

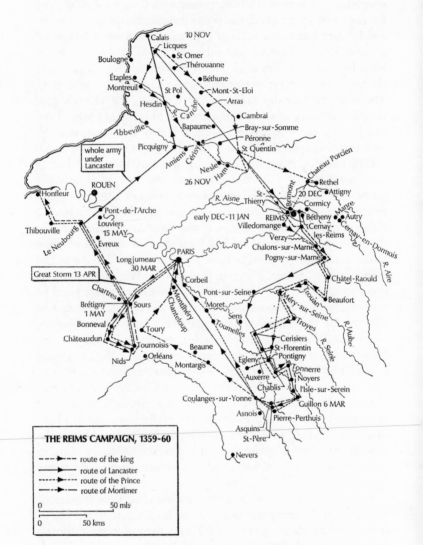

THE REIMS CAMPAIGN, 1359-60

---▶- route of the king
—▶— route of Lancaster
----▶- route of the Prince
—·▶·— route of Mortimer

0 ————————— 50 mls
0 ————————— 50 kms

Map 6. The Rheims campaign

year the captain of Rheims, Gaucher de Châtillon, was able to complete the town's fortifications. Large stocks of weapons and stores had been laid in. Edward, however, was planning to use military force only as a last resort. His chief hope was that, faced with this display of strength, the citizens would open their gates to him, and he particularly relied on the sympathy of Jean de Craon, archbishop of Rheims, who was related to the English royal house and was said to be at odds with king John. As a corollary of this policy, no looting or burning was carried out near Rheims, and friendly relations with the town were carefully cultivated.[16]

As usual, the army was drawn up into three divisions. The first two were commanded by the king and the prince, the third being formed by Lancaster's forces already in the field. This arrangement was all the more essential with such a large force, because adequate supplies would be difficult to find; and the equipment brought over from England included hand mills for grinding corn and small boats for fishing on lakes and rivers, as well as some of the king's hounds and falcons. Lancaster met the king and prince on 10 November, and his report to the king, that provisions were scarce, must have been serious news. The columns dispersed much more widely than on the Crécy campaign, riding 'twenty or thirty leagues apart'. Edward took the most easterly route, along the border of France and Flanders, Brabant and Hainault; Lancaster's forces were in the centre, though nothing is known of their route. The prince and his men rode furthest afield; they set out to the south-east, along the route by which Lancaster had just returned, as far as Hisdin. They then turned due south-east, and closed with the other columns, crossing the Somme and marching to Nesle and Hain on the upper reaches of the river. Here they met the only active resistance of the entire first stage of the campaign on 26 November, when Baldwin Dawkin, said to be master of the dauphin's crossbowmen, attempted to surprise the earl of Stafford by attacking his quarters at night: Dawkin was captured with a number of French knights, and one of his men was killed. At this point there had been no contact between the separate divisions since the beginning of the march, but the prince's men now came up with Lancaster's forces somewhere south of Saint-Quentin. They were within forty miles of Rheims, and the king's division also joined up with them. A council of war was held on 29 and 30 November, as a result of which communications were improved, to avoid loss of contact in future. The prince was directed to approach

Rheims from the north-east; the French having burnt Rethel to prevent him from using its bridge, he had some difficulty in crossing the river Aisne and had to fight his way across at Château-Porcien. Early in December he rejoined the king and Lancaster, and the whole army took up quarters around Rheims.[17]

In pursuance of Edward's policy of persuasion rather than force, the troops were stationed well back from the city, the various commanders being as much as ten miles away. The king occupied the abbey of Saint-Bâle, while the prince was at Villedomange, and Mortimer and John Beauchamp at Bétheny, a mere three miles from Rheims. For the next forty days the army waited outside the city: a loose blockade was set up, and diplomatic efforts to persuade the city to admit the English began. Messengers were still able to pass without difficulty between the dauphin and the garrison of Rheims. The leaders of the English army kept Christmas 'as if they were at home', feasting each other in turn. During the entire time no attempt was made to take the city by assault.[18]

Outside the city, however, the countryside suffered severely at the hands of the English, though operations were only carried out well away from Rheims, at a distance of thirty miles or more; this was probably in order to preserve local resources of food and forage for the army while keeping the troops occupied. On 20 December, Sir Bartholomew Burghersh and Sir Baldwin Botetourt, with many of the prince's and John of Gaunt's men, attacked Cormicy, east of Rheims, by night, scaling the walls and capturing the town. The castle, with a strong keep and a recently reinforced garrison, held out until 6 January, when a mine dug by the English was fired and a general attack launched. The garrison retreated into the keep, but were forced to surrender later that day, the chief captive being the lord of Clermont. Two days later the keep was razed and the town set on fire. While this siege was in progress, a combination of the prince's and Lancaster's men, led by Lancaster, John of Gaunt and Sir John Chandos, attacked other towns to the east of Rheims. Cernay-en-Domnois, a strongly fortified place, was taken on 30 December. Despite a double ditch, strong walls and towers and a good garrison, the first improvised assault succeeded; the castle surrendered, and the town was burnt. The near-by towns of Autry and Manre were approached, the raiders having been joined meanwhile by Eustace d'Abrechicourt; both were taken without opposition and set on fire. The fortunes of war did not always favour the English: a number of the army were taken prisoner,

including William Kingston, a member of the prince's household
staff; Geoffrey Chaucer, then a squire of the king's retinue, was also
captured during the siege.[19]

It was clear that the blockade of Rheims was ineffective, and there
was no sign of any assistance from the archbishop or his men; the
townsmen had taken precautions against possible treachery on their
part. Despite the raids, the morale of the troops was low: the
weather had been very wet, and supplies were running out. To
feed the army, it was essential to move on. Edward had suffered a
major set-back, and there was no very obvious target at which the
campaign could be redirected. His next move was suggested by the
arrival of Burgundian envoys while he was at Rheims, anxious to
avoid the appearance of an English army in Burgundy and offering
to purchase a truce. This was a tactic which was becoming increasingly common in face of the marauding 'free companies', but
which had not been used between major powers before. The
negotiations were still in the preliminary stages when the army was
forced to decamp on 11 January, and Edward therefore moved
southwards to threaten the duchy and improve his bargaining
position. Once more the army divided into three columns, and
headed down the Marne. Near Châlons, the prince was joined by
Sir James Audley and the captal de Buch with a Gascon force.
Châlons was left unscathed, but there were problems over crossing
the river and a week was spent waiting for the bridge at Pogny to
be repaired. The whole army seems to have crossed there, fanning
out again on the west bank, though the distances between the three
divisions were only a few miles. The Seine was crossed at Méry
and Pont-sur-Seine, Lancaster taking a western route to Sens, while
the prince followed his father to Troyes, where the German
contingent were paid off, apparently with the proceeds of a ransom
paid by the duchy of Bar for immunity from attack, and thence to
Pontigny. At Pontigny, the king, the prince and other nobles made
a pilgrimage to the shrine of St Edmund Rich, archbishop of
Canterbury, who had died there in exile in 1240. Strict orders were
given against pillaging. The prince, short of forage for his horses
because he had been following across land already stripped of
fodder, now turned west to Auxerre, establishing himself at
Égleny, in a district which was scattered with well-defended
fortresses. The prince's men

suffered more from the enemy than in any other part of this

expedition hitherto. Several of his knights and esquires were killed at night in their quarters, and his foraging parties taken in the fields, although the country was more deserted before them than in all the other districts, so that they scarcely saw a soldier outside the fortresses.

Five English squires and three archers surprised in a mill by fifty French put up a good defence and captured eleven of them; but many other such skirmishes were evidently less favourable.[20]

The prince seems to have stayed near Auxerre for the next month or so, while the king was at Guillon, on the borders of Burgundy, completing negotiations for the ransom of Burgundy. On 24 February, Roger Mortimer died suddenly at Rouvray, south of Guillon, perhaps killed on a foraging raid. It was only at the beginning of March that the ransom treaty was ready for signature: because the duke was still a minor, the agreement was signed by the nobles and representatives of the chief towns, who assembled at Guillon on 6 March; the actual ceremony took place on the 10th. Edward obtained a ransom of 200,000 gold moutons, payable by Easter 1361 in three instalments, in return for the surrender of the castle of Flavigny and a three years' truce. (Part of the ransom eventually found its way into the prince's purse.) Should king Edward wish to be crowned king of France within that time, and the duke of Burgundy, as one of the twelve peers of France, objected, the treaty was to be void. This was a first step towards accomplishment of his aim, but hardly a fitting reward for so great an expedition.[21]

The king now reverted to more orthodox tactics. Instead of an attempted coronation or diplomatic manoeuvres towards it, he would try to draw the dauphin into battle or to mount an attack on Paris itself. Once again the army formed into three columns, and moved slowly northwards, ravaging the countryside as they went. At Tournelles, near Fontainebleau, the prince came across a manor which had been newly fortified; he surrounded it, set up siege-engines and starved out the garrison after a siege of three or four days, capturing five distinguished knights. The French continued their guerrilla tactics, harassing the army when they could; some German knights of the king's division were killed in a night raid. Furthermore, 'an attack was made on Winchelsea early in March by a French force of about two thousand men, in the hope that the port would be undefended while the army was in France, and much damage was done before the French were driven off'. The landing caused general alarm, and king John was moved to the prince's castle of Berkhamsted, 'for the safe guarding of his person', later that month. On 30 March the English army encamped south of Paris, the king at Chanteloup and the other two divisions between Corbeil and Longjumeau. The captal de Buch was sent to make contact with Charles of Navarre in Normandy, in the hope of mounting a concerted campaign against Paris, where Charles still had many sympathizers.[22]

Since the beginning of the campaign, the Pope had been anxious to achieve a peace settlement, and he had empowered Simon de Langres, master of the Dominicans, and William Lynn, dean of Chichester, to negotiate terms. They were appointed in November, but do not seem to have made contact with Edward until the army reached Guillon. If they did meet him there, nothing came of the talks, and the Pope appointed the abbot of Cluny and the lord of Anthon as additional negotiators on 4 March. Now that the army had encamped outside Paris, it was possible to get representatives of the two sides together; and on Good Friday, 3 April, a conference was held at the leper house at Longjumeau. The constable of France, Robert Fiennes, Boucicaut, Guichard d'Angle and Simon de Bucy represented the French; Lancaster, Northampton, Warwick, Chandos and Sir Walter Muny were the English negotiators. Several of those involved had taken part in the Bordeaux negotiations, but the talks soon broke down; according to the French, 'because of the excessive demands of the enemy'.[23]

Edward's troops ravaged the countryside around Paris during Easter week, burning the villages of Montlhéry and Longjumeau and driving the population inside the walls of the city. A few rash villagers fortified churches and tried to resist the army, but were overcome and slaughtered; at Châtres, a quarrel between the French commander and the villagers led to the burning of the church, with fearful loss of life, while the English looked on. Nearer to Paris, the dauphin ordered the burning of the suburbs of Saint-Germain, Nôtre-Dame-des-Champs and Saint-Marceau lest the English should use them as cover for an attack on the city. Paris was already short of food as a result of the activities of the 'free companies' and the Navarrese in Normandy, and the added influx made conditions chaotic; an eyewitness, Jean de Venette, wrote: 'On Easter Day, I myself saw priests of ten country parishes communicating their people and keeping Easter in various chapels or any spot they could find in the monastery of the Carmelite friars.'[24]

Paris was clearly in no position to stand a siege; but, equally, the English army was not fit to undertake another blockade. However, the English king was anxious to bring matters to a swift conclusion, and the army moved into positions which implied that a siege was about to begin in the hope that the dauphin would attempt to break the encirclement. But there was no response from within the city. On 10 April, the abbot of Cluny succeeded in arranging further talks at the leper house of Tombe-Issoire, between the same negotiators; once more, nothing was agreed. Edward had no choice but to withdraw. Before doing so he made one last attempt to draw out the dauphin, and early on the morning of 12 April drew up the army in full array outside the walls of Paris. Lancaster was in command of the vanguard, the king in the centre, and the prince commanded the rearguard. In honour of the hoped-for conflict, thirty squires were knighted. When, at about mid morning, it was clear that no action would take place, these knights raided the suburbs and a brief skirmish followed with a similar number of French knights; Richard Baskerville, son of one of the prince's companions at Crécy and Poitiers, was unhorsed, but was rescued by his comrades.[25]

The army now headed towards Chartres. Edward's plans at this point are unclear, though his first concern was to find more forage for his horses. A long march was planned for the Monday to bring the army well clear of the ravaged area around Paris. But the weather, which in March had been 'as fair, mild, pleasant and warm as anyone could ever remember having seen it', turned very wintry, and a violent hailstorm swept over the already weary troops. Many of the horses, evidently in poor condition for lack of forage, perished, and much of the baggage train was abandoned. The storm soon became legendary: a London chronicler a century later recorded that it was 'a ffoule Derke day off myste, and off haylle, and so bytter colde, that syttyng on horse bak men dyed. Wherfore, unto this day yt ys called black Monday, and wolle be longe time here affter.' The battered army continued on its way, first south to Châteaudun and then east towards Orléans, as if its leaders were still uncertain about their strategy.[26]

Near Orléans the abbot of Cluny once more met the king and his commanders. This time they were prepared to listen. The English army had been in France for nearly seven months, and had achieved very little, despite its great size and the presence of all the most experienced leaders. The dauphin's tactics of holding only the great cities meant that, without a massive siege, nothing further was likely to be achieved, and the failure at Rheims had underlined the difficulties of a blockade, in that it was easier to hold a well-supplied town than to provision and shelter a large army encamped outside it. It had taken nearly a year to reduce the relatively small fortress of Calais; to take anything larger, except by treachery or a fortunate assault, would be impossible. Furthermore, the army was in poor condition, and although the campaign continued after 'Black Monday', that day's devastation undoubtedly helped to bring the English leaders round to the idea of peace talks. Despite their failure in the field, the English still held a powerful negotiating position and stood to gain a great deal in material terms from any settlement.[27]

There was a delay of some ten days before the talks actually opened, at Brétigny near Chartres, on 1 May. The dauphin sent sixteen representatives, led by the bishop of Beauvais, while Lancaster once more led the English. The treaty was agreed in broad outline by the end of the following week, and its terms were entirely practical. Edward III had been unable to make good his claim to the French crown, despite his great campaign: therefore he renounced it. The French were clearly in no position to drive the English out of Aquitaine: therefore Edward was to have it in full sovereignty, as an independent state. Basically, the terms were those of the ransom treaty of 1358, but the king had to concede some other points, now that the military threat to the French kingdom itself was no longer a powerful bargaining counter: he gave up his claim to sovereignty of Brittany, where the English presence had been a real one for the past two decades, as well as the shadowy claims to the old Angevin territories of Normandy, Anjou, Maine and Touraine. As to king John's ransom, this was to be three million, not four million, florins, and the timetable for the payments was to be slightly longer than that envisaged in 1358. This was the outline of the treaty: the final details, including the vital questions of the mutual renunciation of claims, were to be worked out at a conference between the two kings at Calais, to begin on 15 July, for which a complex timetable was provided, indicating that although the main principles were agreed, there were still many problems to be resolved.[28]

The English army made its way north as soon as the agreement was ready, pausing at Le Neubourg in the Seine valley, where the three divisions, under Lancaster, Mauny and Stafford, were detailed off to make their way separately to Calais to await shipping. The king and his four sons, with a small company of nobles, made their way to Honfleur. Just before they embarked, the prince signed the preliminary agreement, ratified by the dauphin, in the church at Louviers in the Seine valley, on 15 May. On the evening of the 18th the king and the prince landed at Rye: they rode posthaste to London, arriving there the next day, and on the 22nd king John announced his acceptance of the treaty. King Edward himself only promised to abide by the terms on 14 June: John gave a great dinner at the Tower to mark the occasion.[29]

The prince was in England during the summer while the preliminary work for the Calais conference began. At the end of June he escorted king John from London to Dover by way of Canterbury, where the French king offered a jewel valued at £25 at Becket's shrine. On 5 July they left Canterbury for Dover, hunting in the archbishop's park on the way. On the 6th the prince gave a feast for the king at Dover Castle before, on the 7th, John set sail for Calais, where he was to remain until the treaty had been signed and the first instalment of the ransom paid. As was to be expected, the negotiations did not begin on the appointed date, though there was no lack of activity. Early in August, the dauphin arrived at Saint-Omer to supervise the collection of his father's ransom, and a series of officials arrived from England to deal with individual points. Towards the end of August the dauphin moved to Boulogne, and on 24 August, the prince, Lancaster and the other magnates who were to conduct negotiations left for Calais. The actual remaining negotiations were expected to be brief, and Edward was ready to cross by 6 September. But there were difficulties, reported to the council by William 'de Roka' on 9 September; Sir Nicholas Loveigne, one of the prince's knights, crossed on 13 September with letters from the prince to the king; and Sir William Burton, a trusted member of the prince's retinue, came over on 6 October, returning the same day. The difficulties centred on the question of the renunciations: when were these to be made? In the end, a formula was agreed by which these were taken out of the treaty, and a separate agreement made as to when these should take effect. The transfers of lands were to be made as part of the treaty: when this had been done, the formal renunciations of both sides were to be exchanged at Bruges. One side, or both, may have been trying to mitigate the effect of the treaty. Edward III may have hoped to get the renunciation of the French king's rights and sovereignty in Aquitaine made immediately, to be followed by the transfer of territories and lastly his own renunciation; given this demand, the French may have been anxious to separate the renunciations from the main treaty. All we know for certain is that there were 'many altercations' concerning the clauses in the treaty dealing with the transfer of lands. There were also other problems: the hostages for king John were not ready, nor was his ransom, while two of the places to be transferred, Guines and La Rochelle, were causing difficulties. The representatives of La Rochelle had to be summoned to Calais in an attempt to overcome their reluctance, and special provision was made for them at the signing of the treaty. Early in October, a timetable for the various transactions had been agreed, and the supplementary letters dealing with the renunciations were drafted; on 9 October Edward at last left Sandwich to join the prince. Judging by other diplomatic episodes in his career, the prince was probably only indirectly involved in the actual business and technicalities of the talks; Lancaster had far greater experience, and the detailed wording was a question for the clerks on both sides.[30]

All that remained to be completed were the ceremonies and formalities attendant on the signature of a solemn treaty. A feast was given by king John on 12 October at which king Edward, the prince and Lancaster were the guests of honour. On 24 October, at Calais, the two kings solemnly swore to keep the treaty, and early the next day king John was escorted out of Calais by Edward and the prince. Edward returned after three miles; the prince continued with king John to Boulogne, which they reached at about midday. On 26 October, at St Mary's, Boulogne, king John repeated his oath as a free man and the prince and the dauphin also swore to observe the treaty. The prince returned to Calais that afternoon, reaching London on 3 November. The long-awaited peace was made.[31]

Prince of Aquitaine

$\longmapsto$

7

At the end of the expedition of 1359-60, the prince found himself once more without a specific task; unlike the other great magnates, who were often employed on royal business, or who could pursue their own private affairs if they so wished, the prince was both above the routine affairs of state, except as a member of the king's council, and unable to withdraw entirely to the life of a country lord – not that the latter would have been in keeping with his character. Early in 1361 he attended a parliament held at Westminster from 24 January onwards; this was used as a convenient occasion for a number of his tenants to do homage for their estates. In the spring, there was another serious outbreak of plague, which raged so fiercely in London that by 10 May the sittings of the law-courts were suspended for six weeks and finally abandoned until Michaelmas. Among the first victims of this epidemic, known simply as 'the second pestilence' by the chroniclers, was Henry duke of Lancaster, who died on 23 March. Three weeks later he was buried at Newark, in the collegiate church he had founded there; the prince and the rest of the royal family attended the funeral, and the prince covered his bier with two pieces of cloth of gold. There were further deaths from the plague among the knights of the Garter later in the year: Sir Reginald Cobham and Sir William Fitzwarin both died in October. At the Garter feast day on 23 April, which the prince attended, there had been another vacant stall besides Lancaster's, that of Sir Thomas Holland, who had died in Normandy the previous December.[1]

The prince spent the summer at Kennington, Waltham and Byfleet, probably conferring with his father over the settlement and execution of the treaty of Brétigny. In the absence of any council records, it is impossible to date major policy decisions, but there is evidence that it was during this period that plans were made for the prince to take over the government of Aquitaine. First, the appointments of officials in Aquitaine made consequent on its surrender by the French were all of men closely associated with the prince. On 20 January, Sir John Chandos was made the king's lieutenant in France for the transfer of lands, and this was confirmed in a more general letter of 1 July, by which time Sir Richard Stafford, the prince's steward, had been appointed seneschal of Gascony. Sir Nigel Loring, the prince's chamberlain, and Sir Stephen Cosington, one of the prince's retainers, were the other knights among the commissioners. There could be no question of appointing the prince to anything more than a lieutenancy until the provisions of the Calais treaty had been brought into effect, so even if plans were made in the summer of 1361, they were held over until the transfer of territories and the mutual renunciations of claims were completed. But Chandos, who was to do the actual reception of homages, did not start work in Aquitaine until 22 September, having been delayed in Paris for a month waiting for his French colleagues, Boucicaut and Audrehem. Resistance to the change of lordship and further delays because of Audrehem's appointment as lieutenant in Languedoc and Boucicaut's illness meant that the taking of homages was only completed at the end of March 1362, with the result that the exchange of renunciations planned for November at Bruges had to be postponed. None the less, the constable of Bordeaux received £9,350 in October 1361 for the prince's retinue, implying that plans for the prince to go there were to be put in hand as soon as possible. A certain Conrad Dafflen was paid £20 before November 1361, 'in recompense for his expenses about the prince's crossing to Gascony'. On 8 March the following year, Chandos, reporting to London, refers to 'the principality of Aquitaine'; he must therefore have known of plans to make it a fief of the prince's, and had forgotten that the plans were in suspense: equally, in letters patent of 15 February, the prince is styled 'prince of Aquitaine and Wales', though this could have been copied in error at a later date. It would seem that the announcement was planned for February or March, but delayed for reasons unknown to us.[2]

Another reason for the prince passing the summer near London was purely personal, but a personal matter with many implications for affairs of state. The prince was thirty-one in June, and was still unmarried, despite the numerous plans for suitable alliances which had been made for him as part of royal diplomatic manoeuvres in the past. His name had never been linked to any mistresses, and there is good evidence for only one illegitimate son, Sir Roger Clarendon, hanged by order of Henry IV in 1402 because he was regarded as a possible pretender. The prince's life seems to have been that of a bachelor among boon companions; the lists of gifts recorded by his treasurers, apart from occasional presents to his sisters, are all to his companions-in-arms or followers. An arranged marriage would have been entirely in conformity with this pattern, especially in view of the possible diplomatic benefits. The prince chose otherwise, and his choice was in many ways remarkable. Sir Thomas Holland had died in December 1360, leaving a widow, Joan, countess of Kent in her own right. Joan, so Froissart claimed, had been brought up in queen Philippa's household. When she was fifteen or sixteen, she and Holland had exchanged vows in an informal marriage ceremony 'by the words of those present', which was none the less legal and binding in the eyes of the Church. This was kept secret, and during Sir Thomas's absence at Calais in 1347, William Montacute, the young earl of Salisbury, married her, probably with the consent of her guardians, as she was still under age. Faced with such powerful pressure, she said nothing of her affair with Holland, and seems to have acquiesced in the ceremony. But Sir Thomas was undaunted by the prospect of a quarrel with Salisbury, and on his return to England, late in 1347 or early in 1348, set in motion proceedings for the recovery of his wife, reputedly by now one of the most beautiful women in England. He petitioned the Pope for her return, and cardinal Adhémar was instructed to hear the case. He found Sir Thomas's claim valid, and on 13 November 1349 a Bull dissolving the marriage with Salisbury was issued. In 1352 Joan became countess of Kent in her own right, on the death of her brother, and when Sir Thomas died in 1360, she was left as a very wealthy widow, an obvious target for any fortune-hunting knight, and in urgent need of protection in an age when the abduction of heiresses and forcible marriages were far from uncommon. Equally, it was by no means unusual for a woman to remarry several times: Chaucer's Wife of Bath was drawn from life.[3]

All that we know of the prince's wooing (apart from a romantic story in a French chronicle) is that some time during the early summer, his esquire Nicholas Bond was sent to Avignon to obtain the necessary licence for the prince's marriage, at which point the couple had already plighted their troth. Dispensations were needed because they had a common great-grandfather, Edward I, and were therefore related in the second and third degree. Bond had little difficulty in obtaining the dispensation; Innocent VI, like all the Avignon popes, favoured the French cause, and the prince's proposed marriage eliminated an important diplomatic weapon for the English. On 8 September, the necessary letters, directed to the archbishop of Canterbury, were issued. The whole question of Joan's previous marriages was recited, both her marriage to Holland and the annulled contract with Salisbury, and absolution was given in case any penalties were unwittingly incurred by this third match. Dispensation was also required because the prince was godfather to both Joan's sons, and therefore stood in spiritual relationship to her. Because there had been a marriage contract between Joan and the prince before the dispensation was granted, this was dissolved; a suitable penance was imposed for all these various impediments, namely the endowment of two chantry priests, with a stipend of 40 marks a year each. A month later, on 6 October, the prince and Joan plighted their troth once more, in a public ceremony, and on 10 October, at Windsor, Simon Islip, archbishop of Canterbury, together with the bishops of Winchester, Salisbury, Lincoln and Worcester and the abbot of Westminster, celebrated the marriage, in the presence of the king, John of Gaunt, Edmund of Langley, queen Philippa, Joan, queen of Scotland, the prince's sister Isabella, the earls of Warwick and Suffolk, a large number of other lords and ladies, and 'ordinary clergy and laymen in a plentiful multitude'. The king's name is not mentioned in the archbishop's announcement of the marriage, but appears in a con-firmatory Bull issued by the Pope in December as one of those present. There have been speculations that the prince quarrelled with his father over the marriage. However, there is no evidence of discord between the prince and his father afterwards, and the suggestion of French chroniclers that he was exiled to Aquitaine for marrying without permission is unfounded. Otherwise the chroniclers hinted discreetly at the unsuitability of the match, by reciting Joan's previous history or the terms of the dispensation; one writer dared to say that 'this match greatly surprised many people', while another quoted her nickname, 'the virgin of Kent', with evident sarcasm.[4]

The marriage does not seem to have been marked by great festivities, and the prince and his bride spent November to January at Berkhamsted, where the king and queen visited them. In honour of the occasion, the prince suddenly decided on 28 December to give his household new liveries for New Year's Day, and his long-suffering receiver in London, Peter Lacy, was ordered to 'arrange somehow or other to send to Berkhamsted enough cloth for making the said livery'. If the prince's style of living had been extravagant before his marriage, it was not improved by Joan, though she did bring considerable revenue from her lands to help the prince's finances. Early in 1362 there are items such as £200 for a single set of jewelled buttons for the princess, and later the same year the prince's embroiderer was paid £715 for items for the prince, the princess, and the princess's daughter, a reminder that the prince's household had also been enlarged by the addition of three children, the eldest being eleven. The princess was assigned £1,000 a year for her expenses, increased to 2,000 marks in 1363. The prince continued to take part in tournaments: there were two at Smithfield in March and April 1362, at which the king and queen and some of the French captives still in England were present. There was also a proposed tournament in Cheapside, at which the defendants were to appear as the seven deadly sins; the chronicler John of Reading was convinced that this attracted a large number of evil spirits, which hung about all that year.[5]

Apart from two short visits to Peterborough, and a week spent at the prince's manor at Bushey, the prince and princess were at Kennington for much of the summer. Kennington had been the subject of a good deal of expenditure in the previous decade, and was now a palatial establishment.

Recent excavations, combined with frequent entries in the prince's accounts, have produced a fairly detailed picture of what the buildings were like in about 1363. In the 1340s, a hall, prince's chamber and other structures had been built; from 1353 onwards, much of the existing manor was pulled down, including some of the buildings put up in the 1340s, and was replaced by a new hall, with a chamber and wardrobe incorporated in the hall complex. The hall was completed by the great master mason Henry Yevele between 1358 and 1363. It was nearly ninety feet long and fifty feet wide, faced with Reigate stone and decorated with statues; there were three or more fireplaces, but the windows do not appear to have been glazed. The floors were probably covered with glazed tiles (as at Castle Rising, where floor tiles with the prince's arms survive), and the roof was also tiled. The prince's chamber lay at right angles to it, and was only slightly smaller than the hall, though less elaborately finished. A range of half-timbered buildings housed the kitchen and servants' quarters, and there was also a chapel. To the south of the hall lay the great garden, while to the west of the prince's chamber was a private garden; somewhere here vines were grown, as poles to support them were bought in 1362. As there are no specific records of payments to painters for work at Kennington, we can only guess at the decoration of the interior. It may have been elaborately carried out in the manner of the contemporary work at Westminster; on the other hand, the prince possessed a number of sets of tapestries, and the walls may have been covered with these when he was in residence.[6]

The execution of the treaty of Brétigny had run into considerable difficulties. There had been disputes over the lands to be transferred, particularly in some of the border areas, where English claims had never been clearly defined, such as Belleville and Gaure. As a result, when, in October 1361, French commissioners came to ask for Edward's renunciation of his claims and to renounce French sovereignty over Aquitaine, the king refused, and instead sent an embassy to Paris to ask for the transfer of the remaining lands and to receive the French renunciation. His ambassadors, who left in November, were not empowered to make the English side of the renunciation. Not surprisingly, no agreement was reached.

None the less, in July, the long-planned arrangements by which the prince was to become lord of Aquitaine were completed, and on 19 July he did homage to the king at Westminster for his new principality, in the presence of many nobles. The terms on which he was to hold the territory were not dissimilar from those under which he had acted as the king's lieutenant there. The important alteration was in the status of the territory. In the past, the English had ruled in Gascony by consent or conquest: their subjects were either sympathetic to the English cause, or overawed by English arms. Since the treaty of Calais a new situation had arisen: towns were being forcibly but peacefully transferred from French to English suzerainty. Edward had no intention of attempting to suppress any murmurings of discontent by force. His strategy was, as we have already seen in the case of La Rochelle, to woo the

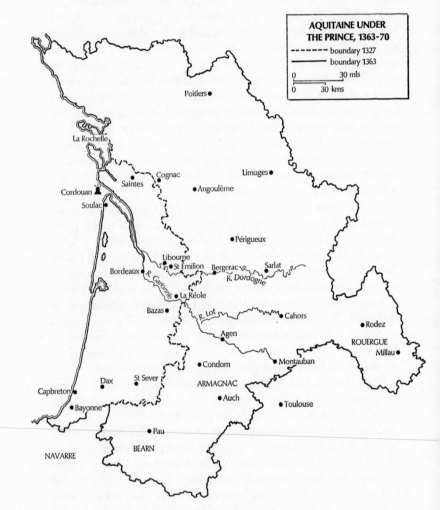

Map 7. Aquitaine under the prince

malcontents with privileges and charters: English rule was to mean new prosperity and freedom from war and its horrors. Many towns were in any case trying to take advantage of the change of lordship: Sir John Chandos, when he arrived at Cahors, had had to face a barrage of demands from the townspeople, to which he was only able to agree in part, before they would accept English rule. One request, which 'astonished' Chandos, was that they were to be liable for war service only in their own province, and never against the king of France. To overcome such diehard loyalists in a time of increasing nationalism, Edward and his council determined to make Aquitaine an independent entity, with its own ruler, under no more than nominal control from England. Furthermore, Aquitaine, which had been a heavy drain on the English exchequer, was to be financially independent: throughout the time of the prince's administration, no exchequer funds were sent out to Bordeaux, whereas the cost of maintaining the officials and troops there had varied from £1,500 to £3,750 per annum in the years since 1356.[7]

The charter by which the principality was granted by Edward to the prince still survives (Plate 4). It was written by John Freton and illuminated by the prince's clerk John Carleton in a style similar to East Anglian manuscripts of the period. The terms of the charter are very wide, particularly when compared with the conditions laid down for the prince's lieutenancy in 1355. After reciting how the king is unable to be personally involved in the affairs of all his lands, and how his eldest son should help him, the grant is made 'by prerogative of royal power', and on the understanding that the prince is to be 'true prince' and to enjoy the name, honour and title of prince of Aquitaine for the rest of his life. Three clauses then define the principality's boundaries, the nature of the prince's lordship (only direct lordship, *superioritas* and *ressort* being reserved to the king) and the prince's powers: all these are framed in the most comprehensive terms. Four supporting documents were also issued: two were to the men of Aquitaine, requiring them to obey the prince, and absolving them from all homages and fees due to the king if these were rendered to the prince. Letters patent were also issued, defining the position regarding the three rights due to the king; and the prince acknowledged the grant, promising to pay as *apport et cens annuel* the sum of one ounce of gold. In fact the only restriction on the prince's power was exactly that on Edward's power in Aquitaine before the French king had renounced his sovereign rights under the treaty of Brétigny. Edward's transfer of powers, even with this exception, reads as though the renunciations had already been made: but they had not, and this was to prove the fatal flaw in the arrangements.[8]

Preparations for the prince's voyage to Gascony began immediately after the act of homage. On 22 July, a small force of Cheshire archers were summoned for 8 September, and £1,000 was borrowed from the earl of Arundel to meet the immediate costs of the expedition. The prince received considerable sums out of the ransom money of king John, partly in payment of the costs of the 1359–60 campaign and partly towards equipping himself for Gascony: out of an instalment paid on 28 July, the prince was given a 'prest' or advance on wages of war of 5,000 marks, and no less than £15,004 19s. 4d. 'for his going towards the parts of Gascony'. Aquitaine's financial independence was being bought at a high price. The prince also made arrangements on 1 September for Lyoun the goldsmith to go with him to Bordeaux, where he was to be provided with a house and living expenses, and was to 'serve the prince and princess before all others in all matters concerning his craft for reasonable payment'. Two embroiderers were also engaged on similar terms. Arrangements were also made for a personal sign to be used by the prince on letters sent from Gascony to England which required special attention, so that his staff in England could identify them during his absence. This consisted of the prince's two mottoes, *Homout*, the German for 'high courage', and the more familiar *ich dene*. The earliest example of such a letter dates from August 1362, within a month of the prince's formal homage for Aquitaine. A 'secret seal' of the prince's feathers, probably used in conjunction with this, was made by John Hiltoft of London about this time.[9]

The prince appears to have hoped to be able to leave for Gascony during the autumn of 1362: ships had been summoned from the coast of France as early as 4 June. On 25 August, he left London for Cornwall, for Restormel and Liskeard, and then spent six weeks at Plympton, apparently either waiting for transport or fair weather for a crossing, or making the necessary arrangements. John Harewell, later constable of Bordeaux, and John Stretelee, who had been constable in 1356, were both with him. The rest of the winter was spent at Restormel, except for a brief journey to Windsor, to see the king, at the end of January; he was back at Restormel by 18 February. Whatever the purpose of his visit to Plymouth the previous autumn, ships had to be summoned by royal writ on 9 February for his crossing; either there had not been enough transport the previous autumn, or arrangements were not completed, as is implied by a summons for 200 archers from Chester on 19 February and a substantial order for arrows and bows on 23 February. But the fleet was slow to gather: at the end of April he paid another visit to Windsor, and it was only at the end of May that preparations were complete. On 9 June, the prince and princess, accompanied by the earl of Warwick and a very considerable retinue, set sail from Plymouth; the prince's party went in the *Saint Mary Cog* of Ipswich, and they landed at Lormont, now a suburb of Bordeaux, on 29 June.[10]

Although Chandos had taken the homages of the leading Gascon towns in 1361-2, the grant of Aquitaine to the prince meant that, as its new lord, the ceremony had to be repeated, and this was to occupy the first six months after his arrival. On 9 July, in a ceremony in the cathedral of Saint-André at Bordeaux similar to that held after his landing in Gascony in 1355, the assembled nobles and citizens heard Guillaume Seris, the constable of Bordeaux, address them in the prince's name. Seris first explained how the prince had been sent as the king's lieutenant to Aquitaine, to receive homage in his father's name; and when the assembly had agreed to do homage in this capacity, he read two grants by which the prince was to hold Aquitaine, 'set out in the vernacular . . . and sealed with the great seal in green wax . . . and in white wax', and then asked that homage should also be done to the prince in person, as lord of Aquitaine, reserving only the sovereignty and *ressort* of the king of England. When this was agreed by the assembly, the actual performance of homage began, each vassal in turn doing homage to the prince as lieutenant; as soon as this was done, Warwick and Chandos, representing the king, cancelled the homage on condition that it was made instead to the prince as lord of Aquitaine in his own right, and the vassal formally assented to this. The first lord to do homage was Arnaud-Amanieu, lord of Albret, and other companions-in-arms of the prince on his 1355-6 campaign followed, including Hélie de Pommiers and Gérard de Tartas. Fifty-eight knights and squires did homage at this first ceremony. On 15 July, five knights did homage in the archbishop's palace, which the prince seems to have used once again as his residence, and there was another public ceremony in the cathedral, at which representatives of towns along the Dordogne and Garonne did homage, as well as deputations from Bayonne, Dax and Saint-Sever in the south-west. The ceremonies at Bordeaux continued on 19, 20, 22, 27 and 30 July, local lords and representatives of places as far afield as Bigorre in the Pyrenees appearing to do homage.[11]

At the beginning of August, the prince set out on his progress through his new domain. On 4 August, the prince was at Bergerac; here the bishop of Sarlat, Austence de Saint-Colombe, did homage, among others. From 10–15 August he was at Périgueux, where a deputation from Quercy and Rouergue, the eastern part of Aquitaine, came to meet him. Three days later, he was at Angoulême, the castle of which was to be one of his favourite residences; on 23 August, he reached Cognac, which later became his headquarters, and continued into Saintonge, arriving at Saintes on 24 August and Saint-Jean-d'Angély on 26 August. He then went to La Rochelle, which had been the most rebellious of all the towns in the area: only sixteen homages are recorded here. In September and October he was at Poitiers, taking the homages of the Poitevin nobles, led by Guillaume Larchevesque, lord of Parthenay; he and many of the other barons of the area were to remain staunchly pro-English.[12]

At the end of November, the prince and his entourage left for Agen, where they spent Christmas. On 26 December, Florimond de Lesparre did homage; important as he was, a still more powerful personage was awaited, Gaston Phoebus of Foix, whom the prince had met in 1355. Foix was renowned as an independent and difficult vassal, to be wooed rather than commanded. On 12 January, in a special ceremony at Agen in the presence of representatives of the king of France, the count did homage, but when Chandos enquired for what lands he was doing homage, Gaston Phoebus replied that it was only for the viscounties of Marsan and Gavaudun, as he had never done homage to anyone for his other land of Béarn itself, but he promised to do homage for Béarn as well if the prince could make good his claim. By mid February, the prince was back at Poitiers, and the few remaining homages were taken there and at Angoulême; although he announced his intention of visiting the Rouergue in March, the visit was cancelled. When the list was closed on 4 April, 1,047 homages had been taken in all. In addition, many charters of privileges had been confirmed or granted to ensure the loyalty of his new subjects: at Cognac in August 1363 the town's old privileges were reiterated, and although the citizens were liable for the repair of its fortifications, the prince agreed to pay for these works. Similar acts were issued to various abbeys round Poitiers while the prince was there; and many more such grants must have been made as what was in effect a new administration took over. In taking the homages and establishing the new regime, the only moments of difficulty had been with Gaston Phoebus and with the higher clergy, who protested that they had never had to swear allegiance before. This led to an acrimonious exchange with the Pope, who was anxious that this should not be a precedent and that the oaths should be withdrawn. The prince had acted in a way which would have been acceptable in England, but was not in accordance with local customs, a complaint which was to recur more and more often.[13]

The prince's administration in Gascony was headed by Sir John Chandos, as constable of Aquitaine, Thomas Felton, the seneschal, and John Harewell, chancellor and constable of Bordeaux, the chief financial officer. Felton had been on the Crécy campaign, and was one of the leading figures on the Poitiers campaign, and was steward of the prince's household for a time after the prince's arrival at Bordeaux. Harewell was a skilled administrator, who later became bishop of Bath and Wells. They were assisted by a council, which included other members of the prince's household, such as Sir Nigel Loring, but was probably informal in its composition. The lords and people of Gascony were represented by the estates, a rather amorphous body, similar to the English parliament in its powers of taxation, but less clearly developed. The various royal lieutenants in the provinces of Aquitaine, analogous to the sheriffs in England, had to ensure that law and order was maintained, relying on the cooperation of the local communities. The difficulty was that the English administration, until recently confined to the area around Bordeaux, had to take on vast new tracts of land, at best friendly towards the English but lacking in any real means of administration, at worst almost openly rebellious. With this imperfect machinery, the prince had not only to govern Aquitaine, but also to tax it: and if the restoration of order was difficult, the raising of taxes in areas where neither the French nor the English had been able to do so for some time was very much more of a problem. The prince had to raise a *fouage*, or hearth tax, in 1364, and this was set at the very high rate of 25 sous, or 1 guyennois d'or, per hearth. It was the most burdensome, and most profitable to the prince, of the various taxes to which he was entitled, but there were immediately murmurs of resistance. Jean d'Armagnac refused to allow it to be levied in the county of Rodez in the Rouergue, claiming ancient privilege; the town of Agen paid, but asked for a charter declaring that it would not be a precedent; but the other territories paid without resistance, indicating that there was considerable goodwill towards the English at this stage.[14]

In the absence of all but a handful of official records and chronicles, we know relatively little about the early years of the prince's administration in Gascony. Equally, there is little information about the prince himself. He travelled round his domains to some extent, much as he had done on his estates in England: after the tour of homage, he was at Limoges in May 1364, Périgueux in July and La Réole in November. The most important event of the year happened elsewhere. King John had returned to captivity in England in January when the ransom due under the treaty of Brétigny had fallen behind and the duc d'Anjou, hostage in his place, had fled. On 8 April John died, and the dauphin became Charles V. John had always been easy-going, inherently friendly towards the English, and lacking in any real determination to treat them as an enemy. Charles, harder and more realistic, saw that there could never be peace between the two kingdoms unless one dominated the other; and he was not prepared to be a puppet of England. His methods were not those of his father, who shared the same ideals as Edward and the prince; he preferred diplomacy and subtlety, which he had learned in his long struggle with the arch-intriguer, Charles of Navarre. Within a few months of the prince's tour of homage, there were signs that Charles's agents were at work. One of the prince's spies informed him of an intrigue between the king of Navarre, Gaston Phoebus, comte de Foix and Charles V, having overheard a conversation between the first two held on 21 June, five months after the count had done homage to the prince. Gaston Phoebus said that Charles V had offered him the lieutenancy of Languedoc, and that he was thinking of making over the lands he held from the prince to his son. He had heard from Charles V's secretary that his master was intending to make war on the English, and would do so as soon as he had recovered the remaining hostages from England. Meanwhile, Charles was trying to secure the allegiance of Arnaud-Amanieu d'Albret, and to make an alliance with the king of Castile. Charles was anxious that Gaston Phoebus should not release Jean d'Armagnac, who was his prisoner after being defeated in a private battle, because if he did so,

Armagnac would ally himself to the prince, 'and they would be two schemers together'. The political and military scene was indeed changing rapidly: the defeat of an Anglo-Navarrese army at Cocherel in May 1364, at which the captal de Buch was captured, led to a peace treaty between Charles of Navarre and Charles V early the following year. The French had at last found a military leader in Bertrand du Guesclin, who, like the prince, became a legend in his own lifetime; but behind the exaggerated exploits attributed to him by his biographer lay many successful campaigns against the so-called 'free companies' who had plagued France for the previous decade. The French were making a remarkable recovery.[15]

The prince had relatively little room for diplomatic manoeuvre; it was in his interest to keep to the terms of the treaty of Brétigny, and to see that it was duly carried out. He did, however, win the allegiance of Jean d'Armagnac by lending him the money to pay his ransom, despite Armagnac's resistance over the *fouage* at Rodez. As to the execution of the treaty itself, the transfer of lands remained in abeyance, and the prince's attitude was therefore one of maintaining the *status quo* until such time as the remaining provisions of the treaty could be carried out. A further difficulty was the consistent underestimation of French resilience by the English, which had led Edward and his advisers to attempt to renegotiate the terms of the main treaty late in 1362, by an agreement made with the principal hostages still held in England. This had been rejected on the initiative of Charles V, then still dauphin: but it was indicative of English thinking.[16]

Negotiations continued over the various outstanding points of the original treaty and over the continuing English support for the king of Navarre during the autumn of 1364. Boucicaut was sent to see the prince during November 1364, partly in his role as commissioner for the transfer of lands under the treaty, but also on other matters. To French complaints about English retention of some areas which should have been transferred, the answer was simple, that if the French completed their side of the treaty, these lands would be handed over. As to other complaints, that revenues due to the French up to the date of the treaty had not been handed over, the prince answered that this was his father's business. Another (now illegible) request, from a mission sent early in 1365, shows that the prince might use such an excuse to evade an awkward question, but was also prepared to admit that he worked closely with Edward and his council, because he says that he is sending Sir John Delves, one of his most trusted councillors and successor to Sir John Wingfield as 'governor of the prince's business', back to England to get advice. On the question of the king of Navarre, the answer is non-committal: 'we have well understood what lord Boucicaut has told us'. The negotiations brought no tangible results.[17]

Meanwhile the prince held court in magnificent style at Bordeaux, Angoulême and elsewhere. In early March 1365, his eldest son, christened Edward, was born at Angoulême, and to celebrate the churching of the princess, the prince held a great tournament on 27 April, on as large a scale as any previous celebration. An eyewitness claimed that there were 154 lords, 706 knights and 18,000 horses, the latter all stabled at the prince's expense. Twenty-four knights and twenty-four lords formed the princess's retinue, and the tourneying, jousting and 'other transitory amusements' lasted for ten days. The cost of candles alone for the occasion was over £400. Sir John Delves took the good news to the king, this being his first grandson in the male line, and was duly rewarded for his tidings. One of the prince's squires was also sent to Charles V, who gave him two silver-gilt enamelled goblets as his reward for bringing the news. Such festivals gave the prince's court a great reputation for extravagance, and there were also stories about the princess's love of luxury. Jean de Beaumanoir, marshal of Brittany, was at Poitiers in November 1363 when a truce between Charles of Blois and Jean de Montfort was signed. While he was there, a lady of the prince's court who was a relative of his wife commented on her unfashionable dress, 'for her hodes, taylles, and sleves be not furred ynowgh after the shape that rennith now'. Jean de Beaumanoir answered that he would be delighted to give her more furs, but he would not let her copy the current fashion at the prince's court, of slit coats and great fringes, because this had been invented by the mistresses of English freebooters. If the princess and her ladies wanted to adopt such fashions, they were welcome to do so: but it would not do their reputation any good.[18]

The prince's 'magnificence' was certainly in part deliberate, in an age which set great store by outward show, an age which would agree with Thomas Hardy: 'who seems most kingly, Is the King'. This policy was reflected in the new coinage issued by him for Gascony. The first coinage of 1363 was very similar to that of his father as lord of Aquitaine, though a new motto was chosen: *Deus judex justus fortis et paciens* ('God is a righteous judge, strong and patient'). The following year, substantial changes were made. A new large gold coin, called the *pavillon* and weighing 85 grains, was struck, showing the prince standing under a Gothic porch, wearing a heraldic prince's crown of roses, and carrying a sword in his right hand, to which he is pointing with his left hand: four ostrich feathers complete the design. All this is based on the French royal coinage, where the largest gold coin showed the king in a similar stance; for the king's sceptre a sword has been substituted, the decoration is more elaborate, and the coin itself larger. The reverse bore a cross with fleur-de-lis and leopards in the angles, and the motto *Dominus aiuto et protectio mei et in ipso speravit cor meum* ('The Lord is my strength and my shield and my heart hath trusted him'). Three years later, a smaller gold coin, the *hardi*, was also introduced. These were pieces for show, which would have a limited circulation among merchants and nobles; but they were none the less a highly effective means of propaganda, proclaiming the prince's power and wealth.[19]

Coinage was also a highly profitable source of revenue, and manipulations of its value in relation to the actual value of metal used was a favourite device of hard-pressed medieval rulers. The prince never resorted to this device: all his coins were of a high intrinsic value, and the *pavillon* actually had to be reduced in weight because its metal value was too high. Furthermore, the prince did not exercise his rights of coinage in purely arbitrary fashion: in 1365, representatives of the towns of Gascony were summoned to Périgueux in September 1365 for a council as to 'what type of money and what value people wanted': it was perhaps as a result of their deliberations that the *hardi* was introduced, no changes being made in the silver coinage. At the same time, a new *fouage* was levied at half the rate exacted in the previous year, apparently without any great opposition. As the surviving records of the tax show only the totals, we have no way of telling whether much of the sum calculated as due remained as an unpaid item; and in 1370 even the overall accounts for the Agenais for 1364–5 had not been made up. What we have is a record of the taxpayers' debt as a result of the *fouage*. The total of £120,808 Bordelais which the *fouage* is shown as yielding is purely a book entry: what actually reached the exchequer we do not know. If English parallels are anything to go by, the real revenue may have been very small indeed: in 1339 a subsidy estimated by parliament, perhaps optimistically, to yield £100,000, actually produced £15,000.[20]

The prince was now beginning to be drawn into a new area of political problems. Castile had long been a thorn in the side of the English in their invasions of France, providing naval aid to the French; and the battle off Winchelsea in 1350 had been fought against a purely Castilian fleet. In 1362, just before the prince had been officially granted Aquitaine, a change of policy on the part of Pedro, king of Castile, had culminated in the signature of an Anglo-Castilian alliance at a formal ceremony in St Paul's cathedral on 22 June. On the English side, John Stretelee, the prince's new chancellor of Aquitaine, had been deeply involved in the negotiations, and the prince gave the two Spanish representatives, Álvaro Sánchez de Cuellar and Diego Sánchez de Terrazas, silver-gilt cups and ewers to mark the occasion, as well as a piece of scarlet cloth. The alliance was intended by Pedro to act as a counterweight to French support for his enemy Pere III of Aragón and for his rival for the Castilian throne, Enrique of Trastamare. In return for English support, which would ensure that the French did not intervene in Castile, he was prepared to break the long-standing alliance with France on the grounds that it had become a dead letter. When the treaties were completed, the prince had copies made of them for his records. The alliance was ratified by Edward in February 1363, but Pedro, unwilling to defy the French openly until he had good reason to do so, waited another year and a half before issuing his ratification.[21]

Although the prince evidently played some part in bringing about the alliance, and it did contain a clause specifying that, despite the treaty of Brétigny, English troops would be used against French invaders within Castile itself, the arrangement was not seen by the English as a serious commitment to involve themselves in affairs in Spain. The war between Castile and Aragón was a local affair, without serious implications for international politics, and there was no likelihood of either side intervening in Aquitaine, even though there was a short common frontier between Castile and Aquitaine in the western Pyrenees. Indeed, there is no evidence of any diplomatic contact between the prince and Castile for nearly three years after he arrived in Aquitaine: in June 1365 he was still far more concerned about the behaviour of the comte de Foix, who was creating difficulties over coming to see the prince to do homage for Béarn, which the English still claimed. The prince, alerted by his agent to Foix's double-dealings, was anxious to secure the

homage, but Foix claimed to have hurt his leg; he told Thomas
Florac, the prince's messenger, that it was 'almost healed' on
3 August, though the prince did not receive the news very graciously, writing on 8 August that he had heard from reliable sources
that Foix was quite fit to travel. Perhaps he was irritated by the
rather familiar tone of Foix's letter, asking that Sir Thomas Felton
or Sir James Audley should come to meet him. Foix also asked that
Chandos's hounds, 'and all the others you can get', should be at
Angoulême or Périgueux, where they were to meet, so that 'I can
show you something of my skill'. Foix was famous as a huntsman,
and his book on hunting was later translated into English by the
prince's nephew, Edward of York, under the title *The Master of
Game*. Nothing came of the projected meeting, and in December
Edward was vainly writing from Westminster to enlist Charles V's
help in obtaining the homage. In June 1366 it still appears not to
have been performed.[22]

Behind these diplomatic sparrings, there is also an occasional
note of more serious matters afoot; in June 1365, reinforcements of
troops were being prepared, and men-at-arms, archers and Welsh
spearmen passed through the ports of Devon and Cornwall during
the summer. These may have been primarily intended to strengthen
the duchy's defences against the 'free companies', the bands of
mercenaries who, deprived of employment, were holding France to
ransom. Aquitaine seems to have remained relatively free of their
ravages, central and southern France being their favourite territory,
where there was no danger of military opposition: indeed, they had
inflicted a serious defeat on a French army sent to attack them at
Brignais in 1362. Many schemes had been devised to rid France of
these marauders; in 1362, there had been a plan to send them to help
the Aragonese king, which had come to nothing because of lack of
funds. This plan was now revived: under the leadership of Bertrand
du Guesclin, a young French commander who had made his name
fighting against these very men, the companies were to go on
crusade against the Moors in southern Spain. This was a trans-
parent fiction: it was tacitly accepted that the real objective was
Castile, and that Pere III and Enrique were the prime movers in the
scheme. The arrangements were completed, in relative secrecy, by
September 1365; in late November, the companies gathered at
Montpellier. The other leaders were Arnoul d'Audrehem, marshal
of France at Poitiers, and Sir Hugh Calveley, a Cheshire knight who
had fought as a member of the companies in Brittany.[23]

The companies crossed into Aragón in the last days of 1365. Pedro had invoked the treaty with England as soon as he heard of their approach, and an embassy went to London in the autumn of 1365. All that was actually done as a result was the issue of a proclamation relating to the clause in the treaty which forbade English subjects to attack Castile; a strongly worded proclamation was issued by the king to Sir John Chandos, and three of the mercenary captains who were actually *en route* for Spain (Calveley, Dagworth and Elmham), threatening that severe reprisals would be taken against anyone who went, or against their families and relations. The expedition was already under way by the time the letters were issued, and the prince himself appears to have done nothing to hinder the departing companies. His only diplomatic activity seems to have been contacts with Charles of Navarre, whose kingdom lay to the north of Castile and Aragón, but these may well have been over French rather than Spanish affairs. The companies marched into Castile early in March: by the end of the month Enrique had made good his claim to the Castilian throne, and had been crowned at Burgos, while Pedro was retreating southwards, his cause rapidly being deserted by the nobles of Castile. By early June he was in exile in Portugal. The companies had performed their tasks only too effectively.[24]

The very swiftness and completeness of the triumph of Enrique and du Guesclin made a reaction inevitable. If the campaign had become a drawn-out war of attrition, little attention would have been paid to it elsewhere. Castile would have been neutralized as an international power, and the intrigues of Spanish politics would have continued much as before. The spectre of an aggressively pro-French monarch in Castile, however, was exactly the spur needed to make the Anglo-Castilian alliance effective. Pedro himself was quick to realize this; and after his first abortive appeal to Portugal for help, he returned to Galicia, the northern part of his kingdom, which was still holding out against Enrique. From here, at the end of July, he left for Bayonne, to put his case in person to the prince in Aquitaine. Within a few days of his arrival, the prince came from Bordeaux to Capbreton, on the north bank of the Adour, to meet him. He had already seen Charles of Navarre at Bordeaux a few days previously, and after the initial meeting with Pedro, he summoned the lords of Gascony to a conference at Bayonne, at which Charles and John of Gaunt, on his way from England with a body of troops, were also to be present.[25]

The English decision to support Pedro was made before the interview between king and prince at Capbreton. Froissart reports that Chandos and other lords strongly opposed the expedition, but there is no other evidence for this; according to Sir John Chandos's herald, the only advice offered was that a treaty with Navarre was essential, since Charles controlled the passes over the Pyrenees into Spain. The practical aspects of the venture seem to have predominated in the August and September negotiations: how it was to be financed, where the troops were to be raised and so on, rather than the broader questions of diplomacy. Any consultations between the prince and Edward and his advisers in England seems to have taken place in April or May, after Enrique had been crowned but before Pedro had come to Gascony. As early as 6 June, ships were being arrested for the transport of troops to Gascony, and on 30 July, just as the Bayonne meeting was taking place, orders were issued for archers to be arrayed for Gascony. The prince was therefore acting on clear instructions from England by the time his part of the negotiations began, and the attempt to restore Pedro was based not on the high-flown principles which Froissart credits to the prince, but on practical politics. A strong pro-French king in Castile was too much of a danger to both England and Aquitaine to be tolerated. But this basic diplomatic need for action was clearly reinforced by the prince's eagerness for a campaign, and for the possible profits that might ensue from it.[26]

Details of the campaign were worked out at Bayonne in September, as planned. In addition to the prince, Pedro and Charles of Navarre, Jean d'Armagnac and the Gascon lords were present, and John of Gaunt arrived from England. The discussions lasted for twelve days, Pedro doing his best to influence their course in his favour by lavish distributions of gifts to all and sundry. The agreements that resulted were long and complex, 'chiefly remarkable, perhaps, for the exceptional burdens they laid upon the Castilian king and for the ill-concealed distrust of him which can be detected behind the numerous precautionary clauses'. Charles of Navarre had much to do with these covering clauses, and his position as party to the agreement greatly complicated the issue. His consent was vital to the prince's plans, and the price was appropriately high: large territorial concessions from Castile and a contribution for damages of 200,000 florins, of which 10 per cent was to be paid in advance by the prince on Pedro's behalf. An advance on war wages of 36,000 florins was also to be paid by the prince. The prince's price was equally high, but unlike that demanded by Charles, it was based on the likely actual costs of the campaign: 250,000 florins for his own men and 300,000 for those of the Gascon lords. This was a preliminary payment, which the prince undertook to make against a notarial obligation by Pedro, by which Pedro's three daughters were to be hostages for the payment. The prince was to meet all costs for the army until January 1367, by which time it ought to be in Castile itself. The final total of the army costs paid by the prince was no less than 1,659,000 florins, or £276,500. It was scarcely surprising that one of the items provided by Edward was 10,000 lb of gold, sent from England in the summer of 1366. The prince also extracted his share of territorial concessions, the chief being the county of Vizcaya on the northern coast. With the territory ceded to Navarre, this meant that the Castilian coast would largely be in foreign hands, and the naval threat to England would be finally removed.[27]

These arrangements were recorded in a series of documents sealed at Libourne on 23 September. The prince and Charles of Navarre have been criticized for the excessive price that they extracted from Pedro; in fact, that the costs of the war should be borne by Pedro was in accordance with the treaty of 1362. Thereafter, the prince looked for a reward for his labours, and some diplomatic advantage. These two objectives were irreconcilable. A strong pro-English government in Castile was the diplomatic aim; but any substantial reward could only be paid in lands, in view of the likely costs of the campaign, and such a grant would weaken Pedro's position among his own people. As he was already cordially detested by his own nobles, to ask for Vizcaya was to invite difficulties. Yet, without some substantial return, the campaign was hardly worth undertaking: the only other possible source was ransoms, and these were indeed specifically reserved to the prince and his followers by the agreement signed at Libourne; but this was an uncertain source of revenue. A further problem lay in the respective characters of the prince, Pedro and Charles. Charles, self-seeking, treacherous and always with an eye to the main chance, was only interested in the immediate benefit to himself and to Navarre; his duplicity and untrustworthiness were all too evident from his deeds in France. The one anxiety which drove him to adhere to the alliance was the presence of a pro-French régime in Castile; despite the fact that he had signed a peace treaty with Charles V in June, his interests and those of France remained irreconcilable. The prince, more at home in warfare than diplomacy, and setting great store by outward forms, was temperamentally very different from Pedro, whose ruling passion was for efficient administration and impartial justice as dispensed by a powerful monarchy, though he had no hesitation in using ruthless means to achieve his ends. His reputation has suffered because the sources for his history and character are all biased against him, ranging from the self-justification of López de Ayala, who went over to Enrique, to a number of stories which are pure propaganda put out by Enrique's followers. But it is clear that he and the prince had relatively little in common, and on many points actively disagreed. Pedro may well have known that he was signing impossible agreements; he was not another king John the Good, to stand on the exact observance of his word once given, but the distrust shown in the provisions of the treaties implies a fundamental failure of understanding between the three leaders of the proposed campaign.[28]

The Spanish Campaign

◄═══►

8

At the end of the meeting at Libourne, the prince's plan seems to have been to set out in the late autumn, as soon as John of Gaunt had returned from England with the additional troops he had been sent to fetch. The main army was to be levied in Gascony: the prince's own retinue would provide the core, but most of the troops would be brought either by Gascon lords or by the free companies. Pedro himself could contribute nothing until they reached Castile, while Charles of Navarre had promised 1,000 horsemen and 1,000 foot. The most likely source of recruits, however, was the very army which had just driven out Pedro. During the summer of 1366, Enrique had dismissed many of the mercenaries, because he could not afford to pay them; they attempted to return via Aragón, were repulsed, and crossed the Pyrenees through Navarre, causing considerable damage as they went. Sir Hugh Calveley, who had ignored Edward's warnings not to serve against Pedro, decided that he could not serve against the prince, and left Enrique's service. Enrique is said to have respected his wish to depart, and to have refrained from hindering him. Calveley did not, however, return to Aquitaine, and his movements during the winter of 1366–7 are uncertain. He may perhaps have joined the forces loyal to Pedro who continued to hold out under Fernando de Castro in Galicia.[1]

Enrique was in no position to fight a new campaign: although he had raised subsidies from the cortes of Castile, these had largely been spent on paying for the previous campaign, and his own military resources were very limited. Du Guesclin was still with him, with a small retinue, but there was little likelihood of aid from either Portugal or Aragón, who had supported his invasion. The probable appearance of a strong force under the prince was enough to make both Dom Pedro of Portugal and Pere III of Aragón adopt a much more cautious attitude towards Enrique, for fear of reprisals if Pedro was restored. They were principally anxious to avoid military involvement once the prince's army had reached Spain: Pere III knew all too well how devastating an incursion by the companies could be, having suffered at their hands when he himself encouraged their entry into Spain; and he also knew that Pedro would be eager to exact revenge. But he was prepared to use every diplomatic weapon available to prevent the invasion, and it was at the instigation of a leading member of his court, the archbishop of Saragossa, that negotiations between Enrique and Charles of Navarre took place early in January. The result was an agreement that Charles would break the treaty made at Libourne, and would actively oppose the passage of the prince's army across the passes into Spain. Charles went so far as to surrender two castles on the border of Castile as pledges of good faith.[2]

When this news reached the prince he was at Bordeaux, where his second son, Richard, had been born on 6 January. Richard was christened in the cathedral by the archbishop three days later. Two distinguished visitors then present in Bordeaux, the claimant to the kingdom of Majorca, Jaime IV, and Richard, king of Armenia, were his godfathers. The prince and Jaime were awaiting the arrival of John of Gaunt from England before going to join the main body of the army at Dax. The prince's reaction to the news from Navarre was swift: knowing that Calveley was still in Castile, on the Navarrese border, he instructed him to invade Charles's kingdom. Although it was now unlikely that an invasion could be mounted before the spring, when the passes leading directly into Castile in the western Pyrenees would be clear, the prince none the less went south to Dax immediately after Richard's christening, on about 13 January. Here he learnt that Calveley's invasion had had the desired effect. Calveley had cut the main roads between the capital of Navarre and Castile, and this had provided an opportunity for those of Charles's councillors who favoured the English alliance to reassert their influence. At the end of the month, Charles met the prince and Pedro at Peyrehorade, and the treaties of Libourne were confirmed. The advantage was now entirely on the English side.

Enrique, confident that his diplomatic manoeuvre had succeeded, had actually given du Guesclin permission to leave Castile, and the latter was trying to enforce various unfulfilled promises made by Pere III early in 1366 by a campaign in Aragón. Pere III was confident that no invasion would take place, until he heard in early February of Charles's journey to Gascony. Within a fortnight the English army was on the move, against an almost completely unprepared enemy.[3]

The army which assembled at Dax was a mixed collection. John of Gaunt had some 800 archers with him, besides his own retinue. The prince's own military resources are pure conjecture. Some English archers may have been serving in Gascony since the previous summer, and 1,600 archers had been summoned in July in England, though these may have been part of John of Gaunt's force. The number of Gascon lords is uncertain: Albret, Armagnac and the captal de Buch were the chief figures, and the names of a number of others are recorded, without any indication of the size of their following. There were also the men from the companies raised by Chandos ('as many as fourteen squadrons'), and the mercenaries who had returned from Spain, including Eustace d'Abrechicourt. In all, there may have been as many as 8,000 men, though in view of the difficult terrain and shortage of supplies in the Pyrenees in winter, the number could well have been less. Once in Castile, there were Fernando de Castro's men in Galicia – a substantial body of troops, who would join the army – and reports coming from Spain suggested that Enrique was not proving a very popular ruler. An Aragonese, writing from the capital of Foix in October, thought that even Enrique's own knights would be unreliable in the event of war, and although the prince had had little direct contact with anyone from Enrique's camp or from Aragón, such rumours must have been common knowledge north of the Pyrenees, and must have formed part of his calculations. If so, the force he took into Spain was to be a catalyst, which would spark off a revolt against Enrique, rather than an army of conquest: and there is good reason to put the total as low as 6,000 men, given such a strategy.[4]

As usual, the army divided into three bodies for the march. The vanguard left Saint-Jean-Pied-du-Port, at the foot of the pass leading to Roncesvalles in Navarre, on 14 February. This was the easiest route into Spain, rising to nearly 4,000 feet at the col de Bentarté and well known to those in the army who had made the pilgrimage to

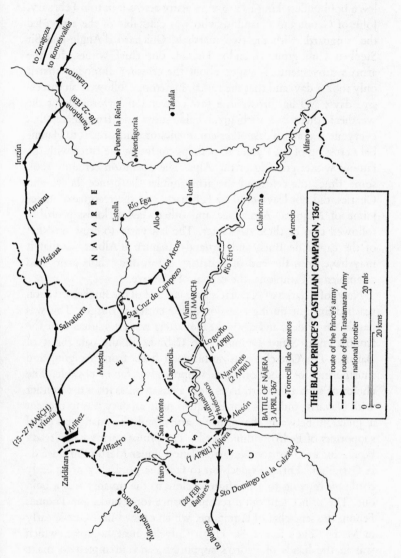

Map 8. The Spanish campaign

Compostela. Even in the depths of winter, the pass is rarely completely blocked by snow for any length of time, but it was none the
less a bold undertaking to move an army across it in mid February.
John of Gaunt and Chandos, who was constable of the army, led
the vanguard, with the two marshals, Guichard d'Angle and Sir
Stephen Cosington. Chandos Herald, our chief witness for the
army's movements, is vague about the crossing, implying that it
only took a day, and that the remaining troops followed on succes-
sive days; and he throws in a few conventional words about the
weather: 'there was such great cold, snow and frost there, that
everyone was afraid'. Another commentator compared it to Hanni-
bal's crossing of the Pyrenees, perhaps confusing the latter with the
famous winter crossing of the Alps. The operation certainly took
some time: the centre of the army, under the prince, Pedro and
Charles, did not leave until 20 February, and the rearguard, under
Jaime of Majorca, Armagnac and other Gascon lords, probably
followed two or three days later. The last party to cross was that
of the captal de Buch and Arnaud-Amanieu d'Albret, so that it
may have been the end of February before the whole army had
assembled at Pamplona, the capital of Navarre.[5]

News of Charles of Navarre's *volte face* and of the English invasion
reached Enrique during a session of the cortes at Burgos. This was
hastily suspended, and a war headquarters was established near the
frontier, near Santo Domingo de Calzada, in the oak forest of
Bañares. Du Guesclin was summoned back from Aragón, and
murmurings of rebellion were suppressed as far as possible. The
choice of such a forward base, only a dozen miles from the frontier
with Navarre, indicates that Enrique's main anxiety was to prevent
a junction between the prince's army and the many potential
supporters of Pedro within Castile. The prince's army had already
been reinforced by 300 Navarrese lances under Martín Enriquez de
la Carra, and Enrique's decision to face the possibility of an early
battle by moving to a position so close to the invader was a bold
one. The prince sent out a reconnaissance force under Sir Thomas
Felton, the seneschal of Aquitaine, which crossed into Castile early
in March. They joined Sir Hugh Calveley near Logroño, which
was in the hands of Pedro's supporters, and attempted to make
contact with the enemy.[6]

The prince's next move is difficult to follow. Instead of marching
directly on Castile by the main road via Logroño – the route which
Felton had taken – he moved northwards and crossed the frontier

near Salvatierra. Two factors may have decided this manoeuvre. The first was Charles of Navarre's latest exploit. Anxious to avoid committing himself further to the prince's cause, in case the fortunes of war went against him, Charles stage-managed his own capture by Olivier de Mauny, a partisan of du Guesclin, on 11 March. Martín Enriquez de la Carra was appointed regent of Navarre, and in view of the uncertain situation, the prince decided to leave Navarre as soon as possible. If Navarre was now uncertain territory, the prince was anxious to maintain communications with Aquitaine, which could only be done by sea, and he therefore kept towards the coast. He may by this point have learnt from Felton where the enemy were, and in this case his move would have enabled him to outflank them and march unopposed on Burgos. A further possibility is that the Navarrese guides were playing a double game, and deliberately led the prince into difficult territory; but this is improbable, as Enriquez de la Carra was with the army, and is consistently portrayed as pro-English.[7]

The prince's route took him through the sparsely populated mountainous terrain of Álava, by the pass of Arruazu, 'a narrow little place, where the army suffered much hardship . . . but he found little in the way of provisions for his army anywhere until he reached Salvatierra'. Salvatierra opened its gates, after a brief resistance in which Sir Richard Burley was wounded. Here the army rested for six days, while news came in of a skirmish between Felton's troops and Enrique's army, which at last gave definite news of the enemy's whereabouts. Both armies now converged on Vitoria, capital of Álava. It was clear that the prince's attempt to surprise and outflank the enemy had failed. Furthermore, Enrique, acting on the advice of du Guesclin, who had now joined him, was evidently trying to fight a guerrilla war of the type which had brought the Rheims campaign of 1359–60 to a stalemate: Charles V had also written to him to urge these tactics. Enrique ensconced himself in the castle of Zaldiarán, and sent companies of light horsemen to attack the prince's foragers. Felton and his men, who had come up to Vitoria in front of the Castilian army, reported Enrique's arrival to the prince; hopeful of a battle, the latter drew up his army outside the town, and made a number of knights, among them King Pedro, who had never been knighted, and his own stepson, Thomas Holland, and Nicholas Bond, who had served him for fourteen years as a squire of his household. But Enrique was not to be drawn; at evening, the army dispersed, and Felton's company took up quarters at Ariñez, four miles south of Vitoria. That night the expected attack materialized, but in a very different form. Two companies of horsemen, under Enrique's brother Don Tello and the marshal d'Audrehem, were sent out to make a night raid on the English encampments. Don Tello and his group came across Sir Hugh Calveley and his men, who were about to join the prince; many of Calveley's soldiers were killed in their beds, and his baggage train badly damaged. Don Tello then rode on to find himself in among the vanguard, but the noise of the attack on Calveley had roused John of Gaunt, who rallied his forces, and when the raiders reached them they were already gathering in battle order, and the centre of the army, under the prince and Chandos, was coming to their aid. The raiders were quickly driven off, but their companions under Audrehem had meanwhile attacked Sir Thomas Felton and his company at Ariñez. Considerably outnumbered, the 400 or so men-at-arms and archers established themselves on a hillock, where the horsemen were unable to charge them; but they were eventually overwhelmed, after a fierce resistance, and Sir William Felton was killed. The others were taken prisoner, including Sir Thomas Felton and Sir Richard Hastings.[8]

The prince's army, unsettled by this attack, was further demoralized by the onset of bad, wet and windy weather. To force the passes southwards in the face of such guerrilla tactics was clearly impossible, and the terrain was unfriendly. The prince therefore decided to retreat, and attempt the route through Logroño which he had initially rejected. In this he was probably encouraged by Calveley's and Felton's reports, which indicated that the countryside there was likely to provide better forage. The route led back into Navarre through barren country, which at least provided no shelter for enemy ambushes; but food was very short, and there were few places to give refuge for the night: Walter of Peterborough describes how he spent one harsh wintry night sleeping in a small copse. At last the army reached the valley of the Ebro, entering Logroño on 1 April. Enrique had made a covering movement, crossing the Ebro at San Vicente and then taking up position at Nájera to prevent the prince from using the bridge over the Najerilla at that town.[9]

Here the prince replied to a formal challenge issued by Enrique a month earlier, in which the latter, after expressing surprise at the invasion, asked the prince to name his proposed route into Castile so that Enrique could meet him in battle. This was precisely what the prince had not wished to do at the time, but he now issued an answer calling on Enrique to give up the throne which he had usurped, in return for which the prince would act as mediator between him and Pedro. The letter, addressed to Enrique as count of Trastamare, had the desired effect of enraging the latter, who replied in an openly insulting manner to 'Edward prince of Wales, who call yourself eldest son of the king of England and prince of Aquitaine', saying that it seemed to all and sundry that he was much attached to vainglory. Enrique demanded that two or three knights from each side should choose a suitable battlefield, and offered safe conduct for up to fifty persons for this to be done. The prince, remembering Poitiers, regarded this as delaying tactics and answered only briefly.[10]

The following day the prince advanced to Navarrete, a small fortress between Logroño and Nájera where Felton had encamped the previous month. Enrique left Nájera to take up a position in the open fields, ready for battle. The plan of guerrilla warfare had evidently been abandoned, partly because Enrique's own temperament was not suited to such a game of cat and mouse, but preferred the traditional style of warfare, and partly because there were indications of disaffection in his army. Already 600 horsemen had gone over to Pedro in mid March; and further defections would have been fatal. On the night of 2 April both armies were prepared for a battle the following day, and councils of war were held. The prince and his advisers decided against a frontal attack on a prepared position held by the enemy, who had established themselves along the bank of a stream which fed the Najerilla, astride the main road to Nájera. Instead, starting in darkness, they took a hillside track leading behind a ridge which rises some 600 feet above the road to the north. Although Enrique sent out scouts to discover the English movements, they failed to make contact and the appearance of the English from the north-east took the Castilian army by surprise; a hasty movement had to be carried out to bring the Castilian line to face the approaching enemy. As the English moved into position, Sir John Chandos's great silk banner was ceremonially unfurled by the prince and handed to him, so that he fought as a banneret, leading his own company of men for the first time.[11]

The vanguard of Enrique's army was undoubtedly its strongest division, with du Guesclin, Audrehem and the French troops as its main component, as well as the *corps d'élite* of Castile, the knights of the Sash, whose banner was carried by Pedro Lopez de Ayala; it is to López de Ayala that we owe the most detailed account of the battle. They fought dismounted, implying that they expected to take up a defensive position, as the prince had done at Poitiers. The centre of the Spanish army was commanded by Enrique himself, placed behind du Guesclin's division, and there were two smaller wings to left and right consisting of light horse from Andalusia called *jinetes*, under Don Tello and the Aragonese count of Denia respectively. There is no mention of any substantial body of cross-bowmen or archers. Enrique's troops were fresh, but some were lightly armed and many were mere footsoldiers of uncertain value; there was also the perennial problem of possible defections if the tide of battle seemed to be going against him. The most experienced commanders were du Guesclin and Audrehem, and they had been placed in the van where they would be unable to direct strategy once battle was joined.[12]

The prince's army consisted of the vanguard, under John of Gaunt and Chandos, with a large proportion of archers, possibly drawn up on either side. Behind this was the main body of the army under the prince himself. The vanguard consisted mainly of English men-at-arms, while the only potentially difficult troops, the Castilian knights, were placed in the centre division, with the Navarrese under Martín Enriquez de la Carra and some of the Gascons under the captal de Buch and the lord of Albret. Both these divisions were dismounted; in the rear was a mounted division, under Jaime of Majorca, Sir Hugh Calveley and the count of Armagnac, similar to the reserve of horse which had been used at Poitiers.[13]

Before the battle actually began, a small group of light horse went over from Enrique's army to join Pedro's men, an ominous start for the Castilians. As they did so, John of Gaunt's men began to advance on foot to attack du Guesclin's division, with heavy covering fire from the archers, carrying shortened lances. After the initial impact, the fighting became a hand-to-hand struggle, and for a time the English were forced back. Fierce and indecisive fighting followed, to cries of 'Guyenne, St George!' and 'Castile, Santiago!' The prince now brought up his main battle: the centre was detailed to support Lancaster, while the two wings were to attack the horsemen under Don Tello and the count of Denia. Don Tello and his men, however, did not await the English onslaught, but fled without taking part in the battle. The right wing, under the count of Denia, also seems to have turned tail, though the count himself was captured

fighting with the vanguard. This left the whole of the English main
battle free to attack the Castilian vanguard, and Enrique now tried
to bring up his main battle to join in the fighting. Enrique himself
charged into the thick of the fight two or three times, to the place
where López de Ayala was defending the standard of the Order of
the Sash; but his men refused to follow him because the English
were fighting strongly, and those on horseback fled, pursued by the
prince's mounted division. The battle was now a foregone conclusion: the Castilian vanguard, which had been the only part of
Enrique's army to engage the enemy seriously, was overwhelmed,
and its leaders either killed or captured. Once again much credit
must go to the English archers, who had not been seen in Spain
before and undoubtedly wrought havoc among the Castilian horsemen. The main cause of Enrique's defeat, however, was the uncertain loyalty of his troops: well over half his army appears to have
left the field without striking a blow. Enrique himself, according to
Fernán Álvarez de Albornoz, whose father helped Enrique's family
to escape, 'was forcibly dragged from the battle by his own men'.[14]

The pursuit took the English horse to the town of Nájera, with its
single bridge over the river Najerilla in front of the town. There
seems to have been some idea of using this as a rallying point, as
many captives were taken in the town itself, while they could easily
have ridden on towards Santo Domingo; but the English quickly
seized the bridge, and many of Enrique's army were killed or
captured along the banks of the river as they tried to cross. In the
town itself the leaders of the three great military orders were
captured, the Grand Master of Calatrava being found in a cellar,
while the prior of the knights of St John and the master of Santiago
yielded when a band of men-at-arms climbed over a high wall
behind which they had taken refuge. The prince waited on the
battlefield with his standards raised until all the pursuers had
returned, and then took up his quarters in the tents where Enrique
had spent the previous night.

The following day, Sunday, 4 April, the prisoners were listed,
and a search made for notable figures among the dead. There was
no sign of Enrique, and neither the prince nor Pedro learnt of his
whereabouts for some time. Otherwise most of the leading
supporters of Enrique could be accounted for, either dead or
captured. For the prince, the best news was the capture of du
Guesclin, who had long been marked out as the best of the French
commanders. He was less pleased to find Audrehem among the

captured, because Audrehem had still not paid him the ransom due after his capture at Poitiers eleven years before, and had sworn not to fight against him until the money had been raised. The prince demanded to know why he had broken his oath, threatening to execute him as a traitor. Audrehem persuaded the prince to listen to him, and then pointed out that both he and the prince were fighting on other men's behalf: he, Audrehem, was fighting not against the prince, but against Pedro, while the prince was not the leader of his army, but merely captain of a company, 'with all reverence to your estate, which is higher than that of any other captain'. Audrehem gained his pardon; but his assessment of the prince's position was all too accurate. As soon as the business of fighting was over and done with, there was an immediate conflict of interest between the prince and Pedro. Pedro needed to secure his position as king of Castile, while the prince was anxious to be paid and to return to Aquitaine. The first clash came over the prisoners: the prince, thinking in chivalric and financial terms, regarded prisoners entirely in terms of ransoms. Pedro saw them as rebels or political opponents, and succeeded in having four of them executed, but only under protest from the prince, who prevented any further killings. Spanish custom with regard to captives, on the evidence of the treatment of English prisoners in 1372, was considerably harsher than that in France and England, where, once the ransom arrangements were made, the prisoner was released on parole, partly to facilitate the collection of the money. The Spanish tended to keep prisoners-of-war in strict custody, relying on the prisoner's friends and relatives to make arrangements for ransom payments. This difference of approach had been the subject of a special clause in the Libourne treaties, under which prisoners were to be retained by the prince. A further complication was that Pedro's only alternative method of acquiring the prisoners, by buying them from their captors, would merely add to the enormous amount owing to the English, and neither the prince nor his followers would be inclined to accept such offers on purely business grounds.[15]

On Monday, 5 April, the prince wrote to Joan at Bordeaux to give her the news of the battle:

My dearest and truest sweetheart and beloved companion . . . as to news, you will want to know that we were encamped in the fields near Navarrete on the second of April, and there we had

news that the Bastard of Spain and all his army were encamped
two leagues from us on the river at Nájera. The next day, very
early in the morning, we moved off towards him, and sent out
our scouts to discover the Bastard's situation, who reported to us
that he had taken up his position and prepared his troops in a good
place and was waiting for us. So we put ourselves into battle
order, and did so well by the will and grace of God that the
Bastard and all his men were defeated, thanks be to our Lord, and
between five and six thousand of those who fought were killed,
and there were plenty of prisoners, whose names we do not know
at present, but among others are Don Sancho, the Bastard's
brother, the count of Denia, Bertrand du Guesclin, the marshal
d'Audrehem, Don Juan Ramírez, 'Johan de Neville', 'Craundon',
Lebègue de Villaines, Señor Carrillo, the Master of Santiago,
the Master of Saint John and various castellans whose names we
do not know, up to two thousand noble prisoners; and as for the
Bastard himself, we do not know at present if he was taken, dead,
or escaped. And after the said battle we lodged that evening in
the Bastard's lodgings, in his own tents and we were more
comfortable there than we have been for four or five days, and
we stayed there all the next day. On the Monday, that is, the day
when this is being written, we moved off and took the road
towards Burgos; and so we shall complete our journey success-
fully with God's help. You will be glad to know, dearest companion, that we, our brother Lancaster and all the nobles of our
army are well, thank God, except only Sir John Ferrers, who did
much fighting.

Soon afterwards one of the prince's servants was sent to London
with one of Enrique's horses, 'taken at the battle of Nájera', just as
Geoffrey Hamelyn had been sent after Poitiers with king John's
tunic and helmet.[16]
The prince's hope that he would complete his journey success-
fully was not to be fulfilled. Pedro re-established himself in his
capital at Burgos two days later, and the prince and his army
encamped outside the town, the prince taking up quarters in the
monastery of Las Huelgas, where the Castilian kings were buried.
Negotiations now began over the payment of the army. The mere
calculation of the sum due took almost a month: it finally came to
2,720,000 gold florins, a sum almost comparable to king John's
ransom. The raising of John's ransom in France, the wealthiest

country in Europe, had caused grave difficulties; in Castile, much poorer and with a fragile, newly established government, the task was clearly impossible. Meanwhile the army waited and the total due increased. Pedro made counter-claims over the jewels he had sold in Gascony, and refused to give Castilian castles as pledges for payment on the grounds that it would weaken his position. As soon as the total had been agreed, a ceremony was arranged at which new deeds of obligation were to be exchanged, in the cathedral at Burgos on 2 May; but the prince's stipulations for the occasion show how much he already distrusted Pedro. A company of English troops was to occupy one of the gates of the city while he was in Burgos, and 1,000 men-at-arms and a company of archers were posted in a near-by square; in addition the prince, though unarmed, was escorted by 500 men-at-arms on foot. A further document, signed at Las Huelgas on 6 May, provided that the first half of the ransom was to be paid within four months, upon which the English army would leave Castile. Pedro left for Toledo soon afterwards to start the work of collecting money, while the English army moved to Valladolid in the hope of finding better supplies of provisions.[17]

Pedro does seem to have made a genuine effort to raise at least part of the money, by loans, taxation and contributions from local communities. From Toledo on 20 May he wrote to the city of Murcia, explaining that 'great quantities of maravedis (i.e. Castilian currency) had to be given to the prince of Wales'. This he could not do, for he had no treasure nor the means to obtain it; 'and the companies of the said prince are going through my kingdom doing damage, as you know, because I cannot pay them the wages due to them'. He appealed to the Murcians to help him by paying all taxes due to him, and also by providing an advance payment on sums due up to the end of the year. Similar letters went out to the other cities, as well as individual letters such as one to the Jewish community at Cuenca asking for a loan. Pedro's attempts to raise money seem to have been perfectly genuine; but over the question of the lands promised to his allies he was certainly unscrupulous. Charters were duly made out for the grant of Vizcaya and Castro Urdiales to the prince, and the county of Soria to Chandos. The prince added his new title to his own deeds, but Chandos found that Pedro's chancery demanded such an exorbitant fee to confirm the grant that he preferred to let the matter drop. As for the transfer of the lands of Vizcaya, the prince's representatives were unable to make any headway; the Basques simply replied that they chose their own lords, as was indeed the case, and that Pedro could not compel them to transfer their allegiance.[18]

As Pedro travelled further south in search of funds, the prince and his men grew increasingly restive. The damage already evident in May increased; the prince himself took Amosco and besieged Medina del Campo in search of provisions. The prince now began to think seriously of other means of rewarding his troops. He opened negotiations, through Sir Hugh Calveley, with Pere III of Aragón at the end of April, and these led to full-scale talks early in July, officially aimed at securing peace between Castile and Aragón, but which in fact led to a secret Anglo-Aragonese draft agreement. The prince's envoys won over Pere III from his pro-French sympathies by suggesting an alliance between the prince, Pere III, Charles of Navarre and Pedro of Portugal, which would partition Castile, thus eliminating both Pedro I and Enrique, settling old Navarrese and Aragonese claims against Castile, and giving the prince the financial compensation he needed. This alliance was to be confirmed at a later meeting, and put into effect if Pedro failed to pay his debts and surrender Vizcaya by April 1368. A truce between Aragón and Castile was also made, which went some way to ensuring that Enrique would not be supported by Pere III if he attempted a new invasion of Castile.[19]

About mid July the prince moved east again, to Soria, where he spent a month before deciding that it was impossible to remain longer in Castile. His men were short of provisions, as they had been throughout the campaign, and the summer had brought serious epidemics, probably malaria and dysentery: 'many of his men died of diseases which they caught because of the unfamiliar climate'. Others were killed in skirmishes with the Castilians. The prince himself was gravely ill, and this may have finally determined his withdrawal. Late in August his men retraced their steps through Navarre, where Charles made much of him and his men, fearing reprisals for his earlier behaviour, and on 29 August the prince took leave of Charles at Saint-Jean-Pied-du-Port after a great feast. At Bayonne the expedition formally ended, with five days of feasting; and early in September the prince entered Bordeaux. He was welcomed by a great procession, and was met at the cathedral by Joan and Edward, his eldest son. He dismounted, and 'they walked together holding hands', to the bishop's palace where they were staying.[20]

The Spanish expedition had achieved its military objective, but had only partly fulfilled its more important diplomatic ends. Pedro was far from being a grateful ally of England, secure on his throne. He was still threatened by Enrique's continued activities, ill-disposed towards the prince and vastly in debt. The prince himself had returned home impoverished and sick, and with his involvement in Spanish politics still unresolved. There was the possibility of another campaign in Castile being needed, if the agreement with Aragón went through. The negotiations with Aragón continued that autumn, but by then the situation had radically changed, because as the prince returned to Aquitaine, Enrique had succeeded in re-entering Castile. The proposals which resulted at the new meeting, held at Tarbes in November and ratified in December by Charles of Navarre and the prince, were Janus-like in the extreme: they seem to have been largely produced by the envoys of Aragón, anxious to secure themselves against Castile. Chandos and Armagnac, the prince's representatives, were deeply involved in the problems of Gascony and unlikely to take any initiative. The partition of Castile, at best a makeshift project, was dropped. Now the Anglo-Navarrese-Aragonese alliance was to be offered to both Enrique and Pedro, the highest bidder to obtain it. However, although the proposals were ratified, the treaty which was to put them into effect was never signed, and as late as February 1369 the government in London were still negotiating with Pedro on the basis of the 1362 treaty. In March 1369, Pedro was murdered by Enrique at Montiel. Despite Aragonese efforts to lure the prince back to Spain by inducing him to claim Pedro's kingdom for himself, the disappearance of the king put an end to the prince's involvement: there was now no hope of claiming his debts. It was only the marriage of John of Gaunt to Pedro's daughter Constanza that revived serious English interest in Castile.[21]

Aquitaine: the Last Years

9

The prince returned to Gascony to find that there were new political problems to be faced. There had been difficulties with the French over the fulfilment of the treaty of Brétigny, but there had been no real indication that the French might try to disrupt the treaty entirely, except for the occasional gossip or report from an agent. Now it was rapidly becoming clear that Charles V was embarking on a diplomatic campaign designed to subvert English authority in Aquitaine, with the object of declaring war once he judged the situation to be sufficiently favourable. The agent who reported in 1364 on Charles's negotiations with Foix had declared that, once the hostages for Brétigny were back in France, Charles would 'make war everywhere against the English and the principality', but this could be taken for no more than an idle threat. In 1365, in negotiations with Pere III of Aragón, Charles's proposals envisaged an early resumption of war with England. Navarre was first to be destroyed and handed over to Aragón; then the Aragonese were to help Charles to drive the English out of Gascony. These were only projects, as insubstantial as the prince's plan to partition Castile, but they showed the end to which Charles's policies were being directed. Far more serious were the declarations in the treaty of Aigues-Mortes drawn up in August 1367 between Enrique and the duc d'Anjou, in which Enrique was to engage in war with England as soon as he had regained the Castilian throne. A specific date, March 1368, was given for the opening of the campaign against England; and the treaty itself contained an unusual piece of very undiplomatic invective against Edward, the prince and his brothers and Charles of Navarre:

> oppressors of men, like new Nimrods . . . following the remnant of fallen angels in their presumptuous pride and unbridled boldness . . . who have entered [France and Castile] but chiefly France, like the sons of Satan, polluting, corrupting, violating and despoiling . . .[1]

Behind these threats of war, Charles used more devious methods. The prince's relationship with the great lords of Gascony was becoming uneasy. He had never succeeded in winning over the fiercely independent Gaston Phoebus of Foix, though the latter had been equally intransigent under French suzerainty. Now relations with other great lords began to sour. Froissart describes a quarrel between Arnaud-Amanieu d'Albret and the prince before the expedition to Spain, because his retinue was reduced from 1,000 lances to 200; but the real problems came after the expedition. The army had set out on a freebooting expedition promising a great reward; they had returned empty-handed. There must have been considerable recriminations among its leaders, because even if the prince paid them eventually, there were no immediate funds to be had. The prince had certainly quarrelled, for one reason or another, with Albret, Armagnac and Chandos within a few months of his return. Traditionally, following Froissart, these quarrels have been put down to the imposition of a new *fouage*; but there are good reasons, to which we shall return, for regarding this as a pretext for an open breach rather than the root of the grievances. In the case of Armagnac and Albret, the real reason for their disenchantment with the prince was purely financial. The prince seems to have been pressing Armagnac for repayment of the loan he had made to him for his ransom from the count of Foix; and Albret had not received payments of the substantial annual pension of £1,000, which had been due to the lords of Albret since the 1350s and were now ten years in arrears. Once again, lack of records for Gascon affairs makes it impossible to arrive at definite conclusions: but the difficulties of the autumn of 1367 seem to have arisen primarily out of the financial plight of the prince after the Spanish expedition. He had no reserve of treasure, such as his father or Charles V held; he had a revenue from his lands in Gascony and elsewhere which was barely sufficient in times of peace. The only recorded payments that he recovered from Pedro or from ransoms were £52,447* from jewels given to him by Pedro, £4,395 from the count of Denia, £1,152 from the marshal d'Audrehem and £1,458 from Bertrand du Guesclin, one eighth of the total sum demanded of 2,720,000 florins, or some £475,000 in sterling guyennois. Furthermore, the entire revenue recorded in Richard Filongley's accounts for 1363–70 is £445,849, not all of which may have been collected; so that the cost of the Spanish expedition was entirely out of proportion to the prince's resources. Even the maintenance of his admittedly lavish household cost only £30,000 per annum during this period, and payments to his own war retinue may well be included in that figure. The prince must have expected to make a substantial profit from the Spanish expedition. As events turned out, he appears to have received a total revenue of nearly £60,000. If that was indeed all, most of the army must have been unpaid.[2]

So behind Chandos Herald's conventional account of feasting at Bayonne to mark the end of a successful expedition, there is the shadow of a much graver situation. The prince's financial weakness was doubly to the French king's advantage. Any remedies the prince might take were bound to be unpopular: it was far easier to raise money before a campaign, with promises of rich booty to be brought home, than during or after an unsuccessful foray, as Edward had learnt to his cost in 1339–40. And discontented and impoverished lords were open to the blandishments of Charles V's purse. The prince's first remedy seems to have been to seek a 'gift' in aid of his expenses, which produced 'from the citizens of the good towns and cities of the principality' a further £14,764. (It is possible that this was raised before the expedition, as a loan – there would have been no need for a gift in view of the anticipated profit – and later converted to a gift.) He then summoned an assembly of the Estates of Gascony to Saint-Émilion on 16 October, but, although the prince went there, this was cancelled, apparently because some of the disbanded troops who had left Bayonne in August were infesting the roads and making travel dangerous. The town of Millau in the Rouergue had difficulty in even getting a message through to the prince to apologize for not sending representatives. A new assembly was therefore summoned to meet at Angoulême in January 1368.[3]

Meanwhile Charles had begun to work on the loyalty of the

* Figures in sterling guyennois, worth about 5 per cent less than English sterling.

Gascon lords. The first, and most obvious, target was Jean, count of Armagnac, the prince's opponent on the campaign of 1355, and an uneasy vassal from the beginning of the prince's rule. He had refused to allow the *fouage* of 1364 and 1365 to be levied on his lands in the Rouergue, and the prince's means of winning his allegiance, by loaning him the ransom money he owed to the comte de Foix, had now become a cause of disaffection. The prince was claiming the balance of the 40,000 crowns he had lent to Armagnac; Armagnac was counter-claiming 200,000 crowns for service in Spain: in 1369 he said that this sum had neither been accounted for nor paid, although other companies had had their claims met in full. Arnaud-Amanieu d'Albret's claim must also have been substantial, if the figure of 200 men-at-arms in his retinue is correct. Charles V's first approaches to these lords were, for obvious reasons, secret; but the rapidity of events in 1368 implies that the ground had already been prepared, and that the settlement of their financial affairs was to be the chief reward for a change of allegiance.[4]

When the estates of Gascony met in January 1368, the prince asked them for a *fouage* of 10 sous per annum for five years. Previous *fouages* had been at the rate of 40d. and 20d. sterling guyennois; this was to be at the rate of 24d., and the total sum raised in five years would be twice the total of the taxation of 1364–5. In other words, the proposal implied a lower rate of annual taxation than had obtained in the past; but an occasional tax was being turned into an annual source of revenue. This tax was agreed by the three estates, nobles, clergy and towns, in the traditional manner. A charter of rights was the price exacted from the prince for the grant of the tax, and it shows the kind of matter which was a cause of grievance. The charter clearly demonstrates that both the towns and the lords cooperated in drawing it up, and it is reasonable to assume that the majority of the Gascon lords consented to the *fouage* for which the prince granted it, though the count of Armagnac later implied that he and other lords had not been at the assembly, saying that 'some of the prince's people' had granted the tax. The main grievances are directed against the excessive activity of central government: they imply that the prince's officers had been over-zealous in asserting the prince's rights, in an area which had been governed on a slack rein for as long as its inhabitants could remember, and where local rights were jealously preserved. Interference in areas which enjoyed rights of 'high justice', that is, of settling all cases except a very few reserved to the crown, was to be abandoned. The prince's *sergents* were not even to live on such territories; the use of safeguards issued by the prince was to be stopped, as this was a means of intervening; and most important of all, the *fouage* and other impositions were not to be levied in future on such areas without the consent of the greater part of those who exercised high justice. This meant that the preponderant voice in any future taxation scheme would be with the great lords, as many of the lesser towns and nobility had no such rights. Even some great towns had no rights of high justice: Poitiers, for instance, did not obtain the necessary charter until October 1369.[5]

The charter of rights reflects the practical difficulties of the prince's administration. Many of the prince's officers were English, used to the relative simplicity of English law, with its scant regard for local custom. The prince and his advisers had already showed, in Cheshire, that they had little time for pleas of local privilege, a cast of mind increasingly common among lawyers both in France and England as they looked towards a revival of the ancient Roman ideal of universal law, centrally enforced. Such ideas were radical enough in England; in Gascony they were unthinkable. Attempts to administer the prince's rights and justice were fraught with difficulty, and in many cases the royal officer had to be summoned to court himself, as in the case of the bishop of Poitiers and the seneschal of Poitou over castle guard at Chauvigny in 1365–7, even though a relatively minor matter was involved. Elsewhere, important nobles were treated as though they were English lords, long inured to a strong central authority: the count of Périgord was arrested for taking up arms against the lord of Mussidan, his vassal; the latter was, admittedly, an English ally of long standing. At a higher level, there was the even more disturbing problem of the ultimate authority in Aquitaine. The Gascons, faced with the prince's attempts to impose a strong legal system on Aquitaine and to exploit his rights to the full, were quite prepared to play at the same game. Appeals from the prince's court to Westminster became frequent as early as January 1365, as did petitions against the prince's ministers. In 1367, a writ to the prince from Westminster recited some of the grievances:

the people of our lordship of Aquitaine, by their quarrels and perpetual complaints, trouble our council continually and increasingly, appealing on the one hand against your seneschals or their lieutenants or other lords subject to you because of the grievances and damage by which, so they say, they are oppressed, against all justice, right and customs of the country . . .

And the writ goes on to complain also of 'novelties' introduced by him and his ministers; these latter are to be suspended while the appeals are heard. The cases were often of tortuous complexity, made worse by legal manoeuvres or illegal seizures of property by main force. Louis de Mauval, having seized the castle of Juliac in the Limousin, not merely appealed to Westminster, but when arbitrators were appointed created chaos by demanding to be represented by the advocate who was presenting his opponents' case. Other litigants used the ignorance of the prince's officers to have property transferred to them, as in the case of the lady of Surgères whose long list of grievances came up at Westminster in October 1366. The Gascon lords chafed under the presence of an administration which, whatever its faults, plainly intended to intervene actively in Gascon affairs, and in asserting local rights and customs, they looked for a more distant, less efficient authority that would not interfere in details. If they could not be ruled from England, might not Paris prove a lighter yoke?[6]

The basis of appeals outside the principality brought into play the still unresolved question of the renunciations of the treaty of Brétigny. Certain lands had not yet been transferred, notably the valuable 'terre de Belleville', which had been the object of a special joint commission in 1366, but was still in dispute. Equally, the ransom due for John II remained partially unpaid. King Edward had therefore refused to make his renunciation of his claim to the kingdom of France. Charles equally refused to make his renunciation of sovereignty and *ressort* over Aquitaine, because the treaty stipulated that both should be made simultaneously, and also because Edward was in breach of the stipulation that the English companies should be withdrawn from France. On the latter point, the English king had little control, as most such bands operated entirely on their own account; but the problem had grown more serious since the end of the prince's Spanish expedition, when a number of troops had re-entered France after the army was disbanded at Bayonne. If Edward had adhered strictly to the treaty, he should not have used the powers of sovereignty and *ressort*, or ultimate appeals, until the renunciations were made, because the

French king had retained these rights pending the making of the renunciations. The fact that he had agreed not to exercise them himself did not entitle Edward to do so. The absence of the renunciations was to be a decisive weapon in the hands of Charles V.[7]

To be fair to the prince, his administration was far from being oppressive if measured in English terms, and many of the Gascon towns would have welcomed a reduction in the powers of the lords and a centralized government for the province, in that this would have encouraged trade. The prince and his council were well aware that the commercial prosperity of Gascony was vital to the English cause. When, in 1368, a statute was passed in England banning English merchants from Bordeaux and Gascons from England in an attempt to reorganize the wine trade, the prince secured its repeal as soon as it became apparent that wine was remaining unsold as a result. He also encouraged such practical measures as the building of a lighthouse at Cordouan (a reef off the mouth of the Gironde estuary) and schemes to improve navigation on the Lot by clearing the channel.[8]

Another criticism that has been levelled at the prince's rule in Aquitaine is that he himself was haughty, proud and unapproachable. There certainly seems to have been a side to his character which enjoyed the excessive flattery offered to him as the victor of Crécy, Poitiers and Nájera, and those who wished to find favour with him exaggerated the trend: Walter of Peterborough, who has left us a poem on the Spanish expedition, says that he wrote an earlier one on Poitiers entitled *Theotecon* (*Son of God*). A curious echo of this is an episode which took place at Périgueux, probably in 1368. The chronicler of the great abbey at Moissac records the story, which he had from the chief protagonist, the bishop of Sarlat himself:

In the time of the said Urban V, Edward prince of Aquitaine, who then ruled the duchy of Aquitaine tranquilly, firmly and peacefully, held a solemn council at Périgueux, at which 22 bishops from the said duchy were present. And a sermon was preached by Austensius, bishop of Sarlat, a great and famous theologian, discreet in temporal and spiritual affairs and richly endowed with worldly wealth. This bishop, in his sermon compared the same prince in certain things to the Son of God. On account of which, certain jealous people who wanted to damage his reputation, cited the bishop to the Roman curia without reasonable cause (unless they wanted to defame him) twisting the meaning of his words, which were perfectly orthodox if rightly understood. Because blows which are anticipated are less harmful, wishing to counter these malicious words and false suggestions, the bishop went to the papal court. And because he was there in person, no-one opposed him either in public or private.

Instead, the bishop dined with the Pope, who was rejoicing over the recent death of Pedro of Castile; and he never had to defend himself against the charges. The chronicler continues:

> The lord bishop told me all this while I had the priory of 'Tanerio', and was a monk in his church. And he added that the prince did not accept gratefully what he had said in praise of him to his face, according to what a friend of his told him; for during a private conversation, the latter said to the prince: 'What did you think of the bishop's sermon today?' He replied that the bishop was doubtless very eloquent and wise, and extremely far-sighted, but that he must have been jesting, because no-one ought to be praised in that fashion to his face, least of all a great prince, who might suddenly be brought low by a stroke of ill-fortune, so that his earlier great deeds would be forgotten, brought to nothing and utterly confounded. This the bishop told me, praising the wisdom of the prince.[9]

The story rings true in several ways. Austence de Saint-Colombe, the bishop of Sarlat, had been a member of an English embassy to the Pope in 1363, and was one of a group of pro-English bishops in an area where many of the clergy, particularly outside the area of Bordeaux and Landes, were under the influence of the pro-French papal court at Avignon: the other bishops might well have cited him, if only for political reasons. He died in about 1370, and the episode would therefore have been fresh in his mind when he told it to Aimeric de Peyrac, who became abbot of Moissac in 1377. The prince's rather world-weary answer conforms well to the general impression of him during the years following the Spanish campaign; his illness was chronic and debilitating, leaving him not so much bedridden as listless and reluctant to act. The disease was almost certainly dysentery: the best description names it as the bloody flux, used at this period with the precise meaning of dysentery.[10]

Such, then, was the background to the prince's last years in
Gascony. After the session of the estates in January 1368 there was
a plan for him to return to England, but he was still at Angoulême
in March. By May, the difficulties ahead were plain. Armagnac,
who was still a member of the prince's council, had once more
refused to allow the *fouage* to be levied in his lands, sending the
lord of Barbazan and Sir Guiraut de Jaulin to inform the prince,
claiming that he and his subjects had always been free of such
obligations. According to Armagnac, the prince, angered by this
refusal, vowed that he would destroy and lay waste the count's
lands unless he paid, and refused to receive any further letters or
messengers. Armagnac then appealed to the king for support. No
reply came from Westminster. He left for Paris, for the marriage
of Arnaud-Amanieu d'Albret, his nephew, to Charles V's sister-in-
law, Marguerite de Bourbon. This marriage was in more than one
way the turning point of Charles V's diplomatic efforts in Gascony.
Until now he had been content to play a waiting game, ensuring
that old antipathies were kept alive, delaying or making difficulties
over the settlement of the peace treaty. How the match between
the lord of Albret and Charles's sister-in-law came to be arranged
is obscure; but the prince could only regard it as an attempt to
undermine any personal influence he might have with the Gascon
lords, particularly as Albret became Charles's vassal, saving his
homage to the English king (but not to the prince) on 1 June.
Once again, it seems that disillusion after the Spanish expedition
was the main cause for Albret's defection. Froissart's complaint that
the prince treated the Gascon lords haughtily, preferring his own
English companions, saying that Armagnac and Albret found a
'hardness' in the prince, rings only partly true. He had trusted them
absolutely at Nájera, and they had come to Spain of their own free
will. If the expedition had also been a financial success, there would
have been no complaint of 'hardness'. The real reason is surely the
lament of the lord of Albret in later years, that he had once made a
good living out of fighting for the English king, and now he had
much less to spend. The turning point had come in 1367. On the
other hand, the prince did not tolerate the pride of the Gascon lords
easily; and once relations began to deteriorate, his intransigence
made matters worse.[11]

Armagnac and the other Gascon lords who came to Paris in May
were therefore very much open to the influence of Charles V. It was
almost certainly in concert with Charles V that Armagnac took the

radical step which was to lead to the renewal of war. At some time between late April and the end of June, he drafted a letter of appeal to the *parlement* at Paris over the question of the *fouage*, on the grounds that since the treaty of Brétigny had never come into effect, Charles V still remained the true overlord of Aquitaine, thus throwing into question the status of the prince's authority there. If the letters were drafted in early May, Charles V did not formally accept them until 30 June; his public acceptance would imply that he, too, regarded the treaty as a dead letter, and, with his usual caution, he may have wished to be sure of his ground, both in legal and practical terms, before taking such a step. On the other hand, there is no evidence that the letter of appeal existed before the end of June; and it therefore seems likely that Armagnac and Charles were working entirely in concert, and that the decision to make and accept the appeal was a mutual one, made during the course of these months. This is all the more probable in that a detailed treaty between Charles and Armagnac, by which they agreed not to negotiate with Edward or the prince over their legal positions without the other party's consent, was also drawn up, and sealed by them and Albret on 30 June. It also provided for the likelihood of the outbreak of war with England, and confirmed the liberties claimed by the Gascon lords.[12]

The treaty, and a contract to give the count of Armagnac additional lands in Gascony, remained secret. The treaty itself provided for the lodging of appeals by the lord of Albret and the count of Périgord; surprisingly, Albret's appeal was only entered on 8 September, although he sealed the treaty, and the count of Périgord did not enter his appeal until the following year. If the prince had recognized the extent of the dissatisfaction and had acted promptly, he might well have seriously undermined Charles's schemes. Instead he chose to regard the affair as a local rebellion in the Rouergue. On 31 May, he instructed the lord of Severac to be ready by 19 June to go to enforce payment. The original date for this summons had been 4 June, but as the prince had not been able to get a reply from those who refused to pay the tax, he was deferring the lord of Severac's mission for a fortnight. The prince was still at Angoulême; apart from a visit on 23 May to the near-by priory of Bouteville, which he had endowed and helped to rebuild, he seems to have remained there throughout this period. A further assembly of the Estates was held at Saintes in August, but the question of the *fouage* does not seem to have been discussed. Such moves as were made seem to have been military: on 18 September, twenty-two ships were retained in England for men-at-arms and archers to be sent shortly to Aquitaine, implying a force of about 1,200 men. During these two years, 1367–8, £26,000 was paid to the prince out of king John's ransom, either for the costs of the Spanish expedition, or for the preparations for a renewal of war in the autumn of 1368.[13]

The transfer of Armagnac's allegiance to Charles must have been known to the prince in late September, when the count repaid the balance of the loan made for his ransom, thus clearing himself of all obligations to the prince. In November, Charles also agreed to pay the arrears of the pension which the lord of Albret was owed by Edward; Albret had already received 10,000 francs in August, and he was now paid the same amount again, as a quarter of the arrears of the pension. In all, Albret received 87,000 francs, or approximately £15,000, over the next four years. Charles had succeeded in replacing the prince as a liberal provider of funds; unlike the prince, however, he did not have to depend on the uncertainties of war in order to raise the money. The actual pensions offered to Armagnac and Albret were £17,000 and £10,000 respectively, as annual payments for their war services: the records show that even Charles was unable to meet these sums in full.[14]

Although the decision to accept the appeal was made in June, the actual summons to the prince was not sent from Paris until November or December. Both sides spent the interval in diplomatic manoeuvres, of which we know only the bare outlines. In mid September, an embassy was sent from London to Paris to demand that the appeals should be rejected by Charles V, and Albret tried to arrange some compromise with them; they took back a new list of grievances from him, which was forwarded to the prince for an answer. Communications with Bordeaux were slow, and hampered by growing mistrust between the prince and the king's councillors, and it was only after the news of the appeals was made public in November that the prince replied, on 7 December. This is almost the only letter from the prince with any personal colour to it, and is worth quoting in full, showing as it does the prince's irritability both with the Gascon lords and with the London councillors, and his dislike of the intricacies of diplomacy:

Most respected lord and father, I commend myself to your highness as best and humbly as I can, asking your blessing.

Most respected lord and father, may it please your highness to know that I have received your honourable letters and the 'creance' which the lord of Albret sent to your lordship at Paris by your messengers the lords Latimer, Neville and John Stretelee; for which, my most respected lord, I thank your highness as humbly as I can for sending copies of the said letters and 'creance' so that I can clear my name [*esclairser mon honeur*] and maintain truly and loyally what before now I have reported to your lordship about the said lord of Albret.

On which, my most respected lord and father, may it please your lordship to know that you are my lord and father and sovereign lord; and what I reported to your highness I did as a son should do to his lord and father, truly and loyally and in no other way, and I will maintain and prove it before your lordship against the said lord of Albret in all the ways that a knight should or that it may please your lordship to command, as before my liege lord and sovereign. And if anyone in England wishes to contradict what I reported to your highness, I will be ready to prove it, and whatever this estate or condition I will find others of the same standing to maintain, for me and in my name, that what I reported to your highness on the said matter was loyally and truly said. And, my most respected lord, without wishing to displease your highness, I am amazed that anyone in your kingdom, whoever he may be, should wish to give credence to reports from anyone, messenger or otherwise, which do me dishonour and discredit my standing; for, most respected lord, I will never report anything to you which will not be found to be true, and which I will not maintain with the grace and help of God against any other subject or vassal of your realm, of whatever standing, without exception. And, most respected lord, do not be displeased that I have written so forwardly [*tant avant*] about this, because it affects me and my honour and standing so closely that it seems to me, my lord, that I must do so, because I would be very aggrieved to be found in such default towards your highness, and I pray that God may keep me from it.

And besides, most honoured lord, I have heard that some people there have believed the excuses of the lord of Albret too easily; but they are not true, as is now plain from the message which Sir Pierre de Curton, who is indeed trustworthy and to be believed, as you yourself know, who has come straight to me from the said Albret in Paris, has expressly told me from him that he has appealed to the king of France as sovereign lord of the principality, and the said Bret told him to tell me that, as he says. And by that, my lord, it appears that the 'creance' which I reported to your lord is indeed proved and found to be true, for that shows it clearly and contradicts expressly the 'creance' and excuses which your messengers brought back to you from the said lord of Albret.

I ask you, most honoured lord, for the sake of such little power I have to serve you, to 'take these matters entirely to heart' and, that you will be pleased to give the bearer of these letters all your orders and pleasures with regard to myself, which, most respected lord, I will always be ready to carry out as best I can.

Most respected lord and father, may the blessed Trinity guard and maintain your highness and give you glorious victory over your enemies.[15]

Meanwhile, Charles sent an embassy to England in a last attempt to compromise and to put into effect the treaty of Brétigny and the schedule of Calais in their entirety. The French embassy arrived in London early in 1369; but it was only a bluff on Charles V's part, because at the same time letters of summons, prepared on 19 November, were already on their way to the prince, citing him to appear at the *parlement* of Paris on 2 May. These letters, which appear to have been circulated to those involved in the appeal before they were sent to the prince – the surviving texts come from the Albret archives – were sent to him via the seneschal of Toulouse. They actually reached the prince early in January 1369, and the prince at once wrote to warn Edward of Charles's duplicity. Froissart's scene of the reception of the French envoys is open to serious doubts: he describes their journey direct from Paris to Bordeaux, gives a text of the letters which is his own invention, and credits the prince with the famous reply: 'We will willingly go to Paris on the day we are cited to be there, since the king of France commands it, but it will be with our helmet on our head and 60,000 men in our company.' In fact, the messengers came from Toulouse, and delivered a rather different letter, in all probability at Angoulême. Chandos Herald says that the prince was ill at the time, and knowledge of his sickness may well have played a part in French calculations. The latter's version of events makes him sit up in bed and say: 'Lords, by my faith, it seems to me that the French think I am dead; but if God gives me comfort, and I can get up from this bed, I will do them a great deal of harm even now, because God knows that they lack a good case, and they will have real cause to complain of me.' Chandos Herald continues by saying that a defiant letter was sent back, and it is the conventional phrasing of this defiance in the poem that Froissart has turned into the prince's reply. The prince's powerlessness added to his fury; the two messengers were seized on their return journey to Toulouse, at Penne d'Agenais, and imprisoned; whether they were later killed is not certain, but seems all too probable. The prince, knowing that the agents of the duc d'Anjou and comte d'Armagnac were active in the Rouergue, sent an invective against Armagnac to Millau, the chief town of the region, accusing Armagnac of breach of his most solemn oaths, of 'great evil and cunning' directed against him, and, in a postscript, of making open war. The letter may have had some effect, as Millau did not go over to the French until November 1369, after an exhaustive inquiry into the legal rights of the two sides.[16]

War was now imminent, and both sides made preparations for a campaign. By 26 February, plans had been made for the earl of Pembroke to go to Aquitaine. The prince did what he could to secure the allegiance of some Gascon lords: the captal de Buch, the most consistent and loyal of his supporters, received a grant of the county of Bigorre on 27 June; the Soudich de la Trau, who had changed sides more than once, was granted the customs of the port of Royan on 10 February, while the city of Poitiers was granted rights of high justice later in the year, on 17 October. The last document gives a list of some of the prince's councillors at this period: the chief was John Harewell, bishop of Bath and Wells and chancellor of Aquitaine, who was blamed for the mishandling of the crisis over the *fouage*. Sir Nigel Loring, his chamberlain, and Sir Arnold Savage were the other two Englishmen named: Savage, a Kentishman, had been mayor of Bordeaux from 1359 to 1363, and was therefore experienced in Gascon affairs. The abbot of Saint-Maxence, chancellor of Aquitaine after Harewell, Arnaud Roche of Saintes and Jean Rival were the leading Gascon figures. In view of the prince's illness, much of the policy-making, as well as the routine administrative work, must have devolved on them.[17]

Despite these spasmodic efforts to rally the pro-English party in Gascony, defections to the French side increased rapidly during the early part of the year. The appellants were joined by the comte de

Périgord; and even in an area such as Poitou, which remained English until a late date, important lords changed to the French side, including the vicomte de Rochechouart, and the lords of Chauvigny and Pons. At the end of March, the French chancery could list over 900 'cities, towns, castles and fortresses' in Gascony which had come over to Charles V. Meanwhile the legal process of hearing the appellants was now close at hand. As expected, the prince did not appear on 2 May before the *parlement*, and its proceedings were concerned with enforcing judgement in his absence. With the general assent of the assembly, which included representatives from the French towns as well as the king's councillors and many nobles, a declaration of war was made: not directly, but implicitly; there was no formal declaration of the opening of hostilities, and indeed a mutual war of harassment and skirmishes had already begun. A reply to the last set of diplomatic demands made by Edward was sent to England; Edward's response was to resume the title of king of France at a parliament held on 3 June. On 19 June, the prince was instructed to publish the king's intention of gaining his land of France by conquest, and to have it proclaimed throughout his principality. On the French side, the duc d'Anjou wrote on 8 June, as Charles's lieutenant in Languedoc, to all his subjects, instructing them to make 'as great war as possible on the English'. The breach was now complete.[18]

The intermittent fighting in the Rouergue which had begun in the spring was transformed into a full-scale French campaign. It was a relatively isolated enclave, surrounded on three sides by French territory, but the importance attached to it by the English was shown by the fact that Chandos, when he returned to Gascony from his Norman lordship of Saint-Sauveur at the end of 1368, went there almost immediately to lead a relief force. He raided deep into French territory, beyond Toulouse, but with little real result: French counter-raids threatened Montauban, the capital of Lower Quercy, which was important enough for the building of a large castle to have been started by the prince. In Périgord, the newly arrived English force under the earl of Pembroke and Edmund of Langley, the prince's younger brother, took the castle of Bourdeilles, but only after a long siege ending in an assault, after which the earl was knighted. Soon afterwards Périgueux itself went over to Charles, while Montauban, although most of the inhabitants were loyal, was handed over by partisans of the French cause during the summer. La Roche-sur-Yon, a small castle which should have been transferred under the treaty of Brétigny, was taken by Edmund of Langley in July, but Sir James Audley, now seneschal of Poitou, died 'of sickness' during the siege. He had been one of the prince's closest companions-in-arms, and the prince is said by Froissart to have attended his funeral at Poitiers. Poitou was a vital area, being on the frontier with France, and Audley was replaced as seneschal by Chandos.[19]

Chandos succeeded in mounting a considerable raid into the duc d'Anjou's territories in October; according to Froissart, he and the earl of Pembroke quarrelled over the plans for this expedition, Pembroke refusing to serve under a mere banneret. Pembroke mounted his own foray, but was ambushed and had to be rescued by Chandos. Certainly there is little sign of coordination in the English military activities in 1369; the prince had still moved no further than Cognac, where he had taken up residence in September. The rest of the year passed without any sign of a major campaign being mounted by either side. The usual minor raids continued, and about this time the great abbey at Saint-Savin near Chauvigny was taken by French troops based at La Roche-Posay on the north-eastern border of Poitou. Chandos, who appears to have been at Poitiers for Christmas, set out to recapture it by night on New Year's Eve with a small band of companions. The attempt failed, and Chandos returned towards Poitiers. At Chauvigny he stopped, saying that he would spend the night there; fires were lit, and he and some of his men stayed there. The others continued towards Poitiers. Early the next morning came news that a small band of French were in the neighbourhood, and Chandos, although he had only forty or so men with him, set off in pursuit. At Lussac-les-Châteaux he came up with the enemy, while the other part of his company, who were also eager to attack the raiders, were still a little way off. Chandos's men dismounted and attacked, but as Chandos moved forward, encumbered by an over-long surcoat embroidered with his arms, he slipped and fell on the frosty ground. A French squire stabbed him in the face with a dagger; he wore no vizor, and was blind in one eye, so failed to avoid the blow. He fell to the ground, while the battle raged around him. The combined English forces were victorious, and hastened to get Chandos to a near-by castle, but he died the next day. Such, in bare outline, is Froissart's account of Chandos's death, embellished by many romantic details and far from certain in its main points. But whatever the actual manoeuvres before and during the skirmish at

Lussac, the loss to the English was very serious. Chandos was the finest English captain of the day, an expert in the affairs of Gascony, whose good relations with the French court made him invaluable as a diplomat; he was also the prince's oldest and closest friend, his constant companion for over thirty years. The English had lost two of their best captains within six months; the prince had lost two of his great comrades-in-arms, and he himself remained bedridden. In the previous year, two other members of the same group of captains who had contributed so much to the prince's successes, the earls of Suffolk and Warwick, had also died. The initiative was now almost entirely with the French.[20]

The measure of French success was that major towns were transferring their allegiance peacefully, such as Agen and Villeneuve in the Garonne and Lot valleys, which represented a serious loss to the English. Even more dangerous was the loss of Bazas, south of the Garonne on the borders of the Landes, and only forty miles from Bordeaux itself, which was handed over in the first quarter of the year. Both sides now prepared for a major and decisive campaign. Charles V, who had formally announced the confiscation of Aquitaine in November 1369, repeated the sentence in June 1370; Edward reiterated his resumption of *ressort* in Aquitaine, to underline his claim to sovereignty there as king of France. After these opening shots of propaganda, the military preparations began. The French persuaded du Guesclin to return from Spain, where he had been since Enrique's successful invasion of Castile in 1368-9. The duc d'Anjou and the duc de Berry, with the comte d'Armagnac, were to mount a double offensive, a pincer movement from north and south: it was said to be directed at Angoulême, in the hope of capturing the prince himself. The English riposte was to be a campaign in Normandy led by the veteran of the wars in Brittany, Sir Robert Knolles, and a campaign in Gascony, on which the prince would be assisted by John of Gaunt. Gaunt was sent with a small retinue only, of 310 men-at-arms and 500 archers. He was also given some political powers; but these were nothing like so wide as those normally given to a king's lieutenant, and the prince's government was evidently regarded by Edward as still capable of functioning in the normal way. Gaunt's commission enabled him to punish rebels or reward loyalty; in other words, he could support military action by a limited range of civil activities, such as exercising justice on rebels or giving charters of privilege to loyal towns. He had no fiscal powers whatever. Gaunt's contingent was not the only one to go to Aquitaine that summer: Sir Walter Huet was sent with 200 men-at-arms and 300 archers.[21]

Gaunt arrived at Bordeaux during July, and joined the prince, probably at Angoulême. The French offensive had not yet begun in earnest, but du Guesclin was active in the area round Limoges, and diplomatic manoeuvres for the surrender of Limoges itself had begun. However, there was a strong English garrison in the castle. On 11 August, the duc de Berry left his headquarters at Bourges, and marched on Limoges, arriving there on 21 August. Limoges consisted, like many French towns, of two distinct quarters, the town, dominated by the castle, and the city, dominated by the cathedral. The town, well walled and garrisoned, made no move to surrender, and the duc de Berry concentrated on the city, which had no English forces in it. Its lord, the bishop of Limoges, Pierre du Cros, was trusted by the prince, and he was godfather to the prince's eldest son Edward. But on receiving the French overtures he made no resistance, and indeed seems to have been enthusiastic about transferring his allegiance; one late chronicle even says that he spread rumours of the prince's death in order to persuade the citizens. On 24 August the city surrendered to the duc de Berry, who entered by the porte Escudière during the morning to cries of 'Montjoie, Saint-Denis!' He left the same day, having installed a small French garrison.[22]

The news of the bishop's defection reached the prince, probably still at Angoulême, just before the end of August. His army was already assembled, and he was able to leave on 7 September, accompanied by Gaunt, Edmund of Langley, the earl of Pembroke and the captal de Buch. Froissart is probably correct in saying that the prince was carried in a litter, because this was his first substantial journey for over two years. The total force seems to have been about 1,200 men-at-arms, 1,000 archers and as many footsoldiers – by no means a large body in the face of a considerable French presence in the area: both du Guesclin and the duc de Berry were near-by. Covering the sixty miles between Angoulême and Limoges in a week of steady marches, the prince and his men arrived outside the city on about 14 September, and made their base in the town, which had not been attacked by the French. The town was by far the largest part of the whole, with some 12,000 inhabitants; the city was about one fifth the size, holding 2,500 people, a number perhaps swelled by refugees from the countryside and by the French garrison to over 3,000. Because of the presence of French troops in the neighbourhood, a quick resolution of the siege was needed before a relief force was brought up. The prince and his fellow-commanders decided to drive a mine under the walls. This was quickly done, and five days later, early on the morning of 19 September, the mine was fired, bringing down a large portion of the wall. The garrison, taken by surprise, fought a defensive action in the streets. By mid morning the resistance had been overcome sufficiently for the leaders of the army to enter the town; but the garrison held out in a position near the cathedral. The bishop was taken prisoner and brought to the prince, who, according to Froissart, threatened to execute him. He was in fact released and allowed to go to Avignon shortly afterwards. At the same time, Gaunt, Edmund and Pembroke were engaged in an attack on the French garrison, who put up a brave resistance. In the end, the two knights and a squire who led the French troops surrendered: all three were held to ransom, and the squire, Roger de Beaufort, remained in captivity until at least 1375, despite the efforts of his uncle, by then elected Pope as Gregory XI, to obtain his release. The main body of English troops were occupied in pillaging the town: Froissart portrays them as engaging in a mass slaughter, but much more reliable sources put the number of dead at about 300, or one in ten of the population. In fact, the number of dead may well have been less than the number of those carrying arms in defence of the city, estimated at about 500. Froissart's vivid picture probably arises from two sources: he is portraying in conventional terms the taking of a city by storm, and his information may have come from a source strongly hostile to the prince. Under the accepted laws of war at the time, a city taken by assault was entirely at the mercy of its conquerors. However, it was extremely rare for a place of the importance of Limoges to be taken in this way, and Froissart is merely depicting what would have been expected to happen under such circumstances. None of the sources which might be expected to make capital, for propaganda purposes, out of such a massacre, even mention it: the references in the papal and French records are purely factual, referring to some destruction of property. The English chronicler Walsingham comes nearest to Froissart, speaking of the prince's wrath and the obstinacy of the inhabitants: he says that after the city was captured, 'the prince almost totally destroyed it and killed all those he found there, a few only being spared their lives and taken prisoner'. Chandos Herald – and here perhaps is the source of both Froissart and Walsingham – says briefly and vaguely: 'But everyone there was killed or taken.'

In terms of those bearing arms in defence of the city, this was probably true. The chronicle in the cartulary of the town of Limoges says that 'all those of the city, men, women and clergy, were taken prisoner, the bishop and the abbot of Saint-Martial, except for the monks of La Règle; and they pillaged the city and then set it on fire'. The Saint-Martial chronicles give the figure of 300 dead quoted above, but do not mention prisoners, while the monk of Uzerche mentions the despoiling of churches and capture of clergy, saying that monasteries and churches were polluted by men being killed in them. The biographer of Urban V mentions the razing of the city and taking of prisoners, but no deaths. In short, the evidence for the famous massacre of civilians is to be found only in Froissart's rhetoric.[23]

Whatever the fate of the inhabitants, the prince took his revenge on the city itself, which was systematically destroyed. Only the abbaye de la Règle and some property belonging to the pro-English canons of the cathedral were left intact. Even the cathedral and its bell tower were damaged: most of the city was literally razed to the ground, either by burning or by actual demolition, while any portable property was carried off. It was to be 150 years before the last repairs were completed. Leaving this monument as an example to other possible rebels, the prince returned to Angoulême. But the very destruction of the city was an admission of weakness, that he could not hope to re-establish his authority and had to content himself with trying to overawe his restless subjects.[24]

This was the prince's last major action as ruler of Aquitaine. The expedition seems to have weakened his health, and to add to his troubles he returned to Angoulême to find that his eldest son, Edward, had died during the campaign. He decided to go back to England and that autumn arrangements for his return were made while he stayed at Cognac. In December the prince's messenger, John Dagenet, who had served him for nearly thirty years, was sent by Edward to Gascony, with letters seeking the prince's approval of a treaty with the king of Navarre which had been negotiated at the beginning of the month at Clarendon. The objects of the alliance were only vaguely stated, but it seems to have been intended as a basis for a new campaign in Normandy. However, the prince refused to ratify the treaty, and as his assent was specifically required by its terms, the project came to nothing. The reasons for this refusal are obscure; Edward, writing to Charles of Navarre to inform him, is naturally vague: 'for certain great and weighty reasons which move him to do so, he neither wishes nor is able, to keep his honour and estate, to assent or agree to the said treaty'. The most likely conjecture is that the prince remembered all too clearly Charles's deceptions during the Spanish campaign, and regarded him as totally untrustworthy.[25]

In January, the prince, Joan and Richard, now four, with a large retinue, sailed for Plymouth; when they arrived, the prince had to spend some weeks at Plympton priory, evidently to recover his strength, before continuing the journey, and the king sent Guy Bryan, one of the admirals of the fleet, to see him there. The prince reached London on 19 April, where he was welcomed by the mayor and citizens and by a band of minstrels. To mark the occasion, the city presented him with a complete service of plate, paid for by a subscription raised in January, to the value of nearly £700.

> Three leading goldsmiths provided it, over 270 items, ranging from handled cups (hanappes) to basins and lavers, from 60 salts to 120 deep plates (esqueles). It was a working outfit for a soldier and administrator, practical, run of the mill stuff, and presumably welcome as such both to the prince and to the suppliers.

The citizens escorted him to John of Gaunt's palace at the Savoy, and then dispersed. The plate was not ready until December, when Peter Lacy accepted it on behalf of the prince; it was the princess who wrote to thank the Londoners for their gift.[26]

The prince returned to a very different England from that he had left eight years earlier. His father was now also an invalid, and since the death of queen Philippa in August 1369 he had come increasingly under the influence of his mistress, Alice Perrers. Edward had lost interest in politics, and spent most of his time in the country. He was only too pleased to let the prince take his place as far as possible; Gaunt, who had acted as his deputy earlier, was still in Gascony. At the end of April, a convocation of the clergy of the see of Canterbury was held at St Paul's, and a difficulty arose over the granting of taxation for the war with France; so at the end of the convocation it was prorogued to the Savoy, where the prince and a number of magnates first begged the clergy to grant £50,000, and then demanded it: the grant was duly made on 3 May. On two other occasions during the following three years, the papal collector of taxes in England, addressing a petition to the king's council, found the prince presiding over the council. On another royal occasion, in February 1372, the prince welcomed John of Gaunt and his new bride, Constanza, claimant to her father Pedro's throne, on their arrival in London, riding out with the mayor and citizens to meet them. They returned through Cheapside, the beauty of Constanza's younger sister Isabel attracting much attention, to Gaunt's palace.[27]

The prince's movements and activities after his return to England are very sparsely documented. The chroniclers give the impression that he was a sick man for much of the time, and there is little evidence to be set against this. He does not seem to have travelled much; there are references to messengers going to and fro between him and the king on urgent business when they were not far apart; and in August 1371, Joan was at Marlborough for queen Philippa's annual memorial service without the prince. He appears to have attended the Garter feast each year from 1372 to 1376, or to have been expected to do so, as robes were always prepared for him. On the other hand, he must have been deeply involved in the plans for a double offensive against France in the year following his return, 1372. In March, plans were set in motion for a campaign by Pembroke in Aquitaine, and a campaign to be led by the king and the prince in northern France. In addition, Gaunt was planning an expedition to Castile. All these plans were brought to nothing when Pembroke's expedition, which was the first to leave, was annihilated by a Castilian fleet off La Rochelle on 22 June, and its leaders, including Pembroke and Guichard d'Angle, captured. Edward ordered Gaunt to join him for a massive naval expedition instead, to gather at Sandwich in mid August. The expedition was originally intended to be purely naval, but French forces were now threatening La Rochelle, and Edward intended to sail to its relief. In addition to Edward, the prince and Gaunt, Edmund of Langley, and the earls of Warwick, Suffolk, Salisbury, March and Hereford were assembled with their retinues when the king went on board his flagship, the *Gracedieu*, on 27 August. The winds were unfavourable, and continued to be so; it took three weeks to get to Winchelsea, and by then news had come of two disasters, the capture of the captal de Buch, one of the most loyal supporters of the English and of the prince, on 23 August, and the surrender of La Rochelle on 7 September. After waiting another fortnight, the force was disbanded on 6 October, an unhappy end to a year that had brought nothing but reverses for the English. It had also been an expensive episode: the prince's advance on war wages alone amounted to £2,000.[28]

The disasters of the summer of 1372 did not improve the political situation at home; a parliament due to meet on 13 October, when the king would have been absent, was delayed until 3 November: the prince's attendance was specially requested: 'as he loves the king and his honour and his own, to attend the parliament . . . as the king would not that business so difficult be treated or directed without the said prince's advice and counsel'. The business in question was the prince's formal surrender of Aquitaine to his father. At a ceremony in the White Chamber on 5 November, Guy Bryan, as spokesman for the prince, explained to the assembled lords – the commons were not present – how the costs of administering Gascony exceeded the revenues, and said that the prince had written to the king to explain this.

And the said prince himself came to England and explained and set out to the king and his council the aforesaid reasons and other later ones, and for the aforesaid reasons and other notable causes the said prince surrendered the principality to the king . . . together with the charters and other deeds in connection with the granting of the principality . . . And the charters and deeds were displayed in the presence of the king and the prelates and magnates and the prince was asked by the said Sir Guy if it was his wish (to surrender the principality) and he said yes, and admitted and acknowledged the charters and deeds.[29]

The parliaments of these years were growing increasingly restless, reflecting the country's discontent: war subsidies for a successful foreign war were one matter, but paying for a series of defeats was another. The parliament of 1371 had led to the replacement of the chancellor and treasurer; that of October 1373 was even more difficult. The king and his advisers tried to obtain a subsidy before the petitions of the parliament were heard, reversing the usual order of proceedings; at which the assembly referred the matter to a committee of eight magnates. Gaunt had led a massive and unsuccessful raid which had marched through France from Calais to Bordeaux with little gain to show for it and the loss of half his men. Gaunt himself, preoccupied with his claim to the Castilian throne, was increasingly inclined towards a peace settlement with France, and there was a growing division between those who, like him, favoured peace, and those who favoured continued war, who looked to the prince for leadership. Beside the problems of royal taxation, there were new difficulties over papal taxes, which Gregory XI was trying to enforce in order to strengthen the papacy, in the hope of eventually launching a new crusade in Palestine. Such taxes were regarded with extreme suspicion by the king and his ministers, as they diminished the ability of the clergy to provide funds for royal demands; and the clerical contribution to royal revenue was a very large proportion of the whole. In 1373, just after Whitsun, a council was held at Westminster to debate the papal demand for this tax, at which the prince presided. A distinguished assembly of spiritual and temporal lords was assembled, together with doctors of theology and canon and civil lawyers. The Pope's demand was to be debated both on theological grounds and on the supposed admission of the Pope as chief of the realm of England by king John. The theological argument was taken first, and the archbishop of Canterbury said that no one could deny the Pope's lordship, and the bishops agreed. The Benedictine monk Uthred of Boldon then quoted the doctrine of the two swords, but John Mardisley, a Franciscan who had been invited to attend by the king, replied by quoting Scripture, 'Put up thy sword into the sheath', to show that Boldon's text was irrelevant, and went on to argue against the Pope's possession of temporal powers of any kind. He was supported by Thomas Ashborne, an Austin friar, who boldly appealed to the prince to intervene: 'You, my lord prince, used to be Paul, bearing the sword; but because you have laid down the Lord's sword, Peter does not know Paul. Lift up your sword and Peter shall know Paul again' – a broad hint that pressure from the temporal authority was needed. When they had finished, the archbishop was dissatisfied: the chronicler makes him say, 'There were good counsels in England before the friars', to which the prince answered that they had only had to come there because of his stupidity: 'We would have lost the kingdom following your advice.' The next day the archbishop tried to escape from his dilemma by saying that he did not know how to reply. The prince insisted that he must give a ruling: 'You ass, it is your duty to guide us all,' are the chronicler's words. Whittlesey then said that he would accept that the Pope should not be lord here, a formula which avoided actually denying the Pope's claim. The bishops and Uthred of Boldon followed suit. 'Where are your two swords then?' the prince is reported to have asked. 'My lord, I am better advised than I was,' came the answer.[30]

The speeches in this episode are undoubtedly fiction; but they indicate the chronicler's assessment of the prince's attitude in such matters. He is represented as practical and forthright, concerned with good government of England rather than theological niceties;

the speech given to Ashborne indicates that he was still regarded as the leader who might yet resolve England's difficulties. One curious text reflecting the admiration for the prince and the hope placed in him for the future has survived, the *Prophecies of Robert of Bridlington* (often attributed to his saintly namesake John). This consists of the usual medieval device of *ex post facto* prophecy – writing a series of verses alluding obscurely to past events, and then adding speculative ones about the future. The whole is then attributed to an author who died before any of the events took place; and the accuracy of the first part guarantees the reliability of the second. The most famous example was Geoffrey of Monmouth's *Prophetia Merlini*, of the mid twelfth century; but in succeeding centuries it was frequently used as a means of writing political pamphlets, partly because such activities could be dangerous. Misuse of the Bridlington prophecies themselves led a doctor of theology to be hanged in 1402. The prophecies are very difficult to date precisely; their obscurity in alluding to past events is deliberate, so that the transition to future events is not readily seen. However, the allusions in the eighth chapter imply that they were written at a time when there were difficulties over the fulfilment of the treaty of Brétigny, and when the king could reasonably be expected to complete fifty years of his reign and celebrate his jubilee, which would give a date of 1365 or later, possibly around 1370. The ninth chapter is undoubtedly prophetic: the writer looks forward to the renewal of England's prosperity after the prince comes to the throne on his father's death. The prince is praised in extravagant terms; his reign would bring abundance of material wealth and renewed martial vigour, and he would lead a new expedition to France which would conquer most of the kingdom. The earlier parts of the poem are quoted in a number of other sources, notably a chronicle from Kirkstall Abbey ending in 1360, but of uncertain date, which refers to the prince as 'our Judas Maccabeus' (after the great Jewish leader), while the king's epithet is the less prominent figure of Mattathias.[31]

But these high hopes were not to be fulfilled. There is so little record of the prince's activities in 1374–5 that it must be assumed that he was seriously ill for much of the time. He was probably at Berkhamsted in February 1374, when a charter was issued by him and his council: John Harewell, the erstwhile chancellor of Gascony, remained his chief adviser, but the other names, with the exception of Nigel Loring and William Spridlington, are all of more recent standing: Aubrey Vere, Hugh Segrave, Arnold Savage,

John Maynard, the last being his steward. John Fordham had been his secretary since at least 1368, but Alan Stokes had only replaced Peter Lacy as receiver-general in 1372. In June 1375 he was at Kennington; a file of over a hundred petitions to his council from about this period, many on very trivial matters, includes a number which are marked 'speak to my lord about this' (soit parler à Monsieur), which indicates that the prince was still able to take an active interest in affairs.[32]

The prince's sickness meant that John of Gaunt was the king's deputy and maker of English policy during these years. The disasters of 1372-3 were followed by a series of lesser defeats, but the cumulative effect was such that it was felt inadvisable to summon parliament in either year. By the end of 1375, both the need for new taxes and an accumulation of judicial business made further postponement impossible; writs were sent out in December for an assembly on 12 February, later prorogued to 28 April. The king attended the official opening, but it was Gaunt who was left to deal with the business of the parliament. The prince was also at the opening, but fell seriously ill again early in May and retired to Kennington. The proceedings of the parliament soon developed into a concerted attack on the management of the war, and those responsible for it, by the commons. They appointed a speaker, Sir Peter de la Mare, who presented a demand to John of Gaunt and the lords that a committee of twelve peers should help the commons, naming four bishops, one of whom may have been the prince's chancellor John Harewell; four earls, all of whom were the sons of the prince's fellow-commanders: Warwick, Suffolk, Stafford and March; and four barons, one of whom was the son of Sir Richard Stafford, another of the prince's close associates. They were 'presumably those who were expected to be most sympathetic to the commons' complaints'; but it is also interesting that they represent exactly the heirs of the great war-leaders of the previous generation, showing how the commons hankered after the victories of previous decades. The failure of the war effort was blamed by both sides on lack of funds, and by the military leaders on John of Gaunt's efforts to make peace at the Bruges conference in 1375, when a truce had been arranged just as a promising offensive had been mounted in Brittany. Scapegoats were needed, and the commons soon found them: they declared that the king's lack of money was due to malpractice by those responsible for the royal finances, naming Lord Latimer and Richard Lyons, a prominent

London merchant, to whom were added the king's favourite, Alice Perrers, who was said to be paid £200 or £300 a year from the treasury, and a number of other administrators. Two of the accused, Richard Lyons and Adam Bury, were creditors of the prince, having lent him £1,300 in or before February 1370. Richard Lyons, who evidently thought that the prince had considerable influence over the proceedings, tried to gain the prince's favour by sending a barrel of gold to him at Kennington; but the prince sent this back with a curt reply, saying that the contents of the barrel were ill-gotten gains, 'for which reason he would not accept such a present nor help the said Richard nor favour his misdeeds, but he was in close council with the commons so as to put in order the state of the kingdom and to amend extortions and wrong-doings'. The prince is said to have regretted turning away the gift, which could have been used to pay 'the knights who work for the kingdom', perhaps meaning the commons. The gift was then offered to the king, who is said to have accepted it cheerfully, on the grounds that it was his in any case. The prince's part in the parliament, despite the claims of the chronicler as to his alliance with the commons and Lyons's evident belief in his influence, does not seem to have been an active one. The roles seem to have been the other way round: the commons looked to the prince to lend authority to their proceedings, just as malcontents had always gathered around the heir to the throne in past reigns. Many knights had served under him, and looked to him as their commander in better days; but the prince seems to have been aloof from the day-to-day affairs of the assembly. There is no firm evidence to show that he had quarrelled with Gaunt in any way.[33]

At the beginning of June, the prince's illness became so grave that he was not expected to live long. He was moved to Westminster; here he made known his last wishes, enjoining the king to respect the gifts he made to his retainers, and Richard, his son, swore to observe them. The rest of the time he spent in prayer and good works; according to the pious account given by Walsingham, as Trinity Sunday approached, a day which he had always held in special reverence, he prayed that he might die on that feast. He made his will in his chamber at Westminster Palace on 7 June, the eve of the festival. Walsingham, who was a monk at St Albans, goes on to give a detailed account of his last hours. This, in view of the prince's particular attachment to that monastery, may have come from an eye-witness, but it contains one almost inexplicable episode.

Walsingham claims that Sir Richard Stury, one of the king's knights of the chamber, had been banished from court in disgrace; he had been appointed to liaise between the king and parliament, but had falsely reported that the commons intended to depose the king, 'as they had deposed his father'. Stury came to the prince on Trinity Sunday to obtain the prince's pardon: the prince told him from his deathbed that he hoped God would make an end of his evil deeds, and to Stury's renewed pleas for forgiveness replied: 'God is just, and will reward you according to your merits. I do not wish you to trouble me longer. Leave my presence and do not come to see me again.' The story sounds plausible enough; but Stury remained in high favour with the princess after his death, and was a knight of Richard II's chamber. In fact, the story probably stems from an attempt to discredit Stury, since he was later a leading member of the 'Lollard knights', who, if not actually followers of Wyclif themselves, were protectors of the heretics. These Walsingham attacked with particular venom; and this story is part of the attack. Walsingham follows by telling how the bishop of Bangor, an ardent opponent of the Lollards, had to exorcize an evil spirit before the prince was able to say more than 'I will' to the bishop's demand that he should forgive his enemies and ask pardon of God and men for his offences. Once the spirit was exorcized, the prince was able to speak properly and died 'in the full catholic faith'. Both episodes show the prince, by implication, as anti-Lollard; but his sympathies were if anything on their side, particularly over their rejection of the Pope's temporal power. The anonymous chronicler of St Mary's Abbey, York, who gives a very detailed account of the parliament, describes the prince's death in conventional terms, saying only that during this period 'he always comforted the good and loyal people of the realm, begging them to be obedient to his father and to govern loyally, and to maintain as best they could the good laws and customs in use to the profit of the kingdom and to put no faith or trust in evildoers or mistreaters of the law'.[34]

The prince died at Westminster on 8 June, Trinity Sunday, as he had wished. His death was universally lamented; not only had one of England's great warriors passed away, but the hopes for the future were dimmed. Men recalled his great victories, and every chronicler found a few high-sounding phrases in which to sum up his career:

Thus died the hope of the English: for while he lived they feared no invasion of the enemy, no onslaught of battle. Never, in his presence, did they do badly or desert the battlefield; and, as is said of Alexander the Great, he never attacked a people whom he did not conquer, he never besieged a city which he did not take.

Walsingham lists as his four great victories, Crécy, Poitiers, Nájera and Limoges. Knighton inserts an eulogy of the prince under the entry for Edward's death in the following year, an interesting indication of the decline in the king's popularity while the prince's star remained undimmed. Another writer speaks of his universal fame: 'his fortune in war during his lifetime all Christian and heathen peoples feared more than any other, as if he had been another Hector'. Thomas Brinton, bishop of Rochester, preached a sermon soon after the prince's death, which is one of the finest examples of eloquence of its day:

Any prince should excel his subjects in power, wisdom and goodness, just as the image of the Holy Trinity represents these, the Father being power, the Son wisdom and the Holy Spirit goodness. But this lord prince had all three qualities in the highest degree.

For his power appears in his glorious victories, for which he is greatly to be commended, according to the scripture, 'Let us now praise powerful and glorious men.' Above all, for his victory at Poitiers, where there was indeed with the French king such a force of armed men that ten armed knights, fighting in their own land, faced each Englishman; yet God favoured the just cause, and the French army was wonderfully scattered by the English army, and the king taken, for which deed the prince might well say of himself, 'Great was my name among the peoples.' Again, because in his deeds in Spain he restored the true king to his throne after his defeat, overthrowing the tyrant and making the kings of Navarre and Majorca almost his subjects, his great power and qualities were such that the Lord could have said to him, as to David, 'I have made thy name great among the names of the great ones of the earth.'

His wisdom appeared in his manner of acting and habit of speaking prudently, because he did not merely talk like the lords of today but was a doer of deeds, so that he never began a great work without bringing it to a praiseworthy end; and again it might be said of him, 'The prince shall be praised of the people for his wisdom.'

His goodness came principally in three things. Where the lords of this world usually oppress and afflict their tenants and land-holders, this lord always cared for his tenants, comforting them in many ways. Where other lords are usually ungrateful to those who serve with them and labour with them in wars, this lord was so generous to his servants that he made them rich and himself poor. And where earthly lords are not usually devout before God, not caring, except for form's sake, whether they hear mass or divine service, this lord was so devout in the service of the Lord that his like has never been seen in such times. And because power without wisdom is like a sword in the hands of a madman, and wisdom without goodness is called calculation, this lord is most praiseworthy because he excelled in power, wisdom and good-ness, which is contained in the image of the Trinity. And that same Trinity he worshipped above all. He is said to have been born on the Feast of the Trinity; on that same feast he paid Nature's debt; and in the church of the Holy Trinity he chose to be buried, in which his praise and remembrance shall dwell for ever; and men shall say with the psalmist, 'in the midst of the congregation I will praise him.'[35]

Brinton's sermon may have been preached when the prince's body was taken from London to Canterbury, early in October. At the end of July, the nobles and clergy were summoned to London for the prince's funeral after Michaelmas; on 22 September the countesses and duchesses of England were notified, and on the 23rd privy seal letters went to five lords, John Montacute, the earl of Salisbury's brother, Lord Luttrell, Sir Bernard Brocas, Sir Simon Burley and Sir Nicholas Dagworth. The burial took place on 5 October. Canterbury was an unusual choice; royal tombs had traditionally been at Westminster since Henry III's day, but the prince's particular devotion to the cathedral, where he had founded the two chantries in 1362 after his marriage, explains the departure from custom, the details being carefully specified in the prince's will:

When our body is taken through the town of Canterbury to the priory, two destriers covered with our arms and two men armed in our arms and in our helms shall go before our body, that is, one with our whole arms of war quartered, and the other with our arms of peace with the badges of ostrich feathers, with four banners of the same suit; each of these who carry the said banners shall have on his head a hat with our arms. He who wears the arms of war shall have an armed man by him carrying a black pennon with ostrich feathers.

His body was to be placed on a hearse between the high altar and the choir, before being interred in the Lady Chapel in the crypt, in a tomb whose details were also carefully specified. Even though the spot chosen for his tomb was directly below the high altar, this was not considered honourable enough, and it was finally erected in the Trinity Chapel beside Becket's shrine, where it has survived the ravages of six centuries remarkably well. The effigy is conventional but none the less striking in its dignity and nobility: the armed figure has a power lacking in the civilian effigy of the prince's father. Around the tomb are the alternate escutcheons of his arms of peace and war, with the two mottoes *Houmout* and *Ich diene*. The effigy looks up at a canopy painted with the image of the Trinity which had been the theme of Bishop Brinton's sermon, and which the prince had so devoutly worshipped. Above, in replica, are the armour and heraldic achievements by which the prince won his fame.[36]

The Legend

10

When all is said and done, the prince remains a shadowy figure. There are very few reliable personal anecdotes about him; there are very few recorded actions which mark him off as a distinctive character. Much of this difficulty arises from the way in which he became a legend in his own lifetime, a legend which was undoubtedly reinforced as men looked back from the domestic troubles of his son's reign to the halcyon days of the great English victories abroad. Leaving aside for the moment the legendary accounts, what can we say about the prince from the factual material, from documents rather than from rhetoric?

First, he seems to have been a very orthodox figure, and in this lay much of his success. The medieval mind was attuned to orthodoxy and rejected the unusual or unaccustomed. Edward II, who despite his bodily strength preferred menial occupations to knightly ones, and Richard II, with his highly developed aesthetic sense and love of refinement, whether in art or cookery, could not share their interests with their barons and courtiers; and on their barons their political power ultimately rested. Edward I, Edward III and the prince all shared these interests; and having a powerful physique, they not only shared but excelled in such matters as tournaments and war. Given that they were at ease in the world of the fourteenth-century knight, they were able to play their part in the expected manner. The prince's immense expenditure on armour, horses and jewels, much of which was given away to his close retainers, was exactly the behaviour expected of him: no question of commissioning great manuscripts, like the duc de Berry, or of employing artists and musicians, like the later Burgundian princes. There is a hint of artistic tastes: he employed Henry Yevele, the greatest architect of the day, and the painter Master Hugh of St Albans; but in overall terms the part they played was slight compared with the *largesse* he distributed, down-to-earth *largesse*, the generosity of a prince. Whether it spilled over into extravagance is hard to assess. The prince did indeed contract large debts; but many of these were either directly or indirectly connected with warfare. As a commander, the prince paid his own retinue; and reimbursement was often slow. This was a problem on the early campaigns; it became critical, as we have seen, on the Spanish campaign, when he himself was effectively a mercenary. In addition, many of his lavish gifts were the rewards of 'past and future good service', as his clerks described it, made to loyal followers.[1]

His successes stemmed from this same background: a world of personal bonds and common ideals. In all the prince's campaigns, a similar group of men accompanied him, men who knew and trusted each other, and who formed a close-knit group. We have already noticed the way in which the English commanders were able to work together where the French commanders did nothing but quarrel. There was one additional factor: both Edward and the prince acquired a reputation for personal courage early in their career, and the prince's chief contribution to the victory at Poitiers may well have been his reputation for bravery and the aura of his leadership. Much of the planning and strategy seems to have been the work of his subordinates; the prince's genius lay not in the detailed planning, but in the ability to hold together and inspire his men.

In matters which required skills other than those of the knight and bonds more subtle than those of comradeship, the prince was not at ease. His diplomatic and administrative record varies from the competent to the disastrous. In England, where he was well served by a loyal and able administrative staff, his estates were, by and large, competently and justly run. When it came to dealing with Spanish politics or the intricacies of Gascon affairs, he and his advisers were out of their depth. Part of the problems were those of background. English diplomacy was still in its infancy: witness Edward's ill-starred efforts at securing alliances in the Low Countries in the early stages of the French war. The French could draw on the intellectual resources of the university of Paris and of the Papal Curia; the English had no such reserves. In terms of administration, the English kings had developed a remarkably advanced administrative machinery, whose shape and workings are much clearer to us with the benefit of hindsight than they may have been to the rulers themselves. Hence the distinction between England and Gascony was not appreciated by the prince and his counsellors: a unified system of regular taxation in return for representation must have seemed a perfectly logical procedure, whereas local customs and privileges were central to the Gascon way of life. There is some indication, too, that the prince's character may have been a handicap: as a successful man of action, he was impatient of diplomatic and administrative details, and tended to respond bluntly to subtleties or evasions. In yet another matter the prince showed his lack of diplomatic skill. However happy his marriage to Joan of Kent may have been, in an age when royal marriages were a valuable and accepted diplomatic weapon it was an astonishing step to have taken. Edward does not seem to have been particularly angry with his son: but it is interesting to notice how the French chroniclers expected him to be, schooled as they were in the ways of a court where such matters were handled more astutely. Again and again Charles V compensated by marriage alliances for the damage caused by the English armies; and in the long run his strategy gave the better results.

Of the prince's private life we know very little: there are no personal letters, no private anecdotes. Only in matters of religion is there a hint of a more than formal attitude. Public piety was required of kings and princes, and it may be that his devotion went no further. Pilgrimages to the great shrines of England before a campaign, magnificent gifts to the abbey of Vale Royal, all these were public and expected acts. The prince's devotion to the Trinity did exceed conventional piety. All the chroniclers insist on his particular devotion to the Trinity. This was a relatively new cult in terms of the Church as a whole, having only been established as a general festival by Pope John XXII in 1333. However, the cult of the Trinity had been established by Becket at Canterbury on his consecration in 1162, and the prince's devotion indicates yet another link between himself and the cathedral there. The earliest portrait of him is a lead 'badge', now in the British Museum, which shows him kneeling before the Trinity, encircled by the garter. The purpose of this remarkable object is unknown: whether it was a funeral badge, a later cast from a mould used to make a gold or silver badge or even a decoration for the plasterwork of a room has not yet been decided. It is, however, striking confirmation of the prince's assertion, when founding the chantry chapels at Canterbury, that he always worshipped the Trinity with special devotion: and the same pose recurs in the frontispiece to one of the manuscripts of Chandos Herald's life of the prince, written some ten years after his death. The prince seems to have held a great feast each year on Trinity Sunday, as witness the sixteen swans ordered for that of 1357. His devotion was widely known: when Bishop Grandisson received news of the victory of Poitiers, he ordered thanksgivings to be celebrated, as the king had requested, but in his letter to his clergy he specifically invoked the name of the Trinity in connection with the victory, and ordered the mass for Trinity Sunday to be celebrated. Finally, there is the superb tester of the Trinity, now much defaced, above the prince's tomb.[2]

The prince also refounded the college of *Boni Homines* at Ashridge in Hertfordshire, originally created by Edmund earl of Cornwall in 1285, increasing the number of canons from seven to twenty. This was done in 1376, shortly before his death; but he had long been interested in the Order. In 1358, he had prevailed on William Edington, bishop of Winchester, who had been in charge of his affairs during his absence in 1355–7, to remodel a new religious foundation at the bishop's native village of Edington into a college of *Boni Homines*. This curious Order, about whose status and origins little is known, never grew beyond these two houses. Their constitutions were similar to those of the Augustine canons, but they wore an unusual sky-blue habit. In his will, the prince left them 'our great table of gold and silver full of precious relics and in the midst a cross of the wood of the True Cross'. He had already waived his rights over elections and over the revenues of the house during a vacancy in the rectorship. These acts of piety, like the provision of a new chaplain at the chantry chapel at Trematon in 1355, or the appointment of a new hermit at Restormel, derived from his responsibilities as duke of Cornwall; but the bequest to Ashridge goes far beyond what was required.[3]

Lastly, there is the prince's friendship for Thomas, abbot of

St Albans from 1349 to 1396. This comes to us from the abbey chronicles, written some time later; it may have been stressed in order to establish a claim to royal favour. The prince is said to have revered him like a father, and to have become a member of the abbey's confraternity; the abbot in turn found him a trusty ally, always willing to listen to problems and to give advice and help. In a quarrel between the abbot and Sir Gerard Witherington, the prince intervened on the abbot's side; his manner is described as 'panting with rage', 'furious'. Equally, when the monks at Canterbury refused to attend a general chapter and imprisoned the messenger from St Albans, the prince was 'horribly enraged' and swore by Our Lady that he would set the man free. However, some suspicion is cast on the warmth of the prince's relationship with the abbey when we find the abbot heading a list of malefactors said to have robbed the prince of £331 in 1353.[4]

The legends which grew up around the prince stem from the spectacular nature of his victories rather than from his character. Before discussing the contemporary versions of such stories, however, there is the problem of his traditional nickname: the Black Prince. This was first used by John Leland in his *Collectanea*, a manuscript anthology of earlier writers on British history dating from the 1530s and 1540s, but not later than 1548. Leland, in summarizing a chronicle by John Warkworth of Peterhouse, Cambridge, refers to how 'the blake prince wan a feld of the frenchmen by Chaveney', and he also gives this name in Latin when summarizing the *Eulogium Historiarum: Ibidem compare Itinerarium Edwardi Principis cog: Nigri*. Neither the *Eulogium* nor the manuscript of Warkworth's chronicle contain the words 'the black prince', nor does Caxton's *Chronicle* from which Warkworth was copying. Many guesses have been made as to the origin of the name, chiefly centring on black armour. All that can be said for certain is that it was sufficiently current in Leland's time for him to recognize it as the usual way of referring to the prince. I would suggest that its true origin may be in pageantry, in that a tradition had grown up of representing the prince in black armour. Furthermore, the likely period for the general use of such name to become established would be under Edward IV. Chronicles contemporary with the prince, including the *Eulogium*, often refer to him as Edward the Fourth, anticipating his succession to the throne. With the coronation of Edward IV, this name became

confusing, and another had to be found. He is also, but less com-
monly, called Edward of Woodstock in contemporary works, and
this evidently failed to catch on. Leland's sources were primarily
English, so that the suggestion that the French called him *le neoir*
seems unlikely.[5]

The traditional character of the Black Prince to be found in most
histories of the period owes most of its colour to the chronicles of
Jean Froissart. I have deliberately used Froissart very sparingly in
the present book. He is a powerful and picturesque writer, but his
substance, in Derek Brewer's phrase, is 'gossip raised to the height
of genius'. It is all too easy to be lured astray by him into a tangle of
half-truths and vivid tableaux. In terms of facts, even when he was
an eyewitness, he is not to be relied on. Two examples will suffice,
because his faults are already well-known. In 1361, he was at
Berkhamsted with the royal household and the prince. He
describes this as the last occasion on which the prince and princess
saw the king and queen before leaving for Aquitaine, and goes on
to place their departure in the following February. This has led most
historians to misdate the feast to 1362, and the prince's departure to
February 1363. In fact, the prince left in June 1363, and had almost
certainly seen the king and queen during that spring. Equally,
Froissart's account of the prince's arrival in Aquitaine is purely
imaginary. Another imaginary itinerary is given for the arrival of
king John in 1357. Knowing that the usual route to London from
the coast was from Dover via Canterbury to the city, this is what
Froissart describes, while in fact the prince and king John landed at
Plymouth and came via Salisbury.[6]

Froissart undoubtedly formed a collection of chronicles, but he
far preferred to record the stories told by knights about their
exploits. Here lies his real value. Monastic chroniclers, often with
access to royal documents, give us official history, perhaps punctu-
ated by a rhetorical outburst or two against the wickedness of the
world. Froissart gives that world as it saw itself: not as it was, but as
it would like to have been. The mirror distorts for lack of distance;
the image is blurred by its very closeness. But there are other factors
at work as well as this lack of perspective. In the absence of
Froissart's 'sources', it is impossible to say how far his stories have
been improved in the telling.[7]

There is however, some evidence that stories in the same vein
were in circulation independently of his chronicle. One of these is
the story of John of Gaunt's fight with one of the captains defending

Limoges in 1370, which is said to have taken place in one of the mines driven under the walls by the besiegers, and ends with the latter becoming Gaunt's brother-in-arms. There is also the story of how Joan of Kent won the prince as her husband, from the same chronicle. This is on the face of it a delightful romantic episode; the chronicler tells how the prince was asked by 'the noble English lord called milord Brocas' (he is possibly thinking of Sir Bernard Brocas who had been with him at Poitiers) to arrange a match between him and Joan of Kent. The prince agreed to do so, but was himself much taken by the countess. When he finally pressed Brocas's suit, the countess declared that she would never remarry, saying that her heart belonged to the most noble knight under heaven. The prince, who had already declared that, were it not for their kinship, he would be very ready to fall in love with her, now pressed her to declare the name of this knight, and after much feigned evasion, was told that it was he himself. At this he vowed that he would take no other wife. But the chronicler goes on to explain that Edward III was furious at his son's betrothal, and banished the pair to Gascony after their marriage, because everyone in England was so incensed that their hero should have been taken in by such a scheming adventuress. In fact, the story is a piece of gossip such as *France-Dimanche* might print about Prince Charles today, but with political overtones designed to discredit the prince and the king's appointment of him as ruler of Aquitaine.[8]

Froissart, had he used the story, might well have discarded the political overtones, from the indications we have of his methods of work. All these point to more considerable reworking of his raw material than is sometimes admitted.

First, there is the question of Froissart's literary background. He tells us himself that his first efforts were in verse, and many of his verses survive, including the huge romance *Meliador*, an Arthurian fantasy in the traditional manner, in which tournaments take up much of the surviving 30,000 lines. The first version of *Meliador* probably antedates the first version of the *Chronicles*, and some of the techniques of composition used in it reappear in the *Chronicles*. Some of them were helpful to Froissart as historian: the 'entrelacement' or intermingling of different themes practised by the writers of romance was valuable when it came to dealing with the enormous panorama of events included in the *Chronicles*: he moves easily from Brittany to Spain, Spain to Scotland, in different chapters, just as the poet would recount the deeds of the various heroes of his romance by moving from one adventure to another completely separate incident, yet always retaining sight of the overall pattern. On the other hand, the poet has liberty to invent detail at will: the historian has not. I would suggest that this is Froissart's weakness, a penchant for the vivid scene wherever his original source permits such an embellishment.

This comes out most clearly in Froissart's reworking of Jean Le Bel. There are three versions of the early part of the *Chronicles*: the standard version, where Jean Le Bel's chronicle is included almost entire, in substance if not *verbatim*, the later Amiens manuscript where Le Bel's contribution is somewhat reduced, and the much reworked Rome manuscript of 1400. Jean Le Bel himself was not only Froissart's major source, but a model for his attitude to his material. Le Bel came from a rich bourgeois family, and was a canon of Saint-Lambert at Liège. Like many canons, including Froissart himself, he lived a largely secular existence; a pen portrait of Le Bel by a contemporary describes him as leading the life of a noble, with a large retinue and great display of wealth. Le Bel's work is written in a fluent, even racy style; he often uses hearsay evidence, admitting that it is only gossip and sometimes querying it, but there is disagreement as to whether he used written sources to any extent. The result is often indistinguishable from Froissart's own work, and only the discovery of a unique manuscript of Le Bel's chronicle has shown how heavily Froissart's first version drew on him.[9]

Froissart's later reworkings, which can be compared and analysed in terms of changing attitudes and patronage, do not concern us here, though they are a fascinating and scarcely explored field. The first version shows us Froissart's attitude to his sources, rather than to what he had previously written. As a first sample, let us take king Philip's movements after the battle of Crécy. Le Bel writes:

This battle, so damaging to the French, went on till midnight, because it was almost night when it began, and the French king and those of his company were unable to reach the scene of combat that day. The king had to leave the field, and his men led him away in great sorrow, despite both him and Sir John of Hainault who was there to guard both his body and his honour, and made them ride on that night until they reached Labroye. There the king rested, very ill at ease, and the next day went to Amiens . . .[10]

Froissart embroiders this by adding a little scene straight out of *Meliador*:

> Very late in the evening, as the light failed, king Philip left, very ill at ease (and with good reason) with only five barons with him: they were Sir John of Hainault, the first and nearest to him, and the lords of Montmorency, Beaujeu, d'Aubigny and Montsaut. The king rode away, lamenting and complaining of his men, as far as the castle of Labroye. When he came to the gate, he found it barred and the drawbridge raised, because it was the dead of night and pitch dark. Then the king called the captain of the castle, because he wished to enter; he was summoned, and came to the watchtower, demanding to know who was knocking at such an hour. King Philip, who heard the voices, answered: 'Open, open, captain, it is the unfortunate king of France.' The captain at once came down, because he recognised the king's voice, and had already heard of the defeat from fugitives who had come past the castle: he lowered the bridge and opened the gate.[11]

That this is an embroidery is confirmed by its deletion in the second version. But other embroideries in the romantic style are retained in all three versions. Let us take three of the chief episodes in the prince's career and see how Froissart deals with them. First, there is the famous episode at Crécy when the commanders with the prince sent to the king to ask for help. The three versions of the conversation between the knight and the king vary considerably:

> And because the prince's guardians and servants saw themselves in danger, they sent a knight from their ranks to the king, who was positioned higher up the slope, on the mound of a windmill, to ask for help. The knight said, when he came to the king: 'My lord, the earl of Warwick, the earl of Oxford and Sir Reginald Cobham who are with your son the prince are hard pressed and the French are fighting bitterly. So they beg you and your division to come and help them to beat off this danger, because if the attack goes on much longer, they fear that your son will not be able to hold them off.' The king replied to the knight, who was called Sir Thomas Norwich, 'Sir Thomas, my son is neither dead nor beaten to the ground nor so badly wounded that he cannot help himself?' 'No, my lord, but he is very hard pressed and badly in need of your help.' 'Sir Thomas', said the

king, 'go back to him and those who sent you and tell them from me that they are not to send to me again for help, whatever happens, so long as my son is alive. Tell them that my orders are that they are to let the boy win his spurs; for I wish the day to be his, if God so wills it, and that he and his companions shall have the honour of it.' [Original version][12]

At one point the prince of Wales' division wavered and was hard pressed. And two English knights came from the prince's division to the king and said: 'Sire, please come and help your son, because he is hard pressed.' Then the king asked if he was wounded or harmed, and they said 'Yes, but not badly.' Then the king replied: 'Go back to him and do not come back to me until he is so harmed that he cannot help himself; let the boy win his spurs.' [Amiens version][13]

. . . and a knight came from the earl of Warwick. He was taken to the king and said: 'Dear lord, I have been sent by the bodyguard of your son the prince, and to let you know that they are afraid that the French attack will overwhelm them, because it is too fierce.' Then the king replied: 'How is my son?' 'In God's name, my lord,' answered the knight, 'he is still strong and healthy and in good condition.' Then the king said, 'Go on, go on, back to those who sent you, and say from me that it is time the boy won his spurs and do not come to seek me again as long as he can hold a sword blade in his hand; if it please God and Saint George, the day shall be his.' [Rome version][14]

The episode of the prince's request for help is well documented in other chronicles. Froissart adds to it three details: the king's position 'on the mound of a windmill' (original and Rome version), a conversation between a knight or knights and the king, and the king's answer. The gist of the conversation centres on two ideas: the prince is to win his spurs, and is to have the glory of the day. Now Froissart does not mention the knighting of the prince at Saint-Vaast at the beginning of the campaign: but he evidently knew that the prince was knighted during the Crécy campaign, and associated it with the prince's valour at the battle itself. Froissart also knew that little or no help was sent to the prince, but preferred to attribute a chivalrous rather than a tactical reason to the king's refusal. Furthermore, he appears to have visited the site of Crécy and to have noted the windmill – or ruins of it, if the *Chronique*

Normande story that it was burnt after the battle is correct. All these details are woven together into a vignette. It can be argued that he had access to eyewitnesses of the battle, and that the anecdote is true: but the chief flaw is that even in the heat of battle, the king was unlikely to speak of his son 'winning his spurs' when he had already been knighted and had fought with some distinction at Caen.

Froissart inherited other traditional devices from historians, notably the longer speeches which he inserts throughout the *Chronicles*. These have a long and respectable ancestry going back to classical historians; even Baker feels obliged to produce a suitable speech for the prince before Poitiers. This is a different, less dramatic, and much more recognizable type of invention than the conversation examined above; it is primarily his reworking of material in a romantic style that produces the most famous scenes. Another example of this is the supper given by the prince for king John after the battle of Poitiers. Here we have a clear but highly rhetorical account of the same events by Geoffrey Baker, writing within three or four years of the battle, to set against Froissart's version.

Among those half dead and scarcely breathing was found Sir James Audley; placed on a broad shield, and carried reverently by his companions in arms, he was borne to the prince's lodgings. His whole household were thankful that he had been found, and the prince left his seat next to the king, with whom he was about to dine; he brought him back to life by his praiseworthy attention, and almost in tears kissed the cold lips, stained with blood, of his scarcely breathing friend. The prince had him stripped of his armour and laid in a soft bed, where he gradually recovered his senses, and the prince comforted him by telling him that he had captured the king, which the wounded man would hardly have believed if anyone except the prince had told him. The prince returned to the king begging him not to consider it an unworthy action of his in leaving him at dinner, because he had gone to attend a man near to death who had spared neither his blood nor his own safety in exposing himself to danger for the prince's honour. The king, learning what arms Sir James bore on his shield, said that the strength and endurance of its owner had stood out even in such a fierce battle. Little else was said at supper except that the king replied to the prince's

efforts to comfort his noble captive in words similar to these:
'Although we have met with an inevitable and sad fate, at least
we have come to it worthily; for although we have been
conquered in battle by our noble cousin, at least we were not
captured like a criminal or cowardly fugitive hiding in a corner,
but, like a stout-hearted soldier ready to live and die for a just
cause, we were taken on the field by the judgement of Mars,
where rich men were held to ransom, cowards fled ignominiously
and the bravest of all gave up their lives heroically.[15]

Froissart's account is too long to quote in full. In the original
version he describes at length Sir James Audley's conversation with
the prince, during which the prince gave Sir James a pension of 500
marks a year. This preceded the king's arrival at the prince's tent.
Just before supper, when Sir James had been suitably tended and
put to bed, he granted the pension given him by the prince to five
knights of his company. Later in the evening, the prince gave a
supper for all the captives:

And the prince served before the king's table and all the other
tables, as humbly as he could; nor would he by any means sit at
the king's table, however much the king requested it, saying
that he was far from being worthy of sitting at table with so great
a prince and such a valiant man as he had shown himself to be
that day. And he constantly kneeled to the king and said: 'Dear
lord, do not be so downcast, even though God has not granted
your wishes today; because my lord father will certainly honour
and befriend you as best he can and will make an agreement with
you in such reasonable terms that you and he will always be good
friends. Indeed I think you have good reason to be cheerful,
even if things have gone against you, because you have won a
great name for prowess today, and have outdone your own
greatest knights. I do not say this to flatter you; everyone on
our side who saw how each one fought agreed about this and
award you the prize and garland if you will wear them.[16]

The revised version omits all mention of Sir James Audley, but
gives an almost identical account of the scene at supper. But I do
not think Froissart's account can be given preference over Baker's
plainer tale. Such a dramatic gesture as Froissart describes would
surely have been remembered among the English army, and
Baker's source seems to have been someone in the prince's close

entourage. The gesture is a purely romantic one, and a careful search of the romances would probably produce the real original. Chandos Herald, always eager to emphasize the prince's virtues, says only that the prince offered to help to take off the king's armour, but the king would not allow him to. The speeches given by Baker and Froissart report the same fact: that it was generally agreed that king John had fought valiantly. It is interesting to note how they clothe the same idea in very different phrases, Baker's a kind of rustic heroic Latin, Froissart's an elegant compliment from the world of tournaments.

So far Froissart and his fellow-chroniclers all concur in praising the prince as a heroic figure. In Froissart's description of the prince's later years he takes a very different view, showing him as haughty, extravagant and cruel. His testimony cannot be lightly set aside, because he had certainly seen the prince at Bordeaux in 1367, and he was writing within a very few years of the events concerned. But after 1369 he no longer had direct contacts with England. With the darkening days of renewed warfare, it was not easy to be impartial, and even if the reports of such episodes as the prince's answer to Charles V's summons in 1369 and the siege of Limoges in 1370 did not come from hostile sources, Froissart seems to have recast them to fit his new sympathies. The question of the relationship between Chandos Herald's poem and Froissart is an interesting and difficult one; it may well be that Froissart used an earlier version of Chandos's material for the Spanish campaign and later years, expanding and recasting it. There are certainly strong points of resemblance, but the Herald's account is briefer and more accurate. It is also possible that Froissart was influenced by that powerful medieval image, the wheel of fortune, in his treatment of the prince's last days, wishing to contrast the brilliance of his youth with his decline into sickness and misfortune.[17]

However Froissart arrived at his portrait of the prince, it is his stories and his judgements that have passed into legend, to give us the resplendent figure of the Black Prince in all his glory, overshadowing even his father in the heroic age of English arms. And when we have sought out the dry facts and dull realities, it is to that legend that we return in the end, more enduring than any mere history.

Notes and References

━━━◆━━━

All works cited are listed in the printed sources. Citations are by author or by title in the case of anonymous works; where two or more works by the same author are listed, the date of publication is also given. In the case of two or more editions of one work, the edition normally used is indicated by a date in bold figures in the bibliography, but is not cited in the references.

Notes refer to the entire preceding paragraph; brief topical indications are given with references where necessary.

ABBREVIATIONS

BEC	*Bibliothèque de l'École de Chartes*
BIHR	*Bulletin of the Institute of Historical Research*
BL	British Library
CCCC	Corpus Christi College, Cambridge
CCCO	Corpus Christi College, Oxford
CCR	Calendar of Close Rolls
CChR	Calendar of Charter Rolls
CPR	Calendar of Patent Rolls
EHR	*English Historical Review*
PRO	Public Record Office
RBP	*Register of the Black Prince*
Rot Parl	*Rotuli Parliamentum*
RS	Rolls Series
SHF	Société de l'Histoire de France
TRHS	*Transactions of the Royal Historical Society*

Chapter I. THE KING'S ELDEST SON

1. Froissart, I, p. 233.
2. Rymer, II, pp. 714–15, 718–19; Stubbs, I, p. 347.

3. Tout, V, p. 314 (Philippa's household). Philippa was the only medieval queen of England not to be crowned within a few weeks of marriage or with her husband. Wharton, I, p. 370;

Barnes, p. 44; Brown, pp. 1015–16; RBP, IV, p. 206; CPR 1345–8, p. 72; CPR 1330–34, p. 2.

4. Stubbs, I, p. 349; Devon, 1847, pp. 143, 144; CPR 1330–4, pp. 16, 74.

5. Tout, V, p. 279; CPR 1330–34, p. 76.

6. CCR 1330–33, p. 517; CPR 1330–1334, p. 523; Riley, p. 189; BL Cotton Galba E III, f. 190; and 183–184ᵛ, 186.

7. CCR 1333–7, p. 350. The earl was at Peterborough at the end of June (CPR 1334–8, p. 128) and Nottingham in early December (ibid., p. 185); for the St Omers, see ibid., p. 247; PRO E 101/387/25 m. 7.

8. CCR 1337–9, pp. 49, 67, 188, 192, 198; CPR 1334–8, p. 536; Holinshed, p. 900.

9. Holinshed, p. 901; John Stow in BL Harleian 545, ff. 128–9.

10. PRO E 101/393/4 f. 8; Scattergood.

11. PRO E 101/387/25 m. 7.

12. PRO E 101/387/25 m. 7, m. 6, m. 5.

Chapter 2.
THE CONFLICT WITH FRANCE

1. For general discussions of the causes of the Hundred Years War I have used: Powicke, Templeman, Cuttino, Perroy, Fowler.

2. Powicke, p. 654.

3. McKisack, p. 112, Foedera, II, p. 813; Perroy, p. 82, cites *this* oath for 1329 and describes it as 'rather vague'.

4. Quoted in Grosjean, p. 19.

5. Le Patourel in Fowler, 1971, p. 28.

6. CCR 1337–9, p. 445; Daumet, p. 6; Sharpe, Letter Book F, p. 28; Barnie, p. 38; Harriss, p. 237.

7. PRO SC 1/39/63, 1/54/29 (letter); E 101/388/12.

8. Avesbury, pp. 305–6.

9. The most recent account of the crisis of 1339–40 is that of Harriss, pp. 253–307, on which this paragraph relies. Tout, *Administrative History*, III, pp. 1339–40; McKisack, pp. 156–64; Tout, II, pp. 293–4; Prince, 1944, p. 147.

10. See Wolffe, pp. 240–41, for useful summary of grants; CCR 1339–41,

p. 529; CCR 1339–41, p. 258.

11. Barnie, p. 7; Palmer in Fowler, p. 57; CSP Venetian I 1202–1509, p. 8; CPR 4 1338–40, p. 510 (marriage); Murimuth, 1889, p. 105.

12. Murimuth, 1889, pp. 208–9; Avesbury, p. 310; Walsingham, 1863, I, p. 226; Minot, p. 15.

13. PRO E 101/389/6, account of expenses of William of Hoo. All details in this paragraph are from m. 1.

14. Nicolas, *History of the Royal Navy*, II, p. 502.

15. *Chronographia*, p. 122; La Roncière, I, p. 446; Knighton, II, p. 18; Dragomanni, III, pp. 338–9; Guisborough, pp. 356–7; La Roncière, I, p. 442.

16. Dragomanni, III, p. 339.

17. *Chronique Normande*, p. 45; Froissart, I, ii, pp. 34–40; Walsingham, *Chronicon Angliae*, p. 11.

18. Luce, 1890, II, pp. 3–15; *Chronique de Pierre Cochon*, p. 65.

19. PRO E 101/389/6 m. 1; details following are from m. 2.

20. PRO E 101/389/6 m. 2; BL Harleian 4304 f. 19; for movements, cf. entries tested by him, CCR 1339–41; McFarlane, 1973, p. 91.

21. Harriss, pp. 294–317.

22. CCR 1339–41, p. 115: John de Lanboun £40, p. 99: Simon de Ruggele £300, p. 622: Robert de Beaupel £230 6s. 8d.; CCR 1341–3, p. 131, William Trussel and John de Legh £1,000; Guy Bryan owed £151 13s. 4d. on 1 May 1344; it was paid in 1350–51; CChR 1341–1417, pp. 11–13; CPR 1340–43, pp. 580–81.

23. PRO E 101/389/3 (summary, 1341–2); BL Harleian 4304 f. 16ᵛ–20 (sixteenth-century copy (1344–5)).

24. CPR 1340–43, p. 527; Avesbury, pp. 341–2.

25. For apparent references to Edward II as Prince of Wales, see Evans, 1925, p. 29; Originalia Rolls II, p. 160; CPR 1338–40, pp. 32–43; Griffiths, p. 13; CPR 1340–43, p. 459 (Peter Gildesburgh surrenders an exchequer post in return for the controllership of the stannary, 24ᵛ, 1342).

26. For this and what follows, see Daumet, pp. 3–12.

27. Murimuth, 1889, pp. 123–7; Nicolas, 1846, p. 6. The Meaux chronicle (p. 52) specifies Arthurian influence, but goes on to quote St George's Day as the date of assembly, probably in confusion with the Order of the Garter. Murimuth, 1889 (Cotton Nero D.X), pp. 231–2 and 155–6. Walsingham, *Chronicon Angliae*, p. 17; PRO SC 40/92; Thomas Hatfield to John Thoresby, requesting the speedy issue of commissions for the hall of the round table, undated, probably autumn 1344; Brown, p. 872.

28. Rymer, III, i, p. 50; the king sailed in the 'floine' *Swallow*, apparently a small ship from which he transferred to the *Katherine*, named as his flagship by Froissart; Rymer, III, i, p. 47; Le Muisit, p. 146; Lucas, p. 521.

29. Rymer, III, pp. 55–6. The storm seems to be a propaganda excuse; Sluys is only fifteen miles from Ghent, and if Edward sailed as soon as the news reached him – probably early on 25 July – this fits perfectly with his arrival in England late the next day. Rymer, III, i, pp. 60, 66 (*et seq.* for postponements).

30. Rymer, III, i, p. 72. Defence measures: CPR 1345–7, pp. 12, 357; will: CPR VII, pp. 129, 131; jewels: RBP IV, p. 69; pilgrimages: RBP IV, pp. 73, 74.

Chapter 3. THE CRÉCY CAMPAIGN

1. Murimuth, 1889, p. 200; Froissart, III, p. 131; Murimuth, 1889, p. 198.

2. *Acta Bellicosa* in Moisant, pp. 157–8; this is the main and most reliable source for the campaign up to 20 August, when the MS. breaks off abruptly. Moisant's edition is inaccurate in some important details cf. notes below; the original MS. is cited wherever it differs from Moisant's text. Viard, 1926, p. 4.

3. CCCC MS. 370, f. 99ᵛ; Murimuth, 1889, p. 199; Baker, p. 79, says that it was Edward who made Montagu, Mortimer and Ros knights.

4. Stephen Birchington in Wharton, *Anglia Sacra*, I, p. 41, says that Bertrand 'tam dictum Portum quam apud

Warflete [Barfleur] cum palis, sicut potuit, obturavit.'

5. Moisant, p. 160.

6. Le Bel, II, pp. 72; confirmed by Northburgh's letter, Avesbury, p. 358, where he speaks of the attackers as *marineres*. But Le Bel also describes the raid on Carentan as sea-borne, which it almost certainly was not (II, pp. 73–4). The port had been blocked with stakes (n. 4 above).

7. Froissart, III, p. 131. Moisant's edition is highly inaccurate at this point (p. 161), names being wrongly given or omitted. The correct text (CCCC MS. 370, f. 100–100ᵛ) is as follows:
'Hec nomina nobilium erigencium vexilla in acie anteriori: Comites Northamptonie et Warewyci memorati, domini Batholomaeus de Burgherssh senior, Johannes de Verdoun, Johannes de Mohoun, Thomas de Outhrech, Johannes le FitzWater, Willelmus de Kerdeston, Reginaldus le Say, Robertus Boursheres, et Willelmus de Seint Amant. In media, Comes Oxonie, domini Edwardus de Monte Acuto, Ricardus Talbot, Reginaldus de Cobham, Robertus de Ferariis, Johannes Darcy junior, Thomas de Bradeston, Johannes senior, Johannes Gray, Willelmus de Kerdeston, Eble Straunge, Michael Ponynges, Moricius de Berkele, Johannes de Stryvelyn, Petrus de Breaucs, Johannes de Chevereston, Boteler de Wem, Godefridus de Harecourt, qui pro terris et possessionibus suis in ducatu Normannie Anglorum regi apud le Hogges homagium faciebat, Willelmus de Kildesby, Walterus de Wetewang, magister Johannes de Thoresby, Philippus de Weston. In postrema insuper acie, Comites Arundellie, Suffolchie, et Huntyngdonie, domini Hugo Despenser, Robertus de Morle, Jacobus Daudele, Johannes Grey, Thomas de Astele, Johannes de Sutton, Willelmus de Cantilupo, Gerardus de Insula, Johannes de Straunge, Robertus de Coleville, et Johannes Botred.'
For Sir Richard Stafford and Sir Richard de la Bere, see Wrottesley, pp. 87, 93; RBP I, p. 48; CPR VII, 1345–8, p. 373.

8. Lescot, p. 71.

9. Cheaux—CCCC MS. 370, f. 101.

10. Prentout, p. 28.

11. Rymer, III, i, p. 126; Murimuth, 1889, p. 203; Stewart-Brown, p. 126: payment of 1,000 marks as a gift, 1347-8.

12. CPR 1345-8, p. 308; Murimuth, 1889, p. 215.

13. The English chroniclers ignore this episode; it appears in the later *Chronographia*, II, p. 225, and *Chronique Normande*, p. 77.

14. *Eulogium*, III, pp. 207-8. The dating at this point is confusing. It is possible that d'Harcourt's reconnaissance was made from Le Neubourg on the 6th (the date given by *Chronique des quatre premiers Valois*, p. 15); but why did the king then go towards Rouen? Alternatively, Cotton Cleopatra D VII makes the king halt at Elbeuf on the 6th; but the *Kitchen Journal* seems more consistent, and when the *Acta Bellicosa* MS. resumes, it agrees with the latter.

15. A madwoman spoke to d'Harcourt, according to Cochon, p. 67; leper hospitals were often used as asylums as well. Baker, p. 80; *Eulogium*, III, p. 208. It is clear from the MS. of *Acta Bellicosa* (though not from Moisant's edition) that the attack on La Roche-Guyon took place on the day on which the army encamped at Freneuse, which is 10 August (cf. Baker, *Kitchen Journal*). The text should read: 'Rocheguyonn aggredit vi armata inexpugnabili quidem apparuit et a pluribus reputabat modernis namque temporibus inde carmina faciebant videlicet le flour de liz perdera sonn nonn quant sera saigne Rocheguyonn.' *Eulogium*, III, p. 208, quotes a similar verse. *Acta Bellicosa* calls de Bois 'Attewode'; but cf. RBP I, p. 13, where an order to Hugh de Hopwas, the prince's escheator in Cheshire, to seize his lands, calls him 'Sir Edward de Boys'. He held in chief of the prince, and was almost certainly a member of his retinue.

16. Richard Wynkeley's letter in Avesbury, p. 362. *Acta Bellicosa* supplies the date for the cardinals' return.

17. Le Muisit, p. 158; CCCC 370, f. 105. 'Transiit princeps versus Mily . . .' After the attack on Oudeuil, 'ad abbathiam Champeux Rex, princeps vero ad Guevylers prosperius pervenerunt.'

18. Northburgh (Avesbury, p. 370) wrongly names Grandvilliers as the king's quarters on the evening of this attack. Given that it was after the capture of Poix, it must have taken place on the 21st, near Airaines. The attack by the king of Bohemia's men then corresponds with Le Muisit's date of the 22nd.

19. I have assumed that the *Kitchen Journal* (PRO E 101/390/11) is correct in giving Acheux (Ossheu) as the halting-place for the king's kitchen on 21 August (no place is given for 22 August, 'ibidem' for 23 August). *Bourgeois de Valenciennes*, p. 226; Wulfard de Ghistels had been on an embassy to Hainault about the queen's inheritance in 1345 (Rymer, III, i, p. 65) and was named 'to treat for alliances' on 28 October 1346 (CPR VII 1345-8, p. 477). Meaux, p. 57: I hope to give details of this in a forthcoming study of the *Acta Bellicosa*; this, the *Eulogium Historiarum* and the Meaux account have many details in common.

20. Froissart, ed. Lettenhove, V, p. 471. Belloc, p. 107 (tide); Meaux, p. 57.

21. Baker, p. 251 (Stowe's tr.).

22. The best sources seem to be as follows: from English side – Baker; independent (possibly based on Genoese fighting at battle and therefore better informed about French) – Giovanni Villani; Flemish (but primarily drawing on French) – Le Bel; French – no one individual source.

23. No satisfactory figure for the English army has yet been given: Sir James Ramsay and Lot, p. 346, give 10,000 men, less perhaps a wastage of 10 per cent during the campaign, i.e. 9,000 at the battle. Burne, 1955, pp. 166-8, favours a rather excessive figure due to the absence of some soldiers from the exchequer rolls, ending with about 15,000.

24. There is very little positive evidence for the actual site. The traditional place seems to have become the accepted site by the time Froissart wrote his account nearly twenty years later, as the windmill which is supposed to have been the king's headquarters is then mentioned for the first time: this is the only positive

feature by which the site can be identified. For the English dispositions, see
Murimuth, 1889, p. 246 (variant version
in BL MS. Cotton Nero D.x). This
agrees with the earlier disposition of the
army given in *Acta Bellicosa*, and is more
reliable than Le Bel's version.

25. *Chronographia*, p. 232; Le Muisit, p.
162. A common story was that the rain
had made their bowstrings useless
(Lescot, p. 74); Venette (p. 43) explains
that this had no effect on the English,
who unstrung their bows and put the
bowstrings under their helmets. But
Venette's account reads very much more
like hearsay than material from eyewitnesses. For the Genoese attack, I have
followed Villani. His account (Dragomanni IV, pp. 110–11) is circumstantial;
I believe it represents the version of one
of the Genoese, who would have seen
only part of the battlefield. Hence his
belief that the whole English army, or at
least the prince of Wales's division, was
within the square of carts. His account
corresponds with that of Baker, pp. 83–4,
as far as the early stages of the battle are
concerned. Villani's version of the later
stages, which makes Edward emerge
from the *laager* and take the enemy from
the rear, is not supported by any other
chronicler. As to the relative rate of fire
of crossbow and longbow, there is no
modern test under scientific conditions;
Hardy, p. 203, deals with the range of
the longbow only – comparative test
figures for crossbows do not seem to
have been compiled.

26. Buchon, XIV, p. 290; *Fontes
Rerum Bohemicarum*, IV, pp. 443, 514;
Baker, p. 84; his account agrees with that
of Le Bourgeois de Valenciennes, p. 233.
The latter's account of FitzSimon's
exploit is possibly confirmed by a grant
of £20 per annum to him just after the
battle, on 1 September (RBP I, p. 14),
'on account of the prince's affection
towards him'; he was also given 100
marks 'as a reward for his labours in the
prince's service during this present
expedition' (RBP I, p. 40). Daniel was
also given a grant, of £20 per annum,
for the raising again of the prince's
banner at Crécy (RBP, I, p. 45).

27. Wynkeley in Murimuth, 1889, p.

216. *Eulogium*, III, p. 310, and *Chronique
Normande*, p. 81, agree that Philip fell,
though the former says he was unseated,
the latter that two horses were killed
under him. Storie Pistoresi, p. 223, says
that he was wounded in the throat,
stomach and hand.

28. Windmill: Cochon, p. 69; this is a
late chronicle (*c.* 1430), but contains
local information and tradition. Galbraith, p. 212; CCCO MS. 78, f. 176: 'Et
le nuyt ensuyvant les francois relievount
et fierent diverses assauts as engleis mes
par leide de dieux toutes ils fuyent de
tout vencuz' (cf. Valenciennes, p. 233).
Meaux, p. 59, gives the detail of the
watchword. Northburgh in Avesbury,
p. 369.

29. Avesbury, p. 369 (number of
dead). Valenciennes, p. 234 ('Et le prince
se teult et fut honteux'). CCCO MS. 78,
f. 175^v. John of Arderne, p. xxvii n. I
have translated *super crestam suam* as
'above his helmet'; *cresta*, 'crest' in the
modern sense, does not appear until *c.*
1400, and in any case does not make
sense. *Winner and Waster*, pp. 101–20: Dr
Derek Brewer tells me that there is little
good reason for the emendation, as 'Yes,
lord' makes perfect sense and scans
better.

30. RBP IV, p. 69; to which day the
phrase, 'bought the same day', refers is
not entirely clear from the context.

31. I would classify the *Acta Bellicosa*'s
account of the battle (now lost but which
influenced later chroniclers) and Geoffrey
Baker as deriving from a member of the
prince's division. Among less reliable
chronicles, Le Bourgeois de Valenciennes
must also have had information from a
similar source. Froissart's version is
considered in Chapter 10 below.

32. Prisoners: Baker, p. 82.

33. Le Bel, p. 106 ('six archers of
Germany, one of whom was master
Races Massures'); the accounts confirm
this: PRO E 25/19 names Rasse Mas-
curiel, Adam de Ederein and Gerard de
Weydenthorp as foreigners serving by
indenture. *Eulogium*, III, p. 211; but there
is some doubt about the incident, as
'Emerie de Rokesle' appears from an
entry on the Memoranda Roll, Q.R., 29.
E.III, to have served 'at the battle of

Crescy and siege of Calais' (Wrottesley, p. 185).

34. On John of Bohemia, see Leger, pp. 329–31; Emler, IV, p. 514 (Benes de Weitmil); Le Bel, p. 102.

35. Lot, p. 348; Dragomanni, IV, p. 111; Burne, 1955, pp. 192–203.

36. Rymer, III, i, pp. 89–90; Viard, 1926, pp. 129–34; Avesbury, p. 369; Rymer, III, i, p. 90; CPR VII 1345–8, p. 136; RBP I, p. 34.

37. The queen was at Calais by 21 September; cf. CPR 1345–7, p. 200. This throws doubt on Le Bel's elaborate account of her arrival 'about All Saints' Day'.

38. Viard, 1926, pp. 192, 142–5; Wrothesley, pp. 102–5; Walsingham, I, p. 269; RBP I, p. 51.

39. Rymer, III, i, pp. 94–5; Meaux, p. 64; Le Bel, II, p. 113; Knighton, p. 48; Baker, p. 90; Avesbury, pp. 386–7; Dragomanni, IV, p. 143; Viard, 1929, pp. 150–51 on French attempts to supply Calais; pp. 163–5 on English levies; pp. 174–7 on attempt of 25 June.

40. Avesbury, p. 386.

41. Quotations are from the king's letter to the Archbishop of Canterbury, Avesbury, pp. 392–3; Viard, 1929, pp. 177–9; summons in RBP I, pp. 82–3: indentures, RBP I, pp. 127–9. For Mauny's imprisonment, see RBP I, p. 33, and Froissart, IV, p. 8.

42. Meaux, pp. 65–6.

43. Villani (IV, p. 145) claims that Philip drew up his men in battle order, and that Edward failed to appear, saying that he would take Calais first and fight him afterwards in Flanders. Viard, 1929, pp. 180–85.

44. Le Bel, II, p. 167; Valenciennes, p. 260, where Edward is said to have wished to kill all the survivors of the siege. Villani (Dragomanni, IV, p. 146) says that the cardinals played the main part in obtaining a pardon for them. Baker, p. 268; Le Patourel, 1951; Rymer, III, i, p. 130, for proclamation; CPR VII 1345–8, pp. 563–5, 567–8, for lists of grants to English; Dragomanni, IV, p. 146 (Flemish proposals).

45. Rymer, III, i, pp. 130, 135.

Chapter 4. THE ORDER OF THE GARTER

1. Baker, p. 96; *Polychronicon*, VIII, p. 344; Harriss, pp. 332–6; CCR 1346–9 VIII, pp. 473, 566; Griffiths, p. 27.

2. Guesnon, pp. 238–9.

3. Baker, p. 97.

4. Rymer, III, i, pp. 128, 153 (1347–8); ibid., pp. 58–9 (1345); ibid., p. 152 (1348).

5. Baker, pp. 108–9.

6. Ashmole, Appendix, f. 1.

7. RBP IV, p. 72; Nicolas, 1846, pp. 33–5; Ashmole, pp. 186–7.

8. CPR VIII, p. 144.

9. Vergil, p. 379; Hay, 1954, pp. 110, 95.

10. Hay, 1954, pp. 110, 95; Ashmole, p. 181; Whiting; Gransden, 1972. Galway, 1947, relies mainly on untrustworthy literary sources; her identification of Joan of Kent with various of Chaucer's heroines, for example, is not accepted by Chaucer scholars, and Gransden's article seriously weakens Galway's arguments, which I find totally unconvincing.

11. Bibbesworth, p. 58 (II, 140 ff); Wright, W. A., p. 22 ('Of thylke men of the garteres'); *Middle English Dictionary*, s.v. garter.

12. Renouard (1949), p. 284; Clement VI, Lettres closes III, iii, pp. 31–8; Barber, pp. 339–44, where the details of the Order of the Sash are set out in full.

13. Villanueva, pp. 553–4; Daumet, pp. 12–13.

14. Alfonso Hernández Coronel, Juan Estevanes, Juan Alfonso Benavides, Sancho Martinez de Leyra (cf. Villanueva, pp. 558–9); Rymer, III, i. p. 47 (offers of aid). It is of course possible that the Castilian Order is a later imitation of the Garter, and that the foundation date was inserted when the *Cronica de Alfonso de Onceno* was revised in 1360–70.

15. Statutes printed in Chevalier, pp. 35–9.

16. Ashmole, Appendix, f. 1, and pp. 642 ff. *Complete Peerage*, I, pp. 339–40, 348.

17. Ashmole, Appendix, f. 1–2; Villanueva, pp. 561–3, 570–72; Renouard.

18. *Winner and Waster*, pp. 61–8, 91–4 (author's translation).

19. Baker, p. 97; for licence to Lancaster to hold tournaments at Lincoln, see Nicolas, 1846, p. 107. Windsor tournament: Baker, p. 101; gifts: RBP IV, pp. 72, 67, 73.

20. Lichfield: Nicolas, pp. 184, 40; Stewart-Brown, p. 121. Canterbury, Bury: Nicolas, pp. 184, 42, 39; gift: RBP IV, p. 67. 'Maule' is perhaps Sir Robert Morley.

21. RBP IV, p. 69.

22. Falconers: RBP IV, p. 38; gambling: RBP IV, p. 76.

23. Reading, p. 88; Meaux, p. 69; Knighton, II, pp. 57-8.

24. Ziegler, passim; Beltz, p. 381.

25. Hatcher, 1970, pp. 104, 119, 127-8; BPR II, pp. 17-18, 8.

26. Polychronicon, p. 355. DNB (III, p. 903) says that St Thomas's heart was kept at Ashridge; for the prince's connection with the latter, see p. 241. Ziegler, p. 195; Baker, p. 102.

27. Baker, p. 103; Rymer, III, i, p. 159.

28. Baker, pp. 104-5; Avesbury, pp. 408-9.

29. CPR VII, p. 465; Baker, p. 108; Rymer, III, i, p. 195; Froissart, IV, pp. 98-9. Le Bel's account (II, pp. 176 ff.), which Froissart uses, is much less convincing than that of the English chroniclers, with which it conflicts in many details. There may, however, be something in the story that Eustace de Ribemont was captured and then released because of his prowess: Baker, p. 107, lists him as a prisoner and then places 'alius Eustacius de Ripplemont' among those who escaped.

30. Rymer, III, i, pp. 195, 200, 201-2.

31. Avesbury, p. 412; Baker, pp. 109-111; Froissart, IV, pp. 88-98. Ships captured: Baker, p. 110 (27), Avesbury, p. 412 (24), Chronicon Angliae, p. 28 (26), Rymer, III, i, pp. 202-3, 206; pardons: CPR IX, pp. 3, 9, 17, 43, 51, 55, 146, 235, 299. On Cosington, see Fowler, pp. 99, 101, 286: there is little evidence that he was actually 'retained' by Lancaster, and the prince's grants to him antedate those by Lancaster. He was employed by the king on diplomatic missions apart from those in which Lancaster was involved – e.g. he escorted princess Joan

to Bordeaux in 1348 – and was in the prince's retinue at Calais (RBP I, p. 80). Ballad: Minot, p. 33; on uncertainty as to victory, Le Muisit, pp. 276-8.

32. Baker, pp. 112-13; Reading, pp. 112, 246-8; Rymer, III, i, p. 205; RBP IV, p. 146; Norfolk Record Office, Norwich bailiffs' account 1349.

33. Fowler, pp. 96-146, gives full details of the diplomatic manoeuvres of 1350-55. Poem: Wright, II, p. 53.

34. C Papal Letters III, p. 394; Harriss, p. 317; Archives Historiques Poitou XLVI, pp. xlix-lii; Avesbury, p. 413.

35. Baker, pp. 116-19; Fowler, p. 100.

36. Tout, 1905; Burne, 1955, pp. 234-243; Baker, p. 120; Renouard, p. 297.

37. Rymer, III, i, pp. 215, 221; RBP II, pp. 9-10.

38. RBP III, pp. 11, 18; CPR IX, p. 81.

39. RBP II, p. 56; IV, pp. 35-6; where letters in the Registers are tested at places other than London, it is reasonable to assume that they come from the prince's personal entourage. The permanent administration was at the wardrobe in Old Jewry, and some letters may have been issued by the prince's exchequer at Westminster; (Berkhamstead), pp. 108-10; RBP IV, p. 47 (Wallingford); IV, p. 54 (Byfleet); IV, p. 10; II, p. 35; IV, p. 164 (saddles); IV, pp. 78, 79, 124; IV, p. 165 (Woodstock tournament); Rymer, III, i, p. 282; RBP IV, p. 100.

40. Booth; RBP IV, p. 113; CPR IX, p. 520; RBP IV, pp. 110-11; Knighton, II, p. 75. The duke may have joined the prince at Macclesfield if an entry in RBP IV, p. 112, refers to 27 Edward III, and not 25 Edward III. 'Rising', McKisack, p. 204.

41. RBP IV, pp. 112-13, 125; charter: CChR V, pp. 313-15 (misdated 1347 – Wauncy, who signs as steward, only became steward after 1349; see Stewart-Brown, p. 240); Morris, pp. 495-9; figures for revenue: Stewart-Brown, pp. 159, 206, 220, 258.

42. Edwards, p. 191; RBP III, pp. 139-140; RBP II, p. 60; Hatcher, 1970, p. 60 n. (Kellygrey); Hatcher, 1973, p. 106; Hatcher, 1970, p. 201; RBP IV, p. 65.

43. Brown, p. 805, from PRO E 120/1 mm 8 and 29; RBP II, p. 60.

44. RBP II, pp. 65, 69; MS. list of officers, D. of C. Office (Sully); RBP II, p. 62.

45. RBP II, p. 67; IV, p. 163; IV, p. 165; IV, pp. 125–6.

46. Fowler, pp. 144–6; Reading p. 120. It is possible that the two pilgrimages are identical, the dating in Reading being open to doubt.

Chapter 5.
AQUITAINE: THE FIRST PERIOD

1. Lodge, 1926, pp. 70 ff.; Hewitt, 1958, ch. I. Any account of the Poitiers campaign must be deeply indebted to Dr Hewitt's book, and this chapter is no exception. I have given references only to those points which are not covered by, or where I differ from, Dr Hewitt's account.

2. Renouard and Capra in Renouard, 1965, p. 359; Fowler, p. 40.

3. Loirette, 1913, pp. 317–18; Boutruche, pp. 382, 80; Delachenal, I, pp. 33–4.

4. Fowler, pp. 62 ff.

5. Darmaillacq, pp. 6–7.

6. Moisant, pp. 28–9; Rymer, III, i, p. 297; BPR II, p. 77.

7. Figures from Hewitt, pp. 20–21, Fowler, p. 50.

8. Sharp in Tout, V, pp. 386–7; RBP IV, p. 31.

9. RBP IV, pp. 143–5; Fowler, pp 230–32; Rymer, III, i, p. 307.

10. Fowler, pp. 147–8.

11. CPR X, p. 464; VIII, p. 562.

12. *Archives municipales de Bordeaux*, V, pp. 439–44.

13. CCCO, MS. 78, f. 179 (author's translation). Knighton, II, p. 80, says that they offered to follow the prince as their liege lord, 'with all their goods and chattels'.

14. See also, on the expedition as a whole, de Santi, Mullot and Poux, Jeanjean. Jeanjean's article is the most recent and reliable.

15. William de Stratton (Gilot, Giliot) – RBP IV, p. 40; Breuils, 1915, p. 120.

16. Baker, pp. 130–31; Avesbury, p. 441 (Wingfield).

17. Devic and Vaissete, IX, p. 649; Roschach, pp. 128–9.

18. Baker, 131; Avesbury, p. 441 (Wingfield).

19. Baker, p. 131. Fossat was certainly among the lords who gathered at Bordeaux in September: see p. 117 above. Jeanjean, p. 28, names Pexiora (anonymous in Baker): Jeanjean, p. 29, identifies Alse as Alzau, not Alzonne.

20. Baker, p. 131; Avesbury, p. 441 (Wingfield) Daneys – above, p. 44; RBP I, p. 119; Fédié, pp. 448–9; Baluze, p. 314.

21. Devic and Vaissete, IX, pp. 653, 655; Mascaro, p. 81.

22. Offering – Henxteworth, f. 5.

23. Capestang – end of expedition: Baker, pp. 134–9; Avesbury, pp. 441–2 (Wingfield); Avesbury, pp. 435–7 (prince).

24. Avesbury, p. 442 (Wingfield).

25. Fowler, pp. 86–7 (1349).

26. Avesbury, pp. 445–7 (Wingfield); Hewitt, p. 89; Avesbury, p. 450 (I have not been able to identify Mirabeau); Avesbury, p. 457.

27. Henxteworth, f. 6ᵛ–11 (9–30 December); Capra, p. 250; Henxteworth ff. 13ᵛ, 21, 25ᵛ, 26 (messages to and from Foix, 4 February, 28 April, 24/25 June), 26ᵛ (Aragón).

28. Avesbury, p. 450 (one of the Durforts was lord of Grignols in the Périgord); Moisant, pp. 46–7; Henxteworth, f. 20 (Chalais).

29. Henxteworth, f. 17, 17ᵛ, 21 (prince at Bordeaux): RBP III, pp. 224, 223; IV, p. 192. Evidence for the king's intentions is slight: the large purchases of bows and arrows and the prince's statement later (Riley, p. 286) that he was expecting his father to cross are the two main points.

30. Henxteworth, f. 23ᵛ, 24 (Soulac, Bordeaux); *Archaeologia*, I, 1754, p. 213 (6 July).

31. Delachenal, I, pp. 140 ff.; Fowler, pp. 151–3; Hewitt, pp. 100–1; Fowler, pp. 154–5.

32. Riley, p. 286. The prince's reason for going to Bourges was not to *get* news of Edward's crossing, but because he should have heard by then that he had crossed – i.e. he was fulfilling his

part of a prearranged plan. Hewitt, pp. 100-1, seems to think that the prince was going to besiege Bourges, whereas nothing of the sort is implied. John of Reading, p. 123; *Eulogium*, III, pp. 215-219; Devic and Vaissete, IX, p. 666.

33. *Eulogium*, III, pp. 216-17 (I have used modern spelling for place-names: Quisser = Quinsac, while Merdan is Marthon rather than Nontron; 'Rochewar' may be Rochefoucauld rather than Rochechouart, on grounds of geography). Denifle, II, p. 119.

34. *Eulogium*, III, pp. 217-18. There is no evidence for an attack on the *suburbs* of Bourges: the document cited by Luce (Froissart, V, iii) to this effect only implies that property in the diocese was destroyed.

35. *Eulogium*, III, pp. 218-19; Baker, p. 140. I would discount Baker's claim that the prince was anxious for battle and hoped that John would try to relieve the siege. Crozet.

36. Riley, p. 286; Delachenal, I, p. 202; Loizeau de Grandmaison; Chevalier; Baker, p. 142 n; Lettenhove, XVIII, p. 386; Goodman, p. 159; Froissart, V, iv; Fowler, p. 155.

37. Delachenal, I, pp. 202-3; *Eulogium*, III, pp. 220-21; Riley, p. 286; Rymer, III, i, pp. 33-4.

38. Lescot, pp. 101-2; *Eulogium*, III, p. 221; Riley, 287; Delachenal, I, pp. 204-5.

39. *Eulogium*, III, pp. 221-2; Riley, p. 287; Baker, p. 142.

40. Douet d'Arcq, C., pp. 27-8; *Eulogium*, III, p. 223. On the battle of Poitiers, I have used the following secondary sources: Hewitt, 1958; Delachenal; Burne, 1938, 1955; Tourneur-Aumont. Hewitt seems to me the best account; the others are all too inclined to try for an exact description of the positions, which is clearly impossible. Galbraith, 1939, is a very useful corrective.

41. *Eulogium*, III, p. 223; Baker, p. 144; Chandos Herald, ll. 905 ff. names Boucicaut among the negotiators, which must be wrong, while *Eulogium* makes the figure eleven from each side instead of eleven in all. Froissart, V, p. 256.

42. Baker, pp. 143-4; Chandos Herald, ll. 995 ff.; Hewitt, p. 114; *Anonimalle Chronicle*, p. 37 (distance between armies); *Eulogium*, III, p. 224, and Baker, p. 146, both imply that the prince could not see the French clearly.

43. Hewitt, p. 114. The shortage of water was only on the Saturday night; Chandos implies that horses were watered in the Miosson on Sunday.

44. Riley, p. 286 (amended in light of Delachenal, I, p. 228: 'preindrions' seems to fit very well as 'to accept battle' - cf. 'la bataille *se prist*' in the next sentence; Fowler, p. 153.

45. Baker, pp. 146-7 (many of Baker's details are very clear - e.g. Warwick's place on the slope down to the marsh, and he is probably the most reliable source though he wrongly ascribes the opening move to the *prince's* column); Chandos Herald, ll. 1103 ff (Abrechicourt); the *Anonimalle Chronicle*, p. 38, is confused, and, not realizing that the French vanguard had separated, makes Salisbury *join* Warwick to beat them off: but its detail about the initial move is valuable. Burne, 1938, p. 45, suggests that the French cavalry divided at the fork of the lane. For a similar use of archers in a defensive position in marshy ground, compare the Calais skirmish of 1350 (p. 98 above).

46. Baker, p. 149; Hardy, 1976 (arrows and armour); Lettenhove, V, p. 286 (fortifications); Delachenal, I, p. 238. On the question of who held the prince's standard, I see no reason to doubt Baker, p. 150 (cf. Hewitt, 1958, p. 130): Shank is stated to have 'attended on the standard', i.e. was part of the guard around it.

47. Delachenal, I, pp. 237-8; Secousse, II, p. 660 (from BN MS. 9618). Knighton, II, p. 90, claims that the earl of Warwick pursued the duc d'Orléans, returning just in time to help to defeat king John's column.

48. Baker, pp. 150-53.

49. Chandos Herald, ll. 1283 ff.; Douet d'Arcq, C., p. 28; I *Archives Historiques Poitou* XLVI, p. 168; Delachenal, I, pp. 239 n., 242-3.

50. Baker, p. 154; Lettenhove, XVIII, p. 387; Goodman, pp. 159, 162; BL MS.

Harleian 4304, f. 17ᵛ; *Eulogium*, III,
p. 224 (Bradeston).

51. Audouin, pp. 164-75; *Archaeologia*,
I, 1754, p. 215.

52. Lettenhove, XVIII, p. 388 (from
BL MS. Cotton Caligula D III, f. 33);
Complainte . . .; Monte-Belluna, p. 131.

53. RBP IV, pp. 254, 333; Fowler, p.
164; Hewitt, pp. 136, 138; *Eulogium*, III,
p. 226; Chandos Herald ll. 1445 ff.;
Rymer, III, i, p. 341. It is very possible
that John Le Cok of Cherbourg was sent
to England with the news brought by
Rede. Rede was paid £2 on 10 October,
so must have arrived on or before that
day, and Cherbourg was the usual
channel of communication between
Edward and Lancaster.

Chapter 6. THE MAKING OF PEACE

1. Rymer, III, i, p. 334; Froissart, V,
p. 69; Baker, p. 155; *Anonimalle Chronicle*, p. 39.

2. Rymer, III, i, p. 348; Baker, p. 155;
Hewitt, p. 139; Delachenal, i, pp. 276-81,
307; Venette, p. 65; *Chronique Jean II*,
p. 107; Fowler, pp. 163-4, seems to
ignore the special clauses.

3. Baker, p. 155; Le Bel, II, pp. 238-9;
Froissart, V, p. 80 (omitted from the
later Amiens version); Hewitt, 1958,
pp. 146-7.

4. Rymer, III, i, p. 348; Capra, p. 249;
Hewitt, p. 149 (details of voyage).
CCCO MS. 78, f. 180ᵛ-181 says that 'ils
eurent graunt encombrere en la meer par
tempestes et ce longement enduira mes
au darrein en le fest de seinte croiz en
Maie [3 May] ils arriverount a Mouse-
hole en Cornewaile'. The voyage home
took twice as long as the outward
voyage, and the fleet may well have been
scattered, but the prince and king John
almost certainly landed at Plymouth.
RBP IV, pp. 204-5; *Anonimalle Chronicle*,
pp. 40-41; *Anonymi Cantuarensis*, pp.
204-6; Knighton, II, p. 93. Henry
Picard loaned money to the prince on
various occasions (RBP IV, pp. 90, 158,
177, 236, 284, 327). Froissart's account of
the prince's return is pure imagination,
despite its precise details; assuming that
the prince landed at Sandwich, he has

simply described a normal journey to
London. Furthermore, the London
citizens are 'all dressed in different
colours' and (V, pp. 82-3) the king is
'very richly dressed'! Many of the
details are suppressed in the Amiens MS.
(V 300), but the prince is still made to
land at Dover.

5. Hewitt, pp. 160-61 summarizes the
rewards: the biographical details are
largely from RBP IV and Wrottesley.

6. Marvaud, II, p. 337; Hewitt, p. 165;
RBP IV, p. 252.

7. Hewitt, pp. 158-9 (summary of
ransoms).

8. Reading, pp. 129, 272; *Eulogium*,
III, p. 227; Reading, p. 130; Knighton,
II, pp. 98-9; *Scalacronica*, pp. 128-9;
RBP IV, pp. 252, 323; Fowler, pp. 197
and n. is doubtful of Lancaster's presence,
but the main chronicles and *Scalacronica* all agree on this. Mortimer
borrowed £1,000 from the prince on
19 February, probably to finance the
tournament (CCR X 489).

9. Reading, p. 131; RBP IV, pp. 284,
324. There were also jousts at Smithfield
on 4 March (Rymer, III, i, p. 421).

10. RBP IV, pp. 248, 252; Stewart-
Brown, pp. 241-7, 248, 260 (records end
in 1360); Brown, pp. 248-57.

11. DNB, sv Isabella; RBP IV, pp.
113, 165, 262.

12. For a general discussion of these
negotiations, see Delachenal, II, pp. 47-
67, and Le Patourel, 1960; details:
Anonymi Cantuarensis, pp. 207-8;
Knighton, II, pp. 94-5.

13. For a full account of events in
France, see Delachenal, I, pp. 245-470;
Le Patourel, 1960, pp. 28-30.

14. Rymer, III, i, p. 424; *Chronique
Jean II*, I, p. 236; RBP III, pp. 331, 347,
350, 354, 356-7; Harriss, pp. 346-7;
RBP IV, pp. 302, 326; Reading, p. 132;
RBP IV, pp. 312-34; Prince, 1931, p.
368 n.; PRO S C1/41/199 (Burghersh)
Scalacronica, p. 148, is probably in error
in describing him as one of Lancaster's
officers, in view of the clear statement
here that he is going with the prince, and
his close association with the latter.
Seven knights are listed in Rymer, III, i,
p. 482.

15. For this campaign I have relied on

Fowler's excellent account (pp. 201–12), Delachenal, II, pp. 146–200; the original sources are *Scalacronica*, pp. 146–62; *Anonimalle Chronicle*, pp. 44–50; Knighton, II, pp. 106–12; *Chronique Jean II*, I, pp. 251–62 (rhymed version in Deschamps, pp. 243–52).

16. Moranvillé, p. 92; Delachenal, II, pp. 160, 155; Knighton, II, p. 107.

17. The only evidence for Lancaster's route until 28 November is *Scalacronica*, p. 148; but see n. 14 above. The attack on Stafford is in Knighton, II, p. 106; *Scalacronica*, pp. 146–7.

18. *Chronique Jean II*, I, pp. 251–2; Delachenal, II, p. 157; *Anonimalle Chronicle*, p. 45; Knighton, II, p. 107.

19. Moranvillé, pp. 94–7; Knighton, II, p. 108; RBP IV, p. 377.

20. Moranvillé, pp. 91–3; Fowler, pp. 204–5; *Scalacronica*, p. 150; *Chronique Jean II*, p. 254. The evidence is confusing: I would read the latter sources to imply that Lancaster travelled separately, the prince following his father to Pontigny.

21. *Scalacronica*, p. 150, implies a stay of some time: Égleny is twenty-five miles from Guillon, and in the light of foraging problems, the conjecture that the whole army was at Guillon is unlikely. Petit, IX, pp. 188–90; Dugdale, *Monasticon*, vi, p. 153 (Mortimer); Rymer, III, i, p. 473; RBP IV, p. 402.

22. *Scalacronica*, pp. 153, 156; *Chronique Jean II*, p. 256; RBP IV, p. 345.

23. Fowler, p. 207; *Chronique Jean II*, p. 257; Lescot, p. 144.

24. Venette, pp. 98–101; *Scalacronica*, p. 157, claims that the English fired the suburbs.

25. *Chronique Jean II*, p. 258; Knighton, II, p. 111; *Scalacronica*, p. 157.

26. Venette, p. 98; *Chronicles of London*, p. 13; Fowler, p. 209.

27. Froissart, VI, p. 4, claims that Lancaster advocated peace; but Chandos Herald makes a similar claim for the prince, and *Chronique Jean II*, p. 259, makes the English sue for peace. All that can be said for certain is that there had been a change of heart since Cluny's previous efforts on 10 April.

28. Le Patourel, pp. 31–3. Le Patourel, to my mind, over-emphasizes the fear of

'imminent disaster' in Edward's mind: the campaign was a stalemate and a diplomatic defeat, but the dauphin could not have hoped to defeat Edward in the field.

29. *Anonimalle Chronicle*, p. 49; *Scalacronica*, p. 161; Rymer, III, i, p. 496; *Chronique Jean II*, p. 319; RBP IV, p. 364 (horse spoiled by hard riding).

30. Douet d'Arcq, L., pp. 270–74; *Anonymi Cantuarensis*, p. 209; Le Patourel, pp. 35–9; Chaplais, 1952, p. 6; Rymer, III, i, p. 508 (plenipotentiary letters); PRO E 101/393/11 f. 63ᵛ (Loveigne); Burton had carried out a delicate errand for the prince in 1351 (RBP IV, p. 12); Rymer, III, i, pp. 512–513 (La Rochelle privileges).

31. *Chronique Jean II*, pp. 320–23; Tout, IV, p. 145.

Chapter 7. PRINCE OF AQUITAINE

1. RBP IV, pp. 372–3; Rymer, III, i, pp. 616, 627; Fowler, p. 218; RBP IV, p. 73; Reading, p. 150.

2. Rymer, III, i, p. 155; ii, p. 638; Bardonnet; Harris, p. 485; RBP IV, p. 403; Sharp, 1930, V, p. 291.

3. Dunn-Pattison, p. 176, and Emerson, 154, refer to 'his little son Edward', in fact his godson – RBP IV, p. 71; Froissart, II, p. 243. Delachenal, II, pp. 8–10, is the best study of Joan's marital affairs: Galway 1947 must be treated with great caution; Clement VI's first Bull is misdated 1347 in *Cal. Papal Letters*, ii, pp. 252–3.

4. RBP IV, p. 427; Rymer, III, ii, pp. 627, 632 and p. 244 below; PRO E 30/180; *Anonymi Cantuarensis*, p. 213; Knighton, II, p. 116; *Polychronicon*, VIII, p. 360; Taylor, 1964, p. 88.

5. RBP, IV, pp. 427, 475–7, 434; tournaments, RBP, IV, pp. 428, 475; Reading, pp. 152 (Smithfield early May, probably in error), 151.

6. Dawson.

7. Chaplais, 1952, p. 8; Rymer, III, ii, p. 668; La Rochelle, p. 169 above; Bardonnet, p. 84; Moisant, p. 70 (Cahors).

8. RBP IV, pp. 484, 144; Rymer, III, ii, pp. 667–70.

9. RBP III, p. 449; Harriss, pp. 494, 476 and n.; Broome, p. 17 (finances); RBP IV, pp. 467, 465, 500.

10. *Archives Historiques Poitou* XLVI, pp. 210–11 (Poitiers); Rymer, III, ii, p. 652; *Anonymi Cantuarensis*, p. 222; RBP IV, pp. 465 ff.; Hingeston-Randolph, p. 1240; Reading, p. 156; *Eulogium*, III, p. 231; RBP III, p. 454. The grant in RBP IV, p. 465, dated Restormel, 24 August, must be an error. Froissart confuses the prince's journey to Bordeaux with the subsequent taking of homage in Saintonge and Poitou. *Saint Mary Cog*: PRO E 61/76 m. 4.

11. Delpit, pp. 86–100; see also *Le Livre des Hommages . . .*, a better but non-chronological text.

12. Delpit, pp. 100–9; *Archives historiques du Poitou,* IV, p. x.

13. Delpit, pp. 117–21; Tucôo-Chala, p. 96; Marvaud, I, p. 153; Archives Vienne I H 15/1, 2 H1/1; letters in favour of mayor of Bourg – *Archives Gironde*, XXXIV, p. 49; *Documents sur la ville de Millau*, 1367, p. 139.

14. Tout, V, p. 349 n.; Delpit, pp. 173–4 (*fouage*); Rouquette, p. 79; *Archives Gironde*, XXXIV, p. 191.

15. *Archives Gironde*, XXXVII, p. 311; XXXIV, pp. 191, 192; Delachenal, III, 551–3.

16. Chaplais, 1952, p. 8; Delachenal, II, pp. 339–45.

17. Lettenhove, XVIII, pp. 481–3; PRO E 30/1274. Both are fragmentary, the latter being in very poor condition. Delachenal, III, pp. 163–4 n., notes Boucicaut's mission, but does not cite these documents. PRO E 30/1274 appears to be later in date, as Delves must have left for England in March 1365; see p. 184 below.

18. Gransden, 1957, p. 276; Lefèvre-Pontalis, p. 62; CPR 1364–7, p. 180. *Eulogium*, III, p. 236, dates the birth 27 January; but this would imply an exceptional interval before the 'churching'. It may have been Delves, or one of his retinue, who told the friars at Lynn about the festivities; the prince had property in the town and at Castle Rising. Delisle, 1874, p. 90 (gift dated 14 March); La Tour Landry, pp. 30, 209 n.; Luce, 1896, p. 350.

19. Beresford-Jones, pp. 25–9; Grueber, pp. 52–4.

20. *Archives historiques Rouergue*, VII, p. 144; Boutruche, p. 202; Filongley's accounts in Delpit, pp. 173–5; Harriss, pp. 279–80.

21. Russell, 1955, pp. 1–11; RBP IV, pp. 476, 484.

22. *Archives historiques Gironde*, IV, pp. 111–12 (misdated by Lodge, 1926, p. 199, to 1363); VI, pp. 370–71. Rymer, III, ii, p. 779.

23. RBP II, pp. 211, 213; Delachenal, II, pp. 319–20; Russell, pp. 27–8, 36–7.

24. Rymer, III, ii, p. 779; Brutails, pp. 85, 89, 108, 139; Castro, pp. 17–18, 74, 96, 137, 175; Russell, 1955, pp. 45–58.

25. Russell, 1955, p. 59, using Froissart, makes the first meeting at Bordeaux; but López de Ayala, p. 548, and Chandos, agree that it was at or near Bayonne. For Charles's presence at Bordeaux, see Castro, p. 210: acknowledgement of a loan of 6,000 'fortz' of gold from the prince, signed by the king. The prince's movements for early 1366 are obscure: he was at St Macaire on 20 March (*Comm. hist. Gironde,* 1849, p. 49) and at Bordeaux in June and July (Delisle, 1874, p. 158).

26. Froissart, VI, pp. 199–200; Chandos Herald, ll. 1914 ff.; Rymer, III, ii, pp. 791, 797.

27. Armitage-Smith, p. 43; Zurita, f. 345; Russell, pp. 63 (quotation), 64–9; Devon, 1847, p. 188.

28. Russell, pp. 67–8, 18–19 (on Pedro's character).

Chapter 8. THE SPANISH CAMPAIGN

1. López de Ayala, p. 551; Russell, 1955, pp. 70–73.

2. López de Ayala, p. 547; Russell, 1955, pp. 75–7.

3. Froissart, VII, p. 1; Russell, 1955, pp. 78–9, 81. The prince was still at Bordeaux on 12 January: grant to R. W. Spridlington, PRO C 61/83 m. 9.

4. Russell, 1955, pp. 79 n.–80 n.; Rymer, III, ii, pp. 797, 799; Chandos Herald, l. 1974; Russell, 1955, p. 77 n.

5. Chandos Herald, ll. 2304–6. For payments to English retainers of the

prince going to Compostela in 1356, see Henxteworth, f. 22. Gloss on Walter of Peterborough in Wright, 1859, i, p. 105; Russell, 1955, pp. 83–5.

6. Russell, 1955, pp. 86–7 follows Froissart in making Sir *William* Felton leader of the expedition; but Chandos Herald is probably Froissart's source, and names Sir *Thomas* as leader.

7. Russell, 1955, pp. 91–2, dates the prince's move before Charles's 'capture'; but Chandos Herald, ll. 2494 ff., says that the prince moved because of the capture.

8. Chandos Herald, ll. 2725 ff.; Wright, 1859, i, p. 109; López de Ayala, pp. 553–4. Chandos Herald's account is clear, but Russell, 1955, p. 91, places the expected battle *after* Tello's attack, following López de Ayala. For Nicholas Bond, RBP IV, p. 102.

9. López de Ayala, pp. 554–5; Wright, 1859, i, p. 112; Chandos Herald, ll. 2878 ff.; Russell, 1955, pp. 92–3.

10. Delachenal, iii, pp. 394, 556–7; Russell, pp. 93–5; López de Ayala, pp. 555–6; Wright, 1859, i, p. 113.

11. López de Ayala, pp. 551, 556–7; Chandos Herald, ll. 3121 ff.; Russell, 1955, pp. 99–101.

12. López de Ayala, p. 552; Russell, 1955, pp. 97–9.

13. Chandos Herald, ll. 3225 ff.: this seems the most reliable account, but cf. Russell, 1955, pp. 96–7, for a different version based on López de Ayala, who is less likely to have known the disposition of the English army.

14. Chandos Herald, ll. 3310 ff.; López de Ayala, pp. 556–7; Russell, 1959, p. 326.

15. Chandos Herald, ll. 3454 ff.; Ayala, p. 558; Russell, 1955, pp. 105–7.

16. Prince, 1926, p. 418; Devon, 1847, p. 191.

17. López de Ayala, pp. 563–6; Russell, 1955, pp. 109–12.

18. Cascales, f. 120; López de Ayala, pp. 571–2; Russell, 1955, pp. 113–14.

19. Zurita, ii, f. 348ᵛ, 349ᵛ; Russell, 1955, pp. 114–26.

20. Chandos Herald, ll. 3644 ff., 3771–2. On the sickness, see Russell, 1959, p. 327, Walsingham, 1874, p. 60.

21. Russell, 1955, pp. 133–8; Castro, VI, pp. 423, 428, 431, 432; Zurita, ii, f. 350–51.

22. Zurita, ii, f. 351–3; Russell, pp. 127–51. Russell emphasizes the prince's 'ambitions', but there is little in the documents he cites to suggest that such ambitions were either very serious or entirely the prince's idea. The draft at Tarbes and the vague proposals of 1369 seem to be much more the work of Aragón than of Chandos and Armagnac.

Chapter 9.
AQUITAINE: THE LAST YEARS

1. Delachenal, IV, pp. 153–6; III, pp. 428–9 n.; above, p. 182; Russell, 1955, pp. 33–4.

2. Froissart, VI, p. 232; Loirette, 1913, pp. 325–6; Delpit, pp. 175–6.

3. Delpit, p. 175; grant to R. Filongley, C 61/83 m. 9; *Archives historiques Rouergue*, VII, pp. 164–5.

4. Moisant, p. 211; Breuils, 1902, p. 77; Loirette, 1931, pp. 13–17.

5. Charter of rights: *Archives municipales Bordeaux*, I, pp. 172–7, and *Bulletin société historique Limousin*, I, pp. 49–52. Clauses xv–xvii of the Bordeaux copy are omitted in the latter, but in the crucial clause xii, the Limoges text reads 'fouages *et* impositions'; I have followed this reading. For the figures for the *fouage*, Delpit, pp. 173–5. The rates of the earlier subsidies are sometimes quoted as 40s. and 20s.; but a brief calculation will show that Filongley's calculations are of the notional yield based on a given number of hearths (with some revision of the total of *feux fiscales* between each taxation), and the proportions for the four taxations in Poitou and Limousin are 40:20:24:24. '40 esterl.' must therefore be 40d., as the latter taxations are stated as 2s. Poitiers Charter: *Archives Historiques Poitou* XLVI, p. 242.

6. Archives Vienne, G 31; Delachenal, IV, p. 180 n.; PRO C 61/78 m. 11; Moisant, pp. 103–4; Rymer, III, ii, pp. 810–11.

7. Delachenal, IV; Chaplais, 1952, p. 54; Delisle, 1874, p. 158.

8. Unwin, pp. 309–10; Rymer, IV, i, p. 156; Moisant, p. 95.

9. Wright, 1859, i, p. 97; Baluze, iv, pp. 411–12; Mollat, pp. 110–12.

10. Delachenal, IV, p. 23; Walsingham, 1874, pp. 88–9.

11. Rymer, III, ii, p. 845; Brutails, p. 161. Moisant, p. 212. Delachenal, IV, p. 74; Froissart, ed. Lettenhove, XI, pp. 226–9.

12. Delachenal, IV, pp. 78 and n., 84–9.

13. Delachenal, IV, p. 79 n.; Denifle, III, p. 279; Rouquette, p. 134; Rymer, III, ii, p. 848; Harriss, p. 494.

14. Breuils, 1902, p. 88; Archives historiques Gironde, I, pp. 157–8; Delachenal, IV, pp. 99–100.

15. Perroy, 1962.

16. Delachenal, IV, pp. 127–33; Breuils, 1902, pp. 88–9; Walsingham, 1874, pp. 61–2; Delachenal, IV, pp. 111–122. The prince was certainly at Angoulême for October, January, February and March; Moisant, p. 210, Archives historiques Gironde, XXXVII, pp. 198, 410; PRO DL 41/10/31; Rymer, III, ii, p. 859; Froissart, VII, pp. 95–9; Chandos Herald, ll. 3877–96; Moisant, pp. 210–12; Chaplais, 1952, pp. 54–5.

17. Rymer, III, ii, pp. 862, 859, 874; Boutruche, p. 235; Archives historiques Poitou, XIV, p. x; XLVI, p. 242.

18. Delachenal, IV, p. 133; Rymer, III, ii, p. 868.

19. Delachenal, IV, pp. 163–87; Momméja; Chandos Herald, ll. 3943–5.

20. Prince at Cognac: Marvaud I, 155; Guinodie I, 382; Archives Vienne 2H1/92. Froissart, VII, pp. 199–204. Froissart's account, convincing in some details, is confused in others, particularly as to the movements on 1 January. Chandos Herald passes over the event in two lines, so cannot help. The improbabilities in Froissart are: two twelve-mile marches (Saint-Savin to Chauvigny, Chauvigny to Lussac) in one night, the presence of an important French commander, Jean de Kerlouet, on a casual raid, and the mysterious reappearance of the other English contingent. In fact, the Saint-Savin episode should probably be ignored: I would think that Chandos was after Kerlouet, and had managed to surround him by dividing his forces before the engagement.

21. Delachenal, IV, pp. 256–8, 278–9; Rymer, III, ii, pp. 883–5, 894; Chandos Herald, ll. 4005–19; Devon, 1835, pp. 119, 130, 141.

22. Leroux, pp. 167–73; Delachenal, IV, pp. 281–6. Texts: Leroux, p. 156; Baluze, IV, p. 376. The only evidence I have found for the prince's whereabouts is a charter dated Angoulême, 3 January. (Archives historiques Gironde, XVI, p. 156) and writs of 28 January (Archives municipales Bordeaux, I, p. 148) and 15 April (PRO C 47/34/1/2). He was at Cognac after the Limoges expedition, on 20 October (ibid., p. 169) and on 8 October (Gaunt's Register, I, pp. 289–290); and see n. 26 below.

23. Leroux, pp. 175–95; C Papal Letters IV, p. 146; Walsingham, p. 67; Chandos Herald, l. 4049; texts as in n. 22 above; Keen, pp. 121–2, on laws of siege, can 'find no legal authority for these rules.' Chroniques quatres premiers Valois, pp. 2, 10, gives some support to Froissart: 'Et moult des citoiens mistrent a mort...' This source (pp. 209–10) also has the story of Gaunt's chivalrous combat with Villemur in the mine.

24. Leroux, pp. 196–227.

25. Delachenal, IV, pp. 364–9; PRO E 101/178/20 (Tonnay-Charente, 5 November 1370); Devon, 1835, pp. 407, 417; Rymer, III, ii, pp. 907–8. For Dagenet's early service: BM Harleian 4304, f. 18. The prince was at Tonnay-Charente on 5 November: PRO E 101/178/20.

26. Anonimalle, pp. 67, 176; PRO E 101/316/6 (Bryan was away from 5 February to 2 March); Sharpe, Letter-book F, p. 275; Riley, pp. 350–52; Reddaway and Walker, 38 (quotation).

27. Wilkins, III, p. 91; Lunt and Graves, p. 477; Holmes, pp. 13, 17; Anonimalle, p. 69.

28. PRO E 101/397/5 f. 34, f. 46; E 403/446/m. 25; Beltz, pp. 9–11; Delachenal, IV, p. 428; Sherborne, pp. 22–4.

29. CCR XIII, p. 463; Rotuli Parliamentorum, II, pp. 309–10; Rymer, III, ii, p. 974.

30. McKisack, p. 385; Eulogium, III, pp. 337–9; Catto; Gwynn, pp. 218–21.

Holmes, p. 14, describes the story as 'of
very doubtful reliability'; Catto, p. 766,
says, 'The value of the *Continuatio*
appears to be fairly high.'

31. Meyvaert; Gwynn, pp. 220–21;
Wright, 1859, pp. xxvii–lii, 123–215;
Kirkstall Abbey Chronicles, pp. 90–91,
etc.

32. Sharp in Tout, V, 312, 328, 379,
398–9; PRO SC 1/50; PRO E 996–1098.

33. Holmes; McKisack, pp. 387–94;
Walsingham, pp. 68–92; *Anonimalle*, pp.
79–95 (quotation, p. 92).

34. Walsingham, 1874, pp. 88–92 (see
pp. 240 and 241 below for the prince's
reverence for the Trinity and attachment
to St Albans); McFarlane, 1972, p. 164;
Amyot, p. 229 n.; *Anonimalle*, p. 95.

35. Walsingham, 1874, p. 91; Knighton, p. 124; *Polychronicon*, VIII, p. 426;
Brinton, i, pp. 355–6.

36. PRO E 403/460 m. 23, 25, 26;
Anonimalle, p. 95; Stanley, pp. 165–82.

Chapter 10. THE LEGEND

1. Yevele was employed at Kennington: see p. 174 above. For Hugh, see
RBP IV, pp. 35, 47.

2. RBP IV, 205; Hingeston-Randolph,
p. 1191; Tristram, pp. 67–9.

3. Todd, p. 3; Stanley, 169; RBP IV,
pp. 105, 128; Chettle; RBP II, pp. 63, 75.

4. Walsingham, 1867, II, 377, 403;
CPR, 1350–54, p. 520.

5. Leland, 1774, II, p. 479; Bodleian
MS. Gen. top. C. 1 f. 689; Cambridge
UL, Peterhouse MS. 190; Caxton,
William, *The Chronicles of England*, 1480;
Eulogium, II, p. 215 (in one MS. *quarti* is
erased); Barnes, p. 363.

6. See pp. 260 and 262 above for
references. Minor facts, too, are a
mixture of plausibility and error:
Froissart (VI, p. 39) says that Foix refused
to come on the Spanish expedition
because he had hurt his leg, but this story
belongs to the 1365 negotiations (p. 187
above).

7. There is no satisfactory full-length
study of Froissart: see Froissart, ed. Luce,
I, i; ed. Lettenhove, I a; Speirs; Dar-
mesteter; Galway, 1959. The best recent
summary is that of Geoffrey Brereton,
introduction to Froissart, *Chronicles*,
Harmondsworth, 1968.

8. *Chroniques quatre premiers Valois*,
pp. 209–10.

9. Le Bel, i, ii ff., pp. xviii, xxiii.

10. Le Bel, ii, pp. 103–4.

11. Froissart, iii, pp. 185–6, 427.

12. Froissart, iii, pp. 182–3.

13. Froissart, iii, p. 423.

14. Froissart, iii, p. 425.

15. Baker, pp. 153–4.

16. Froissart, V, pp. 63–4.

17. Chandos Herald, 1910, p. lvii;
Tyson in her 1975 edition (pp. 30–31)
suggests that the poem in its present form
dates from 1385 and was written for
Richard II, but it clearly includes eyewitness material.

Bibliography

MANUSCRIPT SOURCES
(UNPUBLISHED)

1. Surviving household accounts of the prince:

Public Record Office:
E 101/387/25 (1336–8) (various accounts)
E 101/388/12 (1337–8) (account for clothing)
E 101/389/6 (1340) (expenses roll)
E 101/389/13 (1341–2) (summary accounts)
E 101/389/15 (1341–2) (counter-roll)
E 101/390/3 (1342–4) (summary account)

BL MS. Harleian 4304, ff. 16ᵛ–20 (1344–1345)

Duchy of Cornwall office: Henxteworth's *jornale* or day-book

2. Letters and other documents:

SC 1/39/63
SC 1/40/92
SC 1/54/29
SC 1/41/199
SC 1/50
DL 41/10/31
C 47/34/1/2

3. Other accounts and records:

BL MS. Cotton Galba E III, ff. 178–80

Public Record Office:

E 30/1647
E 30/1274
E 101/385/5
E 101/393/4
E 101/393/11
E 101/178/20
E 101/316/6
C 61/78
C 61/83
E 403/446
E 403/460
E 361/4/23–6

Norfolk Record Office, Norwich: Bailiff's account 1349

Archives de la Vienne, Poitiers:
1 H 15/1
2 H 2/1, 92
G 31

4. Chronicles, etc:

Corpus Christi College, Cambridge MS. 370 ('Hec sunt acta bellicosa . . .'): cited as *Acta Bellicosa*; ed. in Moisant, below.

Corpus Christi College, Oxford MS. 78 (French Brut)

268

British Library MS. Harleian 545 (Notes by John Stow)

BL MS. Harleian 545 (Mondonus Belvaleti, Latin treatise on the Order of the Garter)

The following PRO classes have been checked and found to contain little relevant material not already available in published sources: Issue Rolls (E403), Gascon Rolls (C61), Enrolled Accounts (wardrobe and household) (E367). Items of interest are cited in (3) above.

PRINTED SOURCES

'Accord du prince de Galles avec les prélats, nobles et communes d'Aquitaine (1368)', *Bulletin de la Société Archéologique et historique du Limousin*, I, 1846, pp. 49–52.

Allmand, C. T., *Society at War*, Edinburgh, 1973.

Allou, C. N., 'Notice sur le tombeau de Jean Chandos, près Lussac', *Revue anglo-française*, 3, 1835, pp. 209–22.

Álvarez de Albornoz, Fernando, *Cronica del rey don Pedro*, in Moisant, J., *Le Prince noir en Aquitaine*, q.v.; and see Russell, 1959.

Amyot, Thomas, 'Transcript of a Chronicle in the Harleian Library of MSS. No. 6217, entitled, "An Historical Relation of certain passages about the end of King Edward the Third, and of his Death"', *Archaeologia*, XXII, pp. 204–284. (See also Walsingham, *Chronicon Angliae*, of which this is a tr.)

Anonimalle Chronicle: The Anonimalle Chronicle 1333 to 1381, ed. V. H. Galbraith, Manchester, 1927.

Anonymi Cantuarensis: see Reading, John of.

Archives historiques de la département de la Gironde, Bordeaux 1855 ff. (The following volumes contain relevant material: I, pp. 157–9; II, pp. 111–12; VI, pp. 370–71; XII, XVI, XXI, XXXIV, XXXV, XXXVII.)

Archives municipales de Bordeaux, ed. Henri Barckhausen: I *Livres des bouillons* Bordeaux, 1867; V *Livres des coutumes* Bordeaux, 1890.

Archives Historiques du Poitou, XIII,

Recueil des documents concernant le Poitou contenus dans les registres de la chancellerie de France, ed. Paul Guérin, II: 1330–1347, 1883; XVII, . . . III: 1348–1369, 1886; XIX, . . . IV: 1369–1376, 1888.

ibid., XLVI *Recueil des documents concernant la commune et la ville de Poitiers*, ed. E. Audouin, II: 1328–1380, 1928.

Archives historiques du Rouergue, VII, *Documents sur la ville de Millau*, ed. Jules Artières, Millau, 1930.

Arderne, John, *Treatises of Fistula in Ano . . .*, ed. D'Arcy Power, London, 1910 (EETS OS 139).

Armitage-Smith, Sydney, *John of Gaunt*, 1904.

Armitage-Smith, Sydney (ed.), *John of Gaunt's Register, 1371–5*, London, 1911 (Camden Series, 3rd series, XX–XXI).

Arnould, E. J., 'Un Manuscrit méconnu de *La Vie du Prince Noir*', in *Mélanges . . . offerts à Mario Roques*, II, Paris, 1953, pp. 3–14.

Ashmole, Elias, *The Institutions, Laws and Ceremonies of the Most Noble Order of the Garter*, London, 1672 (reprinted 1971).

Aspin, Isabel S. T. (ed.), *Anglo-Norman Political Songs*, Oxford, 1953 (Anglo-Norman texts, XI).

Audinet, E., 'Les Lois et coutumes de la guerre à l'époque de la guerre de Cent Ans d'après les chroniques de Jean Froissart', *Mémoires de la Société des Antiquaires de l'Ouest*, 3rd series, IX, Poitiers, 1917, pp. lix–cvi.

Avesbury, Robert, *De Gestis Mirabilibus Regis Edwardi Tertii* ed. [with Murimuth] Edward Maunde Thompson, RS 93, London, 1889.

Baker, Galfridi le, de Swynebroke, *Chronicon*, ed. Edward Maunde Thompson, Oxford, 1889.

Baluze, Étienne, *Vitae paparum avenionensium*, ed. G. Mollat, Paris, 1914–27.

Barber, Richard, *The Knight and Chivalry*, London and Ipswich, 1974 (2nd edition).

Bardonnet, A., *Procès-verbal de délivrance à Jean Chandos commissaire du roi d'Angleterre des places françaises*, Niort, 1867.

Barnes, Joshua, *The History of that*

Most Victorious Monarch Edward III . . . Together with That of his Most Renowned Son, Edward Prince of Wales and of Aquitain, sirnamed the Black Prince . . ., Cambridge, 1688.

Barnie, John, *War in Medieval Society: Social Values and the Hundred Years War 1337–99*, London, 1974.

Belloc, H., *Crécy*, London, 1912.

Belloc, H., *Poitiers*, London, 1913.

Beltz, George Frederick, *Memorials of the Most Noble Order of the Garter*, London, 1841.

Bémont, C., *La Guyenne sous la domination anglaise*, London, 1920 (Helps for Students of History, 27).

Beresford-Jones, R. D., *A Manual of Anglo-Gallic Gold Coins*, London, 1964.

Bertrandy-Lacabane, M., *Études sur les Chroniques de Froissart. Guerre de Guienne 1345–1346*, Bordeaux, 1870.

Bibbesworth, Walter de, *Le Traité de Walter de Bibbesworth sur la langue française*, ed. A. Owen, Paris, 1929.

Bock, Friedrich, 'Some New Documents Illustrating the Early Years of the Hundred Years War (1353–1356)', *Bulletin of the John Rylands Library*, xv, pp. 60–99.

Booth, P. H. W., 'Taxation and Public Order: Cheshire in 1353', *Northern History*, XII, 1976, pp. 16–31.

Boutruche, Robert, *La Crise d'une société: seigneurs et paysans du Bordelais pendant la Guerre de Cent Ans*, Paris, 1947.

Bréquigny, L. G. O. F. de, *Lettres de rois, reines et autres personnages . . .*, ed. J. J. Champollion-Figeac, II: *1301–1515*, Paris, 1847.

Breuils, Abbé, 'Histoire de Nogaro, III: XIVᵉ et XVᵉ siècles', *Société Archéologique du Gers (Bulletin)*, 1915, pp. 110–186.

Breuils, A., 'Jean Iᵉʳ Comte d'Armagnac et le mouvement national dans le Midi au temps du prince noir', *Revue des questions historiques*, LIX, 1902, pp. 44–102.

Brie, Friedrich W. D., *Geschichte und Quellen der mittelenglischen Prosachronik The Brute of England oder The Chronicles of England*, Marburg, 1905.

Brinton, Thomas, *The Sermons of Thomas Brinton, Bishop of Rochester (1373–1389)*, ed. Mary Aquinas Devlin, vol. II, Camden Series LXXXVI, London, 1954.

Brissaud, D., *Les Anglais en Guyenne*, London, 1875.

Broome, Dorothy M. (ed.), 'The Ransom of John II, King of France 1360–70', *Camden Miscellany XIV*, 1926 (Camden 3rd Series, XXXVII).

Brown, R. Allen, Colvin, H. M., and Taylor, A. J., *The History of the King's Works*, II: *The Middle Ages*, London, 1963.

Brownbill, John, *The Ledger-Book of Vale Royal Abbey*, The Record Society for . . . Lancashire and Cheshire, LXVIII, 1914.

Bruce, Herbert, *English History in Contemporary Poetry*, I: *The Fourteenth Century*, London, 1914.

The Brut or The Chronicles of England, from MS. Rawl B. 171 Bodleian Library, ed. F. Brie, vol. II, EETS, 1908.

Brush, H. R., 'La Bataille des trente anglois et trente Bretons', *Modern Philology*, 9, 1911, pp. 511–28.

Brutails, Jean-Auguste, *Documents des archives de la Chambre des comptes de Navarre* (1196–1384), Paris, 1890.

Buchon, J. A., *Collection des chroniques nationales françaises: chroniques de Froissart XIV*, Paris, 1826.

Burley, S. J., 'The Victualling of Calais', *BIHR*, xxxi, 1958, pp. 49–57.

Burne, A. H., 'The Battle of Poitiers', *EHR*, 1938, pp. 21–51.

Burne, A. H., 'Cannon at Crécy', *Royal Artillery Journal*, LXXVII, 1939, pp. 335–4.

Burne, A. H., *The Crécy War: A Military History of the Hundred Years' War from 1337 to the Peace of Brétigny, 1360*, London, 1955.

Burne, R. V. H., 'Cheshire under the Black Prince', *Journal of the Archaeological and Historical Society of Cheshire*, NS 44, 1957, pp. 1–18.

Calendar of the Charter Rolls.
Calendar of the Close Rolls.
Calendar of Inquisitions, Miscellaneous.
Calendar of the Patent Rolls.
Calendar of Entries in the Papal Registers relating to Great Britain: Papal Letters.

Calendar of State Papers, Venetian, I: *1202–1509*.

Cambridge Medieval History, VI: Thompson, A. H., *The Art of War to 1400*; VII: Coville, A., *France: the Hundred Years War*.

Capra, Pierre-J., 'Le Séjour du Prince Noir, lieutenant du roi, à l'archevêché de Bordeaux', *Revue historique Bordeaux et département Gironde*, NS 7, 1958, pp. 241–252.

The Caption of Seisin of the Duchy of Cornwall, ed. P. L. Hull, Devon and Cornwall Record Society, NS 17, Torquay, 1971.

Cartier, Normand A., 'The Lost Chronicle', *Speculum*, XXXVI, 1961, pp. 424–34.

Cascales, Francisco, *Discursos historicos de la mui noble i leal ciudad de Murcia*, Murcia, 1621.

Castro, José Ramón, *Catálogo del Archivo General de Navarra: Catálogo de la Sección de Comptos: Documentos VI–VII*, Pamplona, 1954–5.

Catto, J. I., 'An Alleged Great Council of 1374', *EHR*, LXXXII, 1967, pp. 764–771.

Cazelles, Raymond, *La Société politique et la crise de la royauté sous Philippe de Valois*, Paris, 1958.

Chandos, Sir John, The Herald of, *Life of the Black Prince*, ed. Mildred K. Pope and Eleanor C. Lodge, Oxford, 1910; ed. Henry Octavius Coxe, London, 1842; ed. Francisque Michel, London and Paris, 1883; ed. Diana B. Tyson, Tübingen, 1975 (Beihefte zur Zeitschrift für Romanische Philologie, 147).

Chaplais, Pierre, 'The Chancery of Guyenne 1289–1453', *Studies Presented to Sir Hilary Jenkinson*, London, 1957, pp. 61–96.

Chaplais, P., 'English Arguments Concerning the Feudal Status of Aquitaine in the Fourteenth Century', *BIHR*, 21, 1946–8, pp. 203–13.

Chaplais, Pierre, 'Règlement des conflits internationaux franco-anglais au XIVe siècle (1293–1377)', *Le Moyen Âge*, 57, 1951, pp. 269–302.

Chaplais, Pierre, 'Some Documents Regarding the Fulfilment and Interpretation of the Treaty of Brétigny (1361–1369)', *Camden Miscellany XIX* (Camden Third Series, LXXX), London, 1952.

Chettle, H. F., 'The Boni-Homines of Ashridge and Edington', *Downside Review*, lxii, 1944, pp. 40–55.

Chevalier, C., 'Origines de l'église de Tours', *Mémoires de la société archéologique de Touraine*, 1871, XXI, pp. 610–17.

Chevalier, Ulysse, *Documents historiques inédits sur le Dauphiné*, Lyon, 1874.

Chronique des Règnes de Jean II et Charles V, ed. R. Delachenal, I: 1350–64; II: 1364–80, SHF, Paris, 1910, 1916.

Chronique des quatre premiers Valois (1327–1393), ed. S. Luce, SHF, Paris, 1862.

Chronique Normande du XIVe siècle, ed. Auguste and Émile Molinier, SHF, Paris, 1872.

Chronographia Regum Francorum, ed. H. Moranvillé, SHF, Paris, 1893, 1897.

Cirot de la Ville, *Histoire de l'abbaye . . . de la Grande-Sauve*, Paris, 1844.

Clement VI, *Lettres closes . . . se rapportant à la France*, ed. E. Déprez, Paris, 1901–25.

Cobb, John Wolstenholme, *Two Lectures on the History and Antiquities of Berkhamsted*, London, 1883.

Cochon, Pierre, *Chronique normande*, ed. Ch. de Robillard de Beaurepaire, Société de l'histoire de Normandie, Rouen, 1870.

Collins, Arthur, *The Life and Glorious Actions of Edward Prince of Wales*, London, 1740.

Commission des documents et monuments historiques de la Gironde, [Bordeaux] 1849.

Complainte sur la bataille de Poitiers, ed. C. de Beaurepaire, *BEC*, II, 3rd series, Paris, 1851, pp. 257–63.

Cosneau, E., *Traités de la guerre de cent ans*, Paris, 1889.

Contamine, P., *Guerre, état et société à la fin du moyen âge. Études sur les armées des rois de France 1337–1494*, Paris, 1972.

Crozet, René, 'Le Siège de Romorantin par le prince des Galles (août-septembre 1356)', *Mémoires de la société des sciences et lettres de Loir-et-Cher*, 1937, pp. 149–58.

Cuttino, G. P., 'Historical Revision: the Causes of the Hundred Years' War', *Speculum*, 31, 1956, pp. 463–77.

Cuttino, G. P., *English Diplomatic*

Administration 1259–1339, Oxford, 1971 (revised edition).

Cuvelier, *Chronique de Bertrand du Guesclin*, ed. E. Charrière, Paris, 1839.

Darmaillacq, B., 'Le Prince noir contre le comte d'Armagnac', *Revue de Gascogne*, NS 14, 1914, pp. 5–17.

Daumet, Georges, *Étude sur l'alliance de la France et de la Castile au XIVe et au XVe siècles*, Paris, 1898.

Daumet, Georges, 'L'Ordre castillan de l'écharpe', *Bulletin hispanique*, XXV, 1923, pp. 5–32.

Dawson, A. J., 'The Black Prince's Palace at Kennington, Surrey', *British Archaeological Reports*, 26, 1976.

Delachenal, R., *Histoire de Charles V*, Paris, 1909–31.

Delisle, Léopold, *Histoire du château et des sires de Saint-Sauveur-le-Vicomte*, Valognes, 1867.

Delisle, Léopold, *Mandements et actes divers de Charles V 1364–80*, Paris, 1874.

Delpit, Jules, *Collection générale des documents français qui se trouvent en Angleterre*, Paris, 1847.

Denifle, Henri, *La Guerre de Cent Ans et la désolation des églises, monastères et hôpitaux en France*, Paris, 1899.

Déprez, Eugène, *Les Préliminaires de la Guerre de Cent Ans (1328–1342)*, Paris, 1902.

Déprez, Eugène, 'La Bataille de Nájera: le communiqué du prince noir', *Revue historique*, cxxxvi, 1921, pp. 37–59.

De Santi, L., 'L'Expédition du prince noir en 1355 d'après le journal d'un de ses compagnons', *Mémoires de l'Académie des Sciences de Toulouse*, X, 5, 1904, pp. 181–223.

Deschamps, Eustache, *Poésies morales et historiques*, ed. G. A. Crapelet, Paris, 1832.

Devic, C., and Vaissete, J., *Histoire générale de Languedoc*, Toulouse, 1885 (2nd edition).

Devon, Frederick (ed.), *Issue Rolls of Thomas de Brantingham [44 Edward III]*, London, 1835.

Devon, Frederick (ed.), *Issues of the Exchequer [Henry III–Henry VI]*, London, 1847.

Douet d'Arcq, Charles, 'Petite

Chronique Françoise de l'an 1270 à l'an 1356', *Mélanges de la société des bibliophiles*, London, 1867.

Douet d'Arcq, L., *Comptes de l'argenterie des rois de France au XIV siècle*, SHF, Paris, 1851.

Dragomanni, F. G., *Chronica de, Giovanni Villani*, Florence, 1845.

Dugdale, William, *Monasticon*, London 1655–73.

Dunn-Pattison, R. P., *The Black Prince*, London, 1910.

Edwards, J. Goronwy, *Calendar of Ancient Correspondence Concerning Wales*, Cardiff, 1935.

Emerson, Barbara, *The Black Prince*, London, 1976.

Emler, Josef, *Fontes Rerum Bohemicarum IV: Chronicon Francisci Pragensis, Chronicon Benessii de Weitmil*, Prague, 1884.

Eulogium Historiarum sive Temporis, ed. Frank Scott Haydon (RS 9), London, 1863.

Evans, D. L., 'Some Notes on the History of the Principality of Wales in the Time of the Black Prince (1343–1376)', *Transactions of the Honourable Society of Cymmrodrion*, 1925, pp. 25–107.

Evans, D. L. (ed.), *Flintshire Ministers' Accounts 1328–1353*, Flintshire Historical Society (Record Series 2), 1929.

Fédié, L., *Histoire de Carcassonne*, Carcassonne, [1886].

Fillon, Benjamin, 'Jean Chandos, connétable d'Aquitaine et sénéchal de Poitou', *Revue des provinces de l'ouest*, 3, 1855, pp. 193–225.

Fowler, Kenneth, 'Les Finances et la discipline dans les armées anglaises en France au XIVe siècle', *Les Cahiers vernonnais*, 4, 1964, pp. 55–84.

Fowler, Kenneth, *The King's Lieutenant: Henry of Grosmont, 1st Duke of Lancaster*, London, 1959.

Fowler, Kenneth (ed.), *The Hundred Years War*, London, 1971.

Froissart, Jean, *Chroniques*, ed. Siméon Luce, vols. 1– , SHF, Paris, 1870– ; ed. Kervyn de Lettenhove, 1867–77.

Galbraith, V. H., 'The Battle of Poitiers', *EHR*, 1938, pp. 473–5.

Galbraith, V. H., 'Extracts from the Historia Aurea and a French "Brut" (1317–47)', *EHR*, 1928, pp. 203–13.

Galway, Margaret, 'Joan of Kent and the Order of the Garter', *University of Birmingham Historical Journal*, I, 1947, pp. 13–50.

Galway, Margaret, 'Froissart in England', *University of Birmingham Historical Journal*, VII, 1959, pp. 18–35.

Glénisson, Jean, 'Notes d'histoire militaire: quelques lettres de défi du XIVe siècle', *BEC*, CVII, 1947–8, pp. 235–54.

Godéfroy, Frédéric, *Dictionnaire de l'ancienne langue française*, Paris, 1878.

Gollancz, Sir Israel, *A Good Short Debate between Winner and Waster*, London, 1921; Cambridge, 1974.

Gollancz, Sir Israel, *'Ich Dene': some observations on a manuscript of the Life of ... the Black Prince*, London, 1921.

Goodman, A. W., *Chartulary of Winchester Cathedral*, Winchester, 1927.

Gower, John, 'Vox Clamantis', in *Complete Works*, ed. G. C. Macaulay, IV.

Gransden, Antonia, 'A Fourteenth Century Chronicle from the Grey Friars at Lynn', *EHR*, LXXII, 1957, pp. 270–278.

Gransden, Antonia, 'The Alleged Rape by Edward III of the Countess of Salisbury', *EHR*, LXXXVII, 1972, pp. 333–44.

Gransden, Antonia, 'Propaganda in English Medieval Historiography', *Journal of Medieval History*, I, 1975, pp. 363–82.

Gray, Sir Thomas, *Scalacronica*, tr. Sir Herbert Maxwell, Glasgow, 1907.

Green, Louis, *Chronicle into History: An Essay on the Interpretation of History in Florentine Fourteenth-century Chronicles*, Cambridge, 1972.

Griffiths, Ralph A., *The Principality of Wales in the Later Middle Ages: The Structure and Personnel of Government*, I: *South Wales 1277–1536*, Cardiff, 1972.

Grosjean, Georges, *Le Sentiment National dans la Guerre de Cent Ans*, Paris, 1928.

Grueber, Herbert A., *Handbook of the coins of Great Britain and Ireland in the British Museum*, London, 1970 (revised edition).

Gruber, John, 'The Peace Negotiations of the Avignon Popes', *Catholic Historical Review*, 19, 1933–4, pp. 190–99.

Guesnon, A., 'Documents inédits sur l'invasion anglaise', *Bulletin historique et philologique du comité des travaux historiques et scientifiques*, 1897, pp. 208–59.

Guinodie, Raymond, *Histoire de Libourne*, Bordeaux, 1845.

Guisborough, Walter of (Hemingburgh), *Chronicon*, ed. Hans Claude Hamilton, English Historical Society, London, 1848–9.

Gutierrez de Velasco, Antonio, *Los ingleses en España (Siglo XIV)*, Saragossa, 1950.

Gwynn, Aubrey, *The English Austin Friars in the Time of Wyclif*, Oxford, 1940.

Hale, J. R., Highfield, J. R. L., and Smalley, B. (eds.), *Europe in the Later Middle Ages*, London, 1965.

Hardy, Robert, *The Longbow*, Cambridge, 1976.

Harriss, G. L., *King, Parliament, and Public Finance in Medieval England to 1369*, Oxford, 1975.

Harvey, John, *The Black Prince and His Age*, London, 1976.

Hatcher, John, *Rural Economy and Society in the Duchy of Cornwall 1300–1500*, Cambridge, 1970.

Hatcher, John, *English Tin Production and Trade before 1550*, Oxford, 1973.

Hay, Denys, 'The Division of the Spoils of War in Fourteenth-Century England', *TRHS*, Series 5, IV, 1954, pp. 91–109.

Hay, Denys, *Polydore Vergil*, Oxford, 1952.

Hellot, A. (ed.), *Les Cronicques de Normendie 1223–1453*, Société de l'Histoire de Normandie, Rouen, 1881.

Hewitt, H. J., *The Black Prince's Expedition of 1355–1357*, Manchester, 1958.

Hewitt, H. J., *The Organization of War under Edward III 1338–62*, Manchester and New York, 1966.

Hewitt, H. J., *Medieval Cheshire*, Chetham Society, NS 88, Manchester, 1929.

Higden, Ranulph, *Polychronicon*, ed.

Joseph Rawson Lumby, VIII, London, 1882 (RS 41).

Hillgarth, J. N., *The Spanish Kingdoms 1250–1516*, Oxford, 1976.

Hingeston-Randolph, F. C., *The Register of John de Grandisson, Bishop of Exeter*, London, 1897–9.

Hogg, O. F. G., *Artillery: its Origin, Heyday and Decline*, London, 1970.

Holinshed, Raphael, *Chronicles*, London, 1807–9.

Holmes, George A., *The Good Parliament*, Oxford, 1975.

Istore et Croniques de Flandre, ed. Kervyn de Lettenhove, II, Brussels, 1880.

Jeanjean, J. F., *La Guerre de Cent Ans en Pays Audois: incursion du prince noir en 1355*, Carcassonne, 1946.

John of Reading: see Reading.

Johnstone, Hilda, 'The Queen's Household', in Willard and Morris, I, pp. 250–299.

Keen, M. H., *The Laws of War in the Late Middle Ages*, London, 1965.

Kingsford, Charles Lethbridge (ed.), *Chronicles of London*, Oxford, 1905.

Kingsford, Charles Lethbridge, *English Historical Literature in the Fifteenth Century*, Oxford, 1913.

The Kirkstall Abbey Chronicles, ed. John Taylor, Thoresby Society, XLII, Leeds, 1952.

Knighton, Henry, *Chronicon*, ed. Joseph Rawson Lumby, London, 1895 (RS 92).

La Roncière, Charles de, *Histoire de la marine française*, I: *Les origines*, Paris, 1899.

La Tour Landry, *The Book of the Knight of La Tour Landry*, ed. Thomas Wright, Early English Text Society OS 33, London, 1868.

Le Bel, Jehan, *Chronique*, ed. J. Viard and E. Déprez, SHF, Paris, 1904–5.

Lefèvre-Pontalis, Germaine (ed.), 'Petite Chronique de Guyenne', *BEC*, xlvii, 1886, pp. 53–79.

Léger, L., 'Un Poème sur la bataille de Crécy', *Journal des Savants*, 1902, pp. 323–31.

Leland, John. *De rebus Britannicis*

Collectanea, ed. Thomas Hearne, London, 1774 (3rd edition).

Leland, John, *Itinerary*, ed. L. Toulmin-Smith, London, 1910.

Le Muisit, Gilles, *Chronique et Annales*, ed. Henri Lemaître, Paris, 1906.

Le Patourel, J., 'L'Occupation anglaise de Calais au XIVᵉ siècle', *Revue du Nord*, XXXIII, 1951, pp. 228–41.

Le Patourel, John, 'The Treaty of Brétigny, 1360', *TRHS*, Series 5, X, 1960, pp. 19–39.

Leroux, Alfred, 'Le Sac de la cité de Limoges et son relèvement 1370–1464', *Bulletin de la société archéologique et historique du Limousin*, LVI, pp. 155–233.

Lescot, Richard, *Chronique de Richard Lescot*, Paris, 1896.

Lettenhove, Kervyn de, *Froissart: étude littéraire sur le XIVᵐᵉ siècle*, Paris, 1857.

Lewis, N. B., 'The Organization of Indentured Retinues in Fourteenth-century England', *TRHS*, Series 4, XXVII, 1945, pp. 29–38.

Lewis, P. S., *Later Medieval France: the Polity*, London, 1968.

Literae Cantuarienses: The Letter Books of the Monastery of Christ Church, Canterbury, ed. J. Brigstocke Sheppard, London, 1888 (RS 85).

Livre des hommages d'Aquitaine, Le, ed. Jean-Paul Trabut-Cussac, Bordeaux, 1959.

Lodge, Eleanor C., *Gascony under English Rule*, London, 1926.

Lodge, E. C., 'The Relations between England and Gascony 1152–1453', *History*, XIX, 1934, pp. 131–9.

Lodge, E. C., 'The Constables of Bordeaux in the Reign of Edward III', *EHR*, L, 1935, pp. 225–41.

Loirette, Gabriel, 'Arnaud Amanieu, Sire d'Albret et l'appel des seigneurs gascons en 1368', in *Mélanges d'histoire offerts à Charles Bémont*, Paris, 1913.

Loirette, Gabriel, 'Arnaud Amanieu, sire d'Albret et ses rapports avec la monarchie française pendant le règne de Charles V', *Annales du Midi*, 43, 1931, pp. 6–39.

Loizeau de Grandmaison, P. C. A., 'Séjour du prince noir à Montlouis, près Tours', *Bulletin de la Société des Antiquaires de l'Ouest*, 1898.

López de Ayala, Pedro, *Cronicas de les Reyes de Castilla*, Madrid, 1953.

Lot, Ferdinand, *L'Art militaire et les armées au moyen âge en Europe et dans le proche orient*, Paris, 1946.

Louandre, F.-C., *Histoire d'Abbeville et du comte de Ponthieu jusqu'en 1789*, Abbeville, 1883 (3rd edition).

Lucas, Henry Stephen, *The Low Countries and the Hundred Years War 1326–1347*, Ann Arbor, 1929.

Luce, Siméon, *Histoire de Bertrand du Guesclin et de son époque: La jeunesse de Bertrand (1320–1364)*, Paris, 1896.

Luce, Siméon, *La France pendant la Guerre de Cent Ans*, Paris, 1890–93.

Lunt, William E., and Graves, Edgar B., *Accounts Rendered by Papal Collectors in England 1317–1378* (Memoirs of the American Philosophical Society 70), Philadelphia, 1968.

Lyttelton, Dr, 'A Letter from the Black Prince . . . Relating to the Battle of Poitiers', *Archaeologia*, I, 1754, pp. 213–215.

McFarlane, K. B., *Lancastrian Kings and Lollard Knights*, Oxford, 1972.

McFarlane, K. B., *The Nobility of Later Medieval England*, Oxford, 1973.

McFarlane, K. B., 'War, the Economy and Social Change', *Past and Present*, 22, 1962, pp. 3–13.

Mackinnon, J., *History of Edward III*, London, 1900.

McKisack, May, *The Fourteenth Century 1307–1399*, Oxford, 1959.

Marvaud, F., *Études historiques sur la ville de Cognac*, Niort, 1870.

Mascaro, Jacmes, 'Le Libre des memorias', *Bulletin de la Société Archéologique de Beziers*, I, 1836, pp. 67–146.

Mathew, G., 'Ideals of Knighthood in Late Fourteenth Century England', in *Studies in Medieval History presented to F. M. Powicke*, Oxford, 1948.

Meaux, *Chronica Monasterii de Melsa*, ed. Edward A. Bond, London, 1868.

Menéndez Pidal, Ramón, *Historia de España*, XIV: *España Cristiana: Crisis de la Reconquista, Luchas Civiles*, Madrid, 1966.

Mérimée, Prosper, *Histoire de don Pèdre Ier, roi de Castille*, ed. G. Laplane, Paris, 1961.

Meyvaert, Paul, 'John Erghome and the *Vaticinium Roberti Bridlington*', *Speculum*, XLI, 1966, pp. 656–64.

Minot, Laurence, *Poems*, ed. Joseph Hall, Oxford, 1887.

Mirot, L., and Déprez, E., 'Les Ambassades anglaises pendant la guerre de cent ans', *BEC*, LXX, Paris, 1899.

Moisant, J., *Le Prince noir en Aquitaine*, Paris, 1894.

Molinier, Émile, 'Étude sur la vie d'Arnoul d'Audrehem, maréchal de France', *Mémoires presentées à l'Académie des Inscriptions et Belles Lettres (Deuxième Série: Antiquités de la France)*, VI, 1883, pp. 1–359.

Mollat, G., *Étude critique sur les Vitae paparum Avinonensium d'Étienne Baluze*, Paris, 1917.

Mollat, G., 'Innocent VI et les tentatives de paix entre la France et l'Angleterre (1353–1355)', *Revue d'histoire ecclésiastique*, 10, 1909, pp. 729–43.

Momméja, Jules, 'Le Palais inachevé d'Edward, prince de Galles, et la salle du Prince Noir à Montauban', *Bulletin archéologique de Tarn-et-Garonne*, pp. 44–59.

Monte-Belluna, François de, 'Le "Tragicum Argumentum de miserabili statu regni Franciae" ', ed. A. Vernet, *Annuaire-bulletin de la Société de l'Histoire de France*, 1962–3, pp. 101–63.

Montpellier, 'Le Petit Thalamus de, 'Chronique', *Mémoires de la Société Archéologique de Montpellier*, I, 1836.

Moranvillé, H., 'Le Siège de Reims 1359–60', *BEC*, LVI, 1895, pp. 90–98.

Morris, J. E., 'Mounted Infantry in Mediaeval Warfare', *TRHS*, Series 3, VII, 1915, pp. 77–102.

Morris, Rupert H., *Chester during the Plantagenet and Tudor Periods*, Chester, n.d.

Mullot, Henry, and Poux, Joseph, 'Nouvelles recherches sur l'itinéraire du prince noir à travers les pays de l'Aude', *Annales du Midi*, 21, 1909, pp. 297–311.

Murimuth, Adam, *Adami Murimuthensis Chronica . . . cum eorundem continuatione a quodam anonymo*, ed. Thomas Hog, English Historical Society, 1846.

Murimuth, Adam, *Continuatio Chronicarum*, ed. [with Avesbury] Edward Maunde Thompson, London, 1889 (RS 93).

Nicolas, Sir Nicholas Harris, *A History of the Royal Navy*, London, 1847.

Nicolas, Sir Nicholas Harris, 'Observations on the Institution of the Most Noble Order of the Garter', *Archaeologia*, XXXI, 1846, pp. 1–163.

Pantin, W. A., *The English Church in the Fourteenth Century*, Cambridge, 1955.

Perroy, Édouard, *The Hundred Years War*, London, 1962.

Perroy, Édouard, 'Édouard III et les seigneurs gascons en 1368', *Annales du Midi*, LXI, 1948, pp. 91–6.

Petit, Ernest, *Histoire des ducs de Bourgogne de la race capétienne*, Dijon, 1905.

Prentout, E., 'La Prise de Caen par Edouard III 1346', *Mémoires de l'académie nationale . . . de Caen*, 1904, pp. 225–95.

Prince, Albert E., 'The Army and Navy', in Willard and Morris, pp. 332–393.

Prince, A. E., 'The Importance of the Campaign of 1327', *EHR*, L, 1935, pp. 299–302.

Prince, A. E., 'The Indenture System under Edward III', in *Historical Essays in Honour of James Tait*, Manchester, 1933, pp. 283–98.

Prince, A. E., 'A Letter of Edward the Black Prince Describing the Battle of Nájera in 1367', *EHR*, 1926, pp. 415–17.

Prince, A. E., 'The Payment of Army Wages in Edward III's Reign', *Speculum*, XIX, 1944, pp. 137–60.

Prince, A. E., 'The Strength of English Armies in the Reign of Edward III', *EHR*, CLXXXIII, 1931, pp. 353–71.

Ramet, H., *Histoire de Toulouse*, Toulouse, n.d.

Ramsay, Sir James, 'The Strength of English Armies in the Middle Ages', *EHR*, XXIX, 1914, pp. 221–7.

Reading, John of, *Chronica Johannis de Reading et Anonymi Cantuarensis 1346–1367*, ed. James Tait, Manchester, 1914.

'Récit des tribulations d'un Religieux du Diocèse du Sens pendant l'invasion anglaise de 1358', ed. J. Quicherat, *BEC*, III, 4th Series, 1857, pp. 357–60.

Récits d'un bourgeois de Valenciennes, ed. Kervyn de Lettenhove, Louvain, 1877.

Reddaway, T. F., and Walker, Lorna E. M., *The Early History of the Goldsmiths' Company 1327–1509*, London, 1975.

Register of Edward the Black Prince, London, 1930–33.

Renouard, Yves, 'L'Ordre de la Jarretière et l'Ordre de l'Étoile', *Le Moyen Âge*, LV, 1949, pp. 281–30.

Renouard, Yves, *Bordeaux sous les Rois d'Angleterre (Histoire de Bordeaux*, ed. Ch. Higounet, III), Bordeaux, 1965.

Rickert, Margaret, *The Reconstructed Carmelite Missal*, London, 1952.

Riley, H. T., *Memorials of London and London Life*, London, 1868.

Robert of Avesbury, see Avesbury.

Roschach, E., 'Les Quatre Journées du prince noir dans la viguerie de Toulouse', *Mémoires de l'Académie des Sciences de Toulouse X*, V, 1906, pp. 127–41.

Rotuli Parliamentorum [London, *c.* 1777–83].

Rouquette, J., *Le Rouergue sous les anglais*, Millau, 1887.

Runyan, Timothy, 'The Constabulary of Bordeaux: the Accounts of John Ludham and Robert de Wykford', *Medieval Studies*, 1974, pp. 215–58.

Russell, P. E., 'The *Memorias* of Fernán Álvarez de Albornoz, Archbishop of Seville, 1371–80', in *Hispanic Studies in honour of I. González Llubera*, Oxford, 1959, pp. 319–30.

Russell, P. E., *The English Intervention in Spain and Portugal in the Time of Edward III and Richard II*, Oxford, 1955.

Rye, Reginald Arthur, *Catalogue of the Manuscripts . . . in the University Library . . . University of London*, London, 1921.

Rymer, Thomas, *Foedera*, London, 1816–69; IV: The Hague, 1740.

Rymer, Thomas, *Foedera: Appendices to Report on Rymer's Foedera*, London, 1869.

Scalacronica, see Gray, Sir Thomas.

Scattergood, V. J., 'Two Medieval Book Lists', *Library*, 5th series, 23, 1969, pp. 236–9

Sécousse, *Recueil des pièces servant de preuves aux mémoires de l'histoire de Charles II*, Paris, 1755.

Sedgwick, Henry Dwight, *The Life of Edward the Black Prince 1330–1376*, Indianapolis, 1932.

Sharp, Margaret, 'A Jodrell Deed and the Seals of the Black Prince', *Bulletin of the John Rylands Library*, 7, 1922–3, pp. 106–17.

Sharp, Margaret, 'The Administrative Chancery of the Black Prince before 1362', *Essays in Medieval History presented to T. F. Tout*, Manchester, 1925, pp. 321–333.

Sharp, Margaret, 'The Central Administrative System of the Black Prince', in Tout, V, pp. 289–400; 'Diplomatic of the Central Secretarial Departments of the Black Prince', in Tout, V, pp. 400–31.

Sharpe, Reginald R. (ed.), *Calendar of Letter-Books . . . of the City of London: Letterbook G c. A.D. 1352–1374*, London, 1905.

Shaw, Peter, 'The Black Prince', *History*, XXIV, 1939, pp. 1–15.

Shears, F. S., *Froissart: Chronicler and Poet*, London, 1930.

Sherborne, James W., 'The Battle of La Rochelle and the War at Sea 1372–75', *BIHR*, 42, 1969, pp. 22–5.

Smet, J. J. de, *Recueil des Chroniques de Flandre*, Brussels, 1837, 1856.

Stanley, Arthur Penrhyn, *Historical Memorials of Canterbury*, London, 1906.

Stewart-Brown, Ronald, *Accounts of the Chamberlains and Other Officers of the County of Chester 1301–1360*, The Record Society for Lancashire and Cheshire, LIX, Manchester, 1910.

Stillwell, Gardiner, 'Wynnere and Wastoure and the Hundred Years War', *English Literary History*, 8, 1941, pp. 241–247.

'Storie Pistoresi', ed. Silvio Adrasto Barbi, in *Rerum Italicarum Scriptores*, XI, ed. L. A. Muratori, Castello, 1927, p.v.

Stubbs, William (ed.), *Chronicles of the reigns of Edward I and Edward II*, London, 1883 (RS 76).

Taylor, John, 'A Wigmore Chronicle, 1355–77', *Proceedings of the Leeds Philosophical and Literary Society*, II: 1964–6, pp. 81–94.

Taylor, John, *The Universal Chronicle of Ranulf Higden*, Oxford, 1966.

Taylor, John, 'The French "Brut" and the Reign of Edward II', *EHR*, LXXII, 1957, pp. 423–37.

Templeman, G., 'Edward III and the beginnings of the Hundred Years War', *TRHS*, Series 5, II, 1952, pp. 69–88.

Thomas, A. D., and Thornley, I. D. (eds.), *The Great Chronicle of London*, 1939.

Timbal, Pierre-Clément, *La Guerre de Cent Ans vue à travers les registres du parlement (1337–1369)*, Paris, 1961.

Tourneur-Aumont, J. M., *La Bataille de Poitiers (1356) et la construction de la France*, Paris, 1940.

Todd, Henry J., *The History of the College of Bonhommes at Ashridge*, London, 1812.

Tout, T. F., *Chapters in Medieval Administrative History III–VI*, Manchester, 1928–30.

Tout, T. F., 'Firearms in England in the Fourteenth Century', *EHR*, 26, 1911, pp. 666–702.

Tout, T. F., 'Some Neglected Fights between Crécy and Poitiers', *EHR*, XX, 1905, pp. 726–30.

Tristram, E. W., *English Wall Painting of the Fourteenth Century*, London, 1955.

Tucôo-Chala, Pierre, *Gaston Fébus et la vicomté de Béarn*, Bordeaux, 1959.

Unwin, George (ed.), *Finance and Trade under Edward III*, Manchester, 1918.

Venette, Jean de, *The Chronicle of Jean de Venette*, tr. Jean Birdsall, ed. Richard A. Newhall, New York, 1953.

Vergil, Polydore, *Polydori Vergili Historiae anglicanae . . .*, Basle, 1555; reprinted Menston, 1972.

Viard, Jules, 'La Campagne de juillet-août 1346 et la bataille de Crécy', *Le Moyen Âge*, Series 2, XXVII, 1926, pp. 1–84.

Viard, Jules, 'Le Siège de Calais', *Le Moyen Âge*, Series 2, XXX, 1929, pp. 128–89.

Villani, Giovanni, see Dragomanni, F. G.

Villani, Matteo, *Matthaei Villani . . . Historia*, in *Rerum Italicarum Scriptores*, 14, ed. L. A. Muratori, Milan, 1729.

Villanueva, Lorenzo Tadeo, 'Memorial sobre la order de Caballeria de la Banda de Castilla', *Boletín de la real academia de la historia*, lxxii, 1918, pp. 436–65, 552–74.

Wagner, Anthony R., 'The Order of the Garter 1348–1948', *Society of the Friends of St George's, Annual Report*, 1948, pp. 11–18.

[Walsingham, Thomas], *Chronicon Angliae ab anno domini 1328 usque ad 1358*, ed. Edward Maunde Thompson, London, 1874 (RS 64).

[Walsingham, Thomas], *Gesta Abbatium Sancti Albani*, ed. Henry Thomas Riley, London, 1867–9 (RS 52).

[Walsingham, Thomas], *Historia Anglicana*, ed. Henry T. Riley, London, 1863–4 (RS 28).

Wavrin, Jehan de, *Anchiennes Croniques d'Engleterre*, ed. Mlle Dupont, SHF, Paris, 1858.

Weever, John, *Antient Funeral Monuments of Great Britain*, London, 1767.

Wharton, H. (ed.), *Anglia Sacra*, I, pp. 356–83 [*Historia Roffensis 1314–50* by William Dene].

Whiting, B. J., 'The Vows of the Heron', *Speculum*, XX, 1945, pp. 261–78.

Wilkins, D., *Concilia magnae Britanniae et Hiberniae III*, London, 1737.

Willard, James F., and Morris, William A. (eds.), *The English Government at Work 1327–1336*, Cambridge, Mass., 1940.

Withington, Robert, *English Pageantry*, Cambridge, Mass., 1918.

Wolffe, B. P., *The Royal Demesne in English History*, London, 1971.

Wright, Thomas (ed.), *Political Poems and Songs Relating to English History*, London, 1859 (RS 14).

Wright, William Alldis (ed.), *Femina*, Roxburghe Club, 1909.

Wrottesley, George, 'Crécy and Calais from the Public Records', in *Collections for a History of Staffordshire edited by the William Salt Archaeological Society*, XVIII, London, 1897, pp. 1–284.

Ziegler, Phillip, *The Black Death*, London, 1967.

Zurita, Geronimo, *Los cinco libros postreros de la primera parte de los annales de la corona de Aragón*, Saragossa, 1610.

Index

Abbreviations: pr.E. for Edward, prince of Wales and Aquitaine; E.III for king Edward III

Numerals in italic indicate a substantial entry in the Notes and References section; minor entries have not been indexed.

David II, king of Scots (David Bruce), 26, 154
Dawkin, Baldwin, 161
Dax, 193, 194
Delamere forest, 155
Delves, Sir John, 184
Denia, count of, 200–1, 203, 209
Denbigh, 107
Déols, 134
Derby, Henry of Grosmont, earl of, *later* earl *and then* duke of Lancaster, pledge for E.III's debts, 32; at siege of Algeciras, 42, 89; at tournaments, 42; seneschal of England, 43; in Aquitaine, 44, 112, 127; holds Aiguillon, 72; and siege of Calais, 76–7; prestige, 79; and E.III, 82; knight of the Garter, 89–90
as duke of Lancaster: 103–4, 113, 146; tournaments, 92, 93; and Castilian fleet, 99, 100; and negotiations for truce with France, 102; leads raids in Picardy, 103; acts as foreign minister, 103; his Cheshire estate, 106; and expedition in Normandy, 113, 132, 141; contract of service in 1345, 114–15; reinforcements for, 130; pr.E. hopes to join up with, 135, 136; siege of Rennes, 151; his palace, 153; marriage of his daughter, 155; and 1359 expedition, 159, 161, 162, 163, 166; peace negotiations, 165, 167, 168, 169; dies of plague, 170
Despenser family, 13, 14
Despenser, Hugh, 62
Despenser, Philip, 43
Devon, 39, 104, 109
Devonshire, Hugh Courtenay, earl of, 30
Doria, Otto, 65
Dordogne, river, 129, 130
Dorset, 39
Douglas, Sir William, 138
Douve, river, 52
Dover, 74, 168, 243
Doxeye, Richard, 154
Drakelow, 153
dress, of pr.E., 19, 22; Garter robes, 84; garters, 87; of Order of the Sash, 87–8; Hainault influence on, 94; Knighton on dress of wealthy women, 94; fashion at court of pr.E. at Bordeaux, 184
duel, judicial, 101
Dunstable, 42
Durfort, Arnaud, lord of, 112
Durfort, Bertrand de, 130

Durham, Thomas Hatfield, bishop of, 50, 64

Eam, Sir Henry, 90
Ebro, river, 198
Edington, William, Bishop of Winchester, 241
Edward of Angoulême, eldest son of pr.E., 184, 205, 224, 226
Edward the Confessor, king, 85
Edward I, king of England, 27, 77; and confiscation of Gascony, 24; and Amanieu VII of Albret, 111; in Gascony, 113; Vale Royal abbey, 155; ancestor of born pr.E. and Joan of Kent, 173
Edward II, king of England, character and behaviour, 13; deposed and murdered, 14; title of prince of Wales, 41; soldier, 70; tournaments banned, 105; his preference for menial occupations, 238
Edward III, king of England, and his mother, 13, 14; betrothal, 14; king, 14; marriage, 15; and birth of pr.E., 16; and Mortimer, 17; interest in politics, 18; and tournaments, 18, 42–3, 45–6, 92, 93, 155, 174; his claim to crown of France, 23, 25, 28, 44, 102, 110; and duchy of Gascony, 25; does homage to Philip VI, 25–6; relations between Philip VI and, 27; and money for wars, 30, 31, 37–8; war with France, 29, 30, 31, 33; battle of Sluys, 34–7; military expedition in Brittany, 40; collapse of alliances, 41; pilgrimages, 42, 109, 159, 163; Round Table, 43–4; designs on Aquitaine, 44; gambles with pr.E., 46, 94; military experience, 71; and Holy Roman Empire, 82; marriage negotiations for his children, 82–3
Crécy campaign: sets sail for France, 47–8; orders strict discipline, 49, 50, 55; ignorant of terrain, 50; on the march, 50–53, 59–61; takes Caen, 54–5; takes Bayeux, 55; at Lisieux, 56; plans for Rouen, 56–7; two strategies open to, 57; reaches Vernon, 57; rejects Philip's peace terms, 57, 77; Philip challenges, 59; crosses Somme, 61–2; commands centre, 64; battle of Crécy, 67; and king of Bohemia, 68; decides strategy in advance, 70; and siege of Calais, 72–3, 74, 76, 77, 78; returns

288

Ferrers, Robert de, 57
Fiennes, Robert, 165
Filongley, Richard, 209
fiscal matters (*see also entry under* Edward,
prince of Wales and Aquitaine), cost of
alliance with Continental princes, 29,
30; E.III seeks money for French wars,
31; revenue from knighting, 73; profits
and expenditure in Crécy campaign,
80; war expenditure, 81; revenue and
military success, 128; financing of 1359
expedition, 158; ransom of Burgundy,
164; financial independence of Aquitaine, 177; taxation of Aquitaine, 181–2,
185; coinage as source of revenue, 185;
taxation for war with France, 227; papal
taxes, 229–30
FitzSimon, Sir Richard, 67, 90, *255*
Fitzwalter, John, lord 50
Fitzwarin, Sir William, 83, 170
Flanders (*see also* Flemish), 71; Philippa
in, 29; pledges for E.III's debts in, 32;
importance of English wool to, 32, 45;
E.III in alliance with, 32, 41, 44–5, 46;
marriage negotiations with, 81, 102;
independent power, 82; and 1359
campaign, 161
Flanders, counts of, *see* Mâle, Louis de
and Nevers, Louis de
fleet, English, at battle of Sluys, 34–6;
and Crécy campaign, 45, 47, 48; attacks
Boulogne, 73; blockades Calais, 74; to
gather at Sandwich, 99; battle of
Winchelsea against Castilians, 99–100
Flemish, the (*see also* Flanders), at battle
of Sluys, 36; and English, 57; make
raids in Calais area, 74; reinforcements
at Calais, 76; and subsequent English
campaigns, 82
Fleurance, 127
Florac, Thomas, 187
Foix, Gaston III 'Phoebus', count of, his
attack on Nogaro, 119; and pr.E., 125,
208; does homage, 180, 181; intrigues
with Charles V, 182, 207; and homage
for Béarn, 186–7; famous huntsman,
187; Armagnac ransomed from, 208,
210
Fontainebleau, 164
Fontenay-Pesnel, 53
Fordham, John, 232
Fossat, Amanieu de, 117, 122
fouage, 181, 183, 209, 210, *263*
Fountains abbey, 156
France, the French, English domains in,

13, 23–6; peace made with, 14; truce
with England, 22, 78, 97, 101–3; harry
English shipping, 33; and Castile, 41–2,
186; and Flanders, 45; failure to ransom
John II, 157; ravages by 'free companies'
in, 187; proposed partition of, 158
free companies, plague France, 183;
under de Guesclin, 187; cross into
Aragón, 188; success of, 188; troops for
Spanish campaign, 197
Freneuse, 57
Frespech castle, 113
Freton, John, 177
Froissart, Jean, 63; on Edward III and
Philippa, 14–15; and battle of Sluys, 36;
and Chandos, 38; and d'Harcourt, 50;
and surrender of French commanders,
54; and deployment of archers at Crécy,
64; and Order of the Garter, 85; and
capture of Aimeric, 98; and naval battle
off Winchelsea, 100; and removal of
John II to England, 151–2; and Joan of
Kent, 172; and Castilian throne, 189;
and relationship between pr.E. and
Gascon lords, 208; his unreliable reports
of pr.E., 219, 220, 250; and Audley's
funeral, 222; and Pembroke and
Chandos, 222, *264*; and pr.E.'s illness,
224; and massacre at Limoges, 225, 226;
his unreliability, 243, 250, *260, 262*;
value of his work, 243; and contemporary stories, 243–4; literary background, 244; his weakness, 245;
Chronicles, 244, 245, 248; debt to Jean
Le Bel, 245; romantic embroidery by,
246, 247–8; three versions of conversation between knight and E.III at
Crécy, 246–7; and historians' traditional
devices, 248; story of pr.E.'s supper
after Poitiers, 249; and pr.E.'s later
years, 250; and Chandos Herald's poem,
250

Gaddesden, John, 22, 30, 93
Gaillard, lord of, 130
Gaillon, 57
Galiax castle, 120
Galicia, 188, 192, 194
Garonne, river, 122, 125, 129
Garonne valley, 112, 128
Garter, Order of the, foundation of,
83–4; robes, 84; date of foundation,
84–5; motto, 84, 86; Vergil and, 85–6;
and other Orders of Knighthood, 87–9;
original members, 89–90; function, 91;

DATE DUE			
OCT 4 1982			
NO 16 '87			
APR 10 1989			